Indigenous Americas
Robert Warrior, Series Editor

T0395521

continued on page 209

PRODUCING SOVEREIGNTY

Producing Sovereignty

THE RISE OF INDIGENOUS MEDIA IN CANADA

Karrmen Crey

Indigenous Americas

University of Minnesota Press

Minneapolis

London

Portions of chapter 2 are adapted from "The Aboriginal Film and Video Art Alliance: Indigenous Self-Government in Moving Image Media," *JCMS: Journal of Cinema and Media Studies* 60, no. 2 (2021): 175–80, https://doi .org/10.1353/cj.2021.0011. Chapter 4 was originally published as "Screen Text and Institutional Context: Indigenous Film Production and Academic Research Institutions," *Native American and Indigenous Studies* 4, no. 1 (2017): 61–88, muse.jhu.edu/article/661472.

Published by the University of Minnesota Press
111 Third Avenue South, Suite 290
Minneapolis, MN 55401–2520
http://www.upress.umn.edu

ISBN 978-1-5179-1449-3 (hc)
ISBN 978-1-5179-1450-9 (pb)

A Cataloging-in-Publication record for this book is available from the Library of Congress.

The University of Minnesota is an equal-opportunity educator and employer.

UMP LSI

Contents

Introduction

INDIGENOUS POLITICS, THE STATE, AND
MEDIA INSTITUTIONS IN CANADA

In 1982, Canada patriated its Constitution from Britain, officially becoming a sovereign nation. Owing to the efforts of Indigenous groups
across the country, the Constitution included Section 35, which formally recognized and affirmed Indigenous rights. This was a watershed
moment in Indigenous history, nationally and globally, as Section 35
acknowledged that Indigenous peoples possessed legal rights pre-
dating the colonial settler state, and that Indigenous rights and title
had not been extinguished by colonial law and occupation.[1] Acknowl-
edgment in law does not equal acknowledgement in fact, however;
ever since, Indigenous communities, political bodies, and advocates
have struggled to force the Canadian state to abide by their constitutional commitments. In the late 1980s and early 1990s, programs, organizations, and funding supporting Indigenous cultural production
emerged in earnest across the country, much of it through provincial
and national funding and cultural institutions. Against this backdrop,
Indigenous film, television, video, and digital media experienced a
boom across Canada over the past three decades that has resulted in
a rich and diverse body of film, television, video, and digital media.
What made this remarkable surge in production possible? As this brief
sketch indicates, there is a connection between Indigenous relations
with the Canadian state and the surge of Indigenous media that began
in earnest in the early 1990s, but in order to understand this phenomenon, this book examines the complex intersection of factors—social,
political, technological—that coalesced to produce it.

Identifying the 1990s as a key moment in the history of Indigenous
media is not meant to imply that Indigenous media history begins with
this era, but rather to identify that the early 1990s marks a period of

rapid expansion of Indigenous production across Canada that initially and largely took place in the southern, urbanized areas of the country. In the north, Inuit and northern Indigenous broadcasting, which airs television programming produced by northern Inuit and Indigenous communities, was well underway in the 1970s.[2] According to the Inuit Broadcasting Corporation and the Nunavut Media Arts Centre, their holdings consist of some 9,000 hours of programming and footage (Inuit Broadcasting Corporation, n.d.), content that historically was not easily accessible to southern audiences. Attention to the North makes clear that the history of Indigenous media development is a complex and variegated terrain, one that does not resolve into a unified history with a single origin.

Nonetheless, Indigenous media in southern Canada demonstrates exponential growth from the early 1990s onward. Indigenous artists work in all media formats and genres, but nonfiction media—primarily documentary—has by far been the most pervasive form of Indigenous production, and focusing on nonfiction production makes it possible to trace patterns of production over time, genre, format, and region. Prior to 1990, there were some thirty to forty nonfiction works by Indigenous producers in southern Canada, the majority of which were short- and long-form documentaries, and experimental film and video roughly dating back to the late 1960s.[3] Since 1990, the number of nonfiction media texts has grown to hundreds of films, videos, and digital media projects, and hundreds of hours of television production,[4] representing a remarkable surge that has made Canada the site of one of the largest bodies of Indigenous media in the world.

To understand this complex phenomenon, this book draws on scholarship from minoritarian media studies that similarly trace the emergence of identity-based cinemas in the latter part of the twentieth century. Chon A. Noriega and Jun Okada approach Chicano cinema and Asian American film and video respectively not as natural or pregiven categories but rather as historical and political formations debated and shaped through social and ideological forces including state policy, social movements, developments in media technologies, and institutional funding structures and practices (Noriega 2000; Okada 2015). Indigenous media in Canada emerged at the intersection of similar forces: the Indigenous self-determination movement of the latter part of the twentieth century, developments in media technologies and telecommunications, and shifts in national law and policy. Moreover, these forces converge in institutions of media culture that include federal film agencies, national and provincial broadcasters, museums, galleries, postsecondary institutions, and media collectives where programs and funding structures supporting Indigenous production have emerged across the country, in no small part due to the sustained work and pressure from Indigenous artists, advocates, and their allies.

This book focuses on the institutions of media culture that form the backdrop for Indigenous media in Canada, and the Indigenous artists who have produced work in association with them. These sites are deeply enmeshed in Indigenous media history, but their role has been critically underexamined. They are not neutral backdrops or platforms for Indigenous production, but are active and meaning-generating places that interpret and make sense of social, legal, and material shifts in relation to their own institutional identities, cultures, administrative structures, and production practices. This book investigates how Indigenous media practitioners work in and with these institutions and demonstrates that these institutional negotiations shape the textual and discursive strategies of the media texts themselves. These are sophisticated texts that are in critical conversation with institutional discourses, representational conventions, and production cultures, and, this book argues, analysis of the institutional contexts of Indigenous media is a crucial lens for interpreting the textual and aesthetic features of Indigenous media. This approach therefore makes two substantial contributions to Indigenous media studies: first, it proposes that examining these institutions can reveal media practitioners and areas of production that have yet to have sustained attention in scholarly and historical records; second, it theorizes and models institutional analysis of Indigenous media texts through the case studies that are the focus for each chapter.

INDIGENOUS MEDIA AND INSTITUTIONAL CONTEXTS

Institutional analysis counters prevailing tendencies to understand Indigenous media solely in terms of "cultural nationalisms," interpretive approaches that Noriega argues proceed by ascribing to identity-based media a form of cultural aesthetics and politics shaped by exclusion from, and misrepresentation within, dominant society

(2000, 19). Critical discourse has subsequently "followed the well-trodden path of social movement scholarship more generally, looking at the political, aesthetic, and cultural dimensions of contestation without considering its relationships to the state, the political representation system, industry practices, and the market" (19). Within these categories, social phenomena are converted into textual features that come to constitute sets of characteristics through which these media texts are recognized and interpreted. Ultimately, these approaches have tended to organize interpretation around a monolithic cultural nationalism that is set in opposition to the state and which position such cinemas as "outside" of the state. This paradigm raises several issues: it tends to overlook media texts that do not conform to expectations of the "genre," resulting in historical blind spots when it comes to which artists or works get acknowledged and discussed, and interpretation can be circumscribed by these sociocultural markers of difference at the expense of other axes of analysis that contextualize the media texts: state policy, institutional discourses and practices, media formats, and genre conventions. Instead, attention to the institutions of media culture that form the backdrop for Indigenous production provides a framework for opening up sites and bodies of production that have not received much scholarly attention, and builds on analysis of their textual features and discursive interventions by looking at the institutional specificities in which they work.

Institutional analysis of Indigenous media is not a new approach per se, and has been greatly enhanced by the recent monograph *We Interrupt This Program: Indigenous Media Tactics in Canadian Culture* (2017), which also examines the institutional contexts for Indigenous media practices in Canada and is an important forerunner for this book. Miranda J. Brady and John M. H. Kelly (Haida)[5] focus on sites that produce public discourses about Indigeneity, which include the Truth and Reconciliation Commission, performance- and media-based art institutions, the imagineNATIVE Film + Media Arts Festival, and Indigenous journalism, tracing "media tactics" developed by Indigenous artists and activists to engage and intervene in "established frameworks" of these cultural institutions as a form of resistance to create space for Indigenous perspectives (10). Brady and Kelly (2017) provide an invaluable precedent to my own work, identifying institutional contexts as a critical axis for the analysis of Indigenous media, and attending to the specificities of each institution in order to contex-tualize the particular strategies used by Indigenous artists, ultimately linking these strategies to what ends up on screen. They also bring attention to sites that have not had much scholarly attention, which this book expands by examining the Banff Centre for Arts and Crea-tivity, provincial broadcasters, independent television production companies, and postsecondary programs. This book also provides a historical, political, and cultural framework for understanding the rapid expansion of Indigenous media across the country in order to bring attention to the forces behind institutional responsiveness to Indigenous media-making initiatives and programs.

Historically, where there has been address of institutional contexts for Indigenous media in Canada, the National Film Board of Canada (NFB) has occupied much of the attention, owing to the significant role that this public film agency has played in Indigenous media his-tory (Gauthier 2010; Abbott 1998; Druick 2007; Pick 1999; Lewis 2006; White 2002; Silverman 2002; Steven 1993). Since the 1960s, the NFB has developed training programs and resources in support of Indigenous production, including the Indian Film Crew in 1967 (Stewart 2007) and Studio One in 1991 (Cardinal, n.d.), which be-came the Aboriginal Filmmaking Program in 1996 (White 2006, 135). As a result, the NFB has become a home to an extensive body of Indigenous documentary, animation, and web-based media. Further-more, the institutional emphasis on the NFB can be attributed in no small part to the groundbreaking and unparalleled career of Abenaki filmmaker Alanis Obomsawin, who has produced dozens of documen-taries and film-based projects since she began working with the NFB in 1967 (Lewis 2006), in the process becoming one of the world's most well-regarded Indigenous filmmakers and contributing to the agency's renown as a major center for Indigenous film in the world. Scholarship on Obomsawin's work tends to compare it to NFB docu-mentary traditions of the "Griersonian documentary style," which Jennifer Gauthier explains embodies characteristics of the expository documentary: it seeks objectivity in the construction of an argument, relies on the authority of the filmmaker/narrator as the representative of a governing body or social group, and employs evidentiary editing where images are placed as illustration of the argument (2010, 28). In other words, NFB documentaries in this tradition have sought to "speak for" their subjects (2010, 28) in the process of making these subjects "legible" to the state that the NFB represents. The NFB and its filmmaking style are therefore deeply implicated in the project of colonial nation building in Canada as an apparatus through which the state attempts to extend control over populations within its bounds.

Scholarship has been responsive to such critiques, and tends to proceed by examining how Indigenous people, once in control of the NFB film apparatus, innovate on its documentary conventions to overturn its colonial roots, a significant focus of which has been Obomsawin's documentary approach. This scholarship argues that Obomsawin's films "rework documentary conventions and place representation at the service of a Native political and aesthetic agenda" (Pick 1999, 77) and employ theoretical frameworks from literature on the radical politics of minority media to interpret her filmmaking style and ethic. Zuzana Pick and Tia Wong, for example, draw on critical models from Latin American cinema and Third Cinema for understanding Obomsawin's representational strategies: Pick utilizes Chon Noriega's definition of interviews as a form of "testimonial narrative" that "gives voice" to a community or social group via communication between filmmaker and subject(s) (1999, 78), while Wong tests the applications of Third Cinema's "revolutionary, combative, and decolonizing cinema that attacks the political and legal apparatuses of the dominant nation-state" in her examination of Obomsawin's documentaries focusing on conflicts between Indigenous communities and the Canadian state (2009). These theoretical frameworks make sense of the political and formal techniques Obomsawin's films employ to challenge the authority of the settler state, which include subverting the objectivity of the didactic documentary by using a first-person voiceover that foregrounds the filmmaker's subjective point of view and relationship to Indigenous communities, historical segments narrating histories of Canada's oppression of Indigenous peoples, ironic editing that undermines the claims and authority of state representatives, and interviews in which she is shown with the interviewees, clearly sympathetic to their positions (Lewis 2006; Steven 1993; White 2002). By examining how Obomsawin challenges NFB institutional discourses and practices, this scholarship traces the stylistic and ideological negotiations that she undertakes to produce her work, which are inscribed in the film texts.

"VISUAL SOVEREIGNTY": FOURTH CINEMAS AND MEDIA INDUSTRIES

It is worth lingering on the example of Obomsawin's institutional engagement with the NFB and her transformation of its documentary traditions, as it illustrates the concept of "visual sovereignty" as theorized by Michelle Raheja (Seneca), a framework that guides this book. In *Reservation Reelism: Redfacing, Visual Sovereignty, and Representations of Native Americans in Film* (2013), Raheja examines Indigenous participation in early Hollywood and ethnographic films both on- and off-screen, arguing that Indigenous actors and production consultants demonstrate "visual sovereignty" by disrupting the "surfaces" of stereotypical roles and narratives through their performances on-screen, and by advising and guiding the production offscreen (194).Raheja effectively asks why Indigenous people would participate in systems and industries shaped by colonial ideology that reproduce demeaning Indigenous representations, and develops a framework for interpreting their participation that examines the pressure they place on their screen performances and on film productions themselves. In doing so, Raheja identifies manifestations of Indigenous agency within colonial film productions and industries, pointing to ways that Indigenous people participate in and transform film industry activities and norms.

Indigenous agency in media production is often defined in terms of control of the cinematic apparatus (beginning in North America in earnest in the 1970s onward), but Raheja's model for visual sovereignty also traces Indigenous agency to the very beginnings of cinema's history, and traces an Indigenous engagement with and participation in cinema and media industries that seeks to transform their structures and resources in order to make them meaningful for Indigenous participants and Indigenous priorities. "Visual sovereignty" is a guiding framework for this study, as it can be extended to examine the transformation that Indigenous media practitioners create while working within dominant systems and institutions. Rather than see these individuals and their work as "capitulating" to these regimes, or simply ruffling their edges, I argue that their work is engaged in complex and critical ways with these political, social, and cultural arenas both on-screen and off.

This approach is indebted to anthropological studies of Indigenous media, particularly ethnographic studies of the social contexts of Indigenous production. Faye Ginsburg cites the "reinvention" of anthropology in between the 1960s and 1980s as context for this scholarly approach. She traces the reflexive turn in anthropology that took place in the 1960s and 1970s that stemmed from an increased awareness of the power relations embedded in ethnographic research, which instigated a shift toward more collaborative practices between researchers and subjects; by the 1980s, Indigenous and other groups increasingly took control of their own image-making (Ginsburg 1994a, 1995). Since that time, there has been greater attention to Indigenous production contexts by anthropologists including Eric Michaels (1986, 1994), Ginsburg (1991, 1993, 1994a, 1994b, 1995, 2007, 2012), and Kristin Dowell (2013), who have examined Indigenous peoples' use of media technologies and the material contexts of its production. These authors approach Indigenous media as a form of mediation that enables and revitalizes Indigenous social relations, which Ginsburg terms "embedded aesthetics," which she theorizes in order to "draw attention to a system of evaluation that refuses a separation of textual production and circulation from broader arenas of social relations" (1994b, 368). Embedded aesthetics focuses on media-making activities as ways in which Indigenous relations and communities can be maintained and cultivated. In the process, Ginsburg highlights the social and material dimensions of media production as a site of investigation, which I build on by focusing on institutional contexts as a part of these social and material dimensions, and by illustrating how the media text itself is marked by the social activities of its production.

The scholarship of Ginsburg and others is oriented by questions about how Indigenous artists and communities engage and use media technologies, and what priorities, interests, and purposes guide the screen content of Indigenous media and the production practices used to create it. These are central questions that Indigenous artists and theorists reflect on and debate, speaking more often than not from the specificities of their social position informed by their lived Indigenous experience as a starting point for their reflections on Indigenous media practice. Cree/Métis filmmaker Loretta Todd has argued that Indigenous control of the cinematic apparatus is an extension of Indigenous self-determination, as are artists' critical appropriation of Western representational modes in their work (1990, 1992, 2005b; Abbott 1998; Eisner 2003). Victor Masayesva Jr. (Hopi) and Barry

Barclay (Maori) have also theorized the specificities of Indigenous media in terms of "Indigenous experimentalism" (2005) and "Fourth Cinema" (2003) respectively. Masayesva conceptualizes the "third arm" of video production: the instinct to make the "edit cut" motivated by an Indigenous filmmaker's particular cultural and social experience and history (2005). Barclay (2003) considers Indigenous cinematic specificity beyond the textual, relating a story of a visit to Athens wherein he encountered a row of soldiers' headstones, the meaning and significance of which would be impossible to discern without a curator's expertise and interpretation. Barclay's analogy centers the Indigenous filmmaker ("curator") as the source of knowledge, the interpreter who imbues the text with meaning; by implication, the viewer's task is to seek to understand this history and context as an interpretive framework. Both Masayesva and Barclay cite the irreducibility of the filmmaker and their social and cultural milieu in the cinema and media production process, which ultimately guides their aesthetic choices. These arguments point to the realities of dominant media industries, which have historically excluded Indigenous people both behind the camera as creatives and on-screen, where Indigenous roles are often played by non-Indigenous performers or rely on stereotypes that project colonial fantasies. They also link aesthetic features to cultural forms and narratives, a relationship discussed and debated in scholarship from art history and cinema studies (Leuthold 1998; Pick 2003; Ryan 1999). However, questions of the political economy of Indigenous media are never far from these discussions. For instance, Barclay asks:

> Can there be said to be a Fourth Cinema in the sense of dedicated buildings and attendances and box office takings? Perhaps there can, albeit in a fledgling way, via a loyal festival following, or via an interested and regular faithful—Indigenous and non-Indigenous—who attend screenings of Indigenous features when they appear at downtown cinemas. In this sense, there is already a cinema of Indigenous features—very small, but significant. (2003, 11)

In addition to opening up audiences and screening circuits as aspects of Fourth Cinema, Barclay also considers an infrastructure for financial support that is not based in mainstream box office terms but rather through a philosophy of social value proven by the "interested and regular faithful" audiences, both Indigenous and non-Indigenous. Indigenous media therefore cannot be considered in terms of aesthetic features alone; these are tied to the materiality of production: its economic and industrial conditions, and the people doing the work.

A caveat should be made here: while Todd, Barclay, Masayesva, and others theorize what has over time come to be broadly understood as "Fourth Cinema," they are not making claims that specific aesthetic features or thematic/political concerns irreducibly define Fourth Cinema as a cultural category. They base their theories in the specificities of their own lived histories and cultures, which do include a shared experience of colonization. However, this shared experience does not resolve into a unified perspective; rather, as Barclay argues, it has cultivated a shared critical perspective of colonial history and settler colonial society. He uses the metaphor of the colonizers' ship approaching a shore, on which stands the Indigenous peoples of that territory. While the perspective from the ship is that of the colonizers, Barclay argues that Fourth Cinema is produced by the perspective of the Indigenous people from the shore, looking back critically at the ship and its inhabitants (2003, 10). Thus, while Indigenous cinema has in common a critical perspective borne of the experience of colonization, the histories, cultural contexts, and material production conditions of the filmmakers ultimately shape what ends up on-screen.

RISE UP: CONTEXTUALIZING THE RISE OF INDIGENOUS MEDIA IN CANADA

Broadly speaking, three major intersecting social and political factors form the context for the rise of Indigenous media in Canada: the Indigenous self-determination movement in the latter part of the twentieth century; the events surrounding Canada's celebrations of 1992, the 125th anniversary of the Confederation of the Dominion of Canada; and a succession of conflicts and standoffs between Indigenous communities and the Canadian state that happened across the country in the 1980s early 1990s.

Until the late 1960s, Indigenous-state relations in Canada were best characterized as assimilationist, with law and policy designed to result in the Indigenous legal and social termination as distinct peoples. Canada entered the 1960s on the currents of the civil rights era, electing Liberal Party leader Pierre Trudeau as prime minister, whose administration ushered in the rhetoric of the "just society," a platform for participatory democracy based on human rights and equality (McMillan and Yellowhorn 2009, 324). Trudeau's government implemented universal healthcare, promoted greater regional political representation, and formalized a federal policy of "multiculturalism" that sought to reconcile Canada's diverse and not always harmonious constituencies by officially recognizing cultural and social plurality. Seeking to dismantle what his administration perceived as mechanisms of social inequality, Trudeau in 1969 presented the "Statement of the Government of Canada on Indian Policy," or as it would become known more notoriously, "the White Paper," which initiated a turning point in Indigenous-state relations. The White Paper proposed abolishing the Indian Act and with it the distinct legal status of Indigenous peoples in Canada, arguing that the Indian Act was the source of socioeconomic barriers and impoverished conditions facing Indigenous peoples (Asch 1993). Dismantling this piece of legislation, Trudeau's government reasoned, would remove the key apparatus preventing Indigenous peoples from equal participation in Canadian society. These assumptions stemmed from the 1963 Report, "A Survey of the Contemporary Indians of Canada: Economic, Political, Educational Needs and Policies," or the "Hawthorn Report." The Hawthorn Report was commissioned by the federal government to investigate the social welfare of Indigenous peoples across Canada. The report concluded that Indigenous peoples were Canada's most disadvantaged group, and that the history of residential schools and government policy had failed to prepare Indigenous people to participate in Canadian society. Unlike the White Paper's rhetoric of social well-being, the Hawthorn Report framed its findings in more explicitly economic terms, identifying the conditions contributing to Indigenous "economic inferiority" that hindered their ability to participate in the Canadian economy (Hawthorn and Tremblay 1967, 24). When weighing social welfare expenditures for Indigenous peoples with Crown fiduciary obligations to Indigenous peoples guaranteed by the Indian Act, the federal treasury was spending C\$72 million annually on services for Indigenous peoples (or over C\$707 million in 2023 dollars). While the White Paper does not foreground these imperatives as a part of its logic, dismantling the Indian Act would not only bolster Canada's image as a participatory democracy, but it would also absolve the state of much of its financial responsibility for Indigenous peoples, serving state interests.

The White Paper was met with outrage from Indigenous groups across the country. Despite Indigenous people's participation in consultations as a part of the Hawthorn Report, the White Paper did not reflect their perspectives and therefore represented the state's interests rather than those of Indigenous peoples. Moreover, the Indian Act was the only piece of federal legislation that formally recognized Canada's unique relationship with and obligations to Indigenous peoples. Abolishing the Indian Act was seen as an extension of Canada's assimilation policies, as it would dismantle the main piece of federal legislation that acknowledged Indigenous peoples' unique status, rights, and historical relationship with Canada (Indigenous Foundations 2009). The resulting outrage and protests across Canada ultimately led to the White Paper's demise, but not before it had catalyzed a national Indigenous political movement dedicated to Indigenous sovereignty. The principles for sovereignty were expressed in the Indian Chiefs of Alberta's response to the White Paper, entitled "Citizen Plus" (1970), later popularly known as the "Red Paper." The Red Paper argued that the Indian Act should not be dismantled but rather amended to eliminate its paternalism by supporting principles of Indigenous self-government, the basis for an equitable relationship with Indigenous peoples (1970, 200). Here "self-government" is defined as the internal autonomy of Indigenous groups to govern their own affairs without interference from "outsiders,"[6] premised on community and federal resources guaranteed by provisions of the Indian Act. As a capstone measure, the Red Paper called for the legal entrenchment of Indigenous rights in the Canadian Constitution to further formalize acknowledgement of these rights as the basis for Indigenous self-government and guarantee that they could not be threatened by any legal maneuverings. The Red Paper was subsequently adopted as the national Indigenous position on the White Paper and provided a framework for Indigenous self-government that would guide the Indigenous political agenda in Canada for the following decades.

Political and legal scholars have characterized Indigenous peoples' negotiations with the Canadian state from the 1970s onward as attempts to enact "nation-to-nation" relationships between Indigenous groups and Canada, based on mutual recognition that Indigenous communities and their rights historically preceded Canadian statehood and are the basis for Indigenous nationhood and right to self-determination and equal footing in Canadian state activities and processes (Cardinal 1974; Cairns 2000; Russell 2011; Schouls 2005). As discussed by Ian Peach, the 1980s and early 1990s was a vital period of Indigenous political organization and demonstration: Indigenous groups demanded participation in constitutional amendment processes; Member of Legislative Assembly Elijah Harper (Oji-Cree) undertook a filibuster in 1990 that contributed to the defeat of the Meech Lake Accord; and, as will be discussed further below, the Mohawk people of Kanehsatake, Quebec, stood off against the Canadian military for 78 days in 1990 to protect their traditional territories from municipal development (2011). In 1991, the Royal Commission on Aboriginal Peoples was established to investigate the relationship between Indigenous peoples and the government of Canada, Indian and Northern Affairs Canada, and Canadian culture and society more broadly. The commission's final report explicitly identifies that Indigenous participation in "mainstream institutions" was crucial for providing Indigenous peoples with access to the resources and training necessary for building "Aboriginal institutions" (Dussault and Erasmus 1996), pointing to the development of a discourse describing Indigenous participation at the state level, which would be realized by state support for creating space for Indigenous participation in its institutional apparatuses.

If it seems either generous or disinguous that the Canadian state would seek to support Indigenous institutions and representation at a national level, which would ostensibly be critical of the state, this maneuvering can be understood as a form of governmentality, by which liberal democratic states "manage" populations that fall within its boundaries. Liberal democratic states seek domain not (primarily) through the top-down force of despotic regimes, but as Michel Foucault argues, through administration (2007). Foucault theorizes "governmentality" to examine the histories of state governance, explaining that it means three things: First, it is "the ensemble formed by institutions, procedures, analyses and reflections, calculations, and tactics that allow the exercise of this very specific, albeit very complex, power that has the population as its target." Second, it is "the tendency . . . for a long time, and throughout the West, [that] has constantly led towards the pre-eminence . . . of the type of power that we can call 'government' and which has led to the development of a series of specific governmental apparatuses." And third, that "we should understand the process, or rather, the result of the process by which the state . . . became the administrative state in the fifteenth and sixteenth centuries and was gradually 'governmentalized'" (2007, 108–9). Within the liberal democratic state, populations are "disciplined" or "managed" through the state's administrative apparatuses through which it sustains its authority. Governmentality is the rationale for the Canadian state's response to the Indigenous sovereignty movement in the latter part of the twentieth century. By recognizing Indigenous rights and representation within its legislative and policy structures, the state sought to incorporate Indigenous difference within its national identity and institutions, thereby stabilizing its authority and legitimacy.

The managerial dimensions of the state's efforts have not been lost on Indigenous peoples and political theorists. Glen Sean Coulthard (Yellowknives Dene) and Jodi Byrd (Chickasaw) offer trenchant and timely critiques of contemporary Indigenous-state relations, arguing that state recognition of Indigenous rights and the treaty process are a form of late colonialism. They argue that the treaty process converts Indigenous traditional political and economic structures—which are based in a relationship to territory—into Western governance and economic models: Indigenous territories become private property and are administered like municipalities, severing traditional relationships to the land and undermining the very principles through which Indigenous sovereignty exists (Coulthard 2014; Byrd 2011). These territorial relationships are the basis for Indigenous nationhood, distinguishing Indigenous peoples from other ethnic and social minorities. Byrd argues that the strategies by which the liberal multicultural state seeks restitution with Indigenous peoples actually "reinscribe the original colonial injury" by attaching the legitimacy of Indigenous nationhood to the colonial state in the form of "domestic dependent nationhood," despite the fact that Indigenous nations historically have held nation-to-nation treaties with European nations, as well as Canada and the United States (2011, xxii–xxiii). Addressing the U.S. context, Byrd asserts that Indigenous recognition actually requires that

> American Indian national assertions of sovereignty, self-determination, and land rights disappear into U.S. territoriality as indigenous identity becomes a racial identity and citizens of

colonized indigenous nations become internal ethnic minorities within the colonizing nation-state. (xxiv)

Such critiques identify the ways in which federal acknowledgement of Indigenous rights can bolster state authority by undermining the traditions and place-based relationships that distinguish Indigenous peoples from other designated ethnic groups. Byrd's analysis is not premised on Indigenous political or cultural balkanization as a condition of sovereignty, but rather argues that

> indigenous critical theory could be said to exist in its best form when it centers itself within indigenous epistemologies and the specificities of the communities and cultures from which it emerges and then looks outward to engage European philosophical, legal, and cultural traditions in order to build upon all the allied tools available. (xxx)

Byrd's framework for critical theory is invaluable for understanding the orientation of Indigenous engagement with the state during this period. Indigenous peoples draw on Western traditions and apparatuses in the process of working toward self-determination, an orientation contextualizing Indigenous intervention and participation in state-sponsored programs and services for cultural production that accelerated in Canada through the 1990s (Cardinal 1974).

As already mentioned, the late 1980s and early 1990s was also a period of massive Indigenous organizing, political demonstrations, and conflicts with the state. Despite the constitutional amendments of 1982 affirming Aboriginal and treaty rights, Indigenous-state relations through the 1980s declined as the state refused to take Indigenous rights seriously. Tensions reached a high-water mark with the armed confrontations of the Oka Crisis in 1990 in Kanehsatake, Quebec, and the Gustafsen Lake (Ts'Peten) standoff in 1995 near 100 Mile House in British Columbia (Cardinal 1974, viii).[7] Both conflicts stemmed from long-standing disputes about non-Indigenous settlers occupying Indigenous traditional territories, and were covered extensively by the media. The Oka Crisis in particular is often referred to as a historic turning point in Indigenous cultural politics, critical discourse, and cultural production in Canada. In the summer of 1990, a territorial dispute arose between the Mohawk people of Kanehsatake and the municipality of Oka, Quebec. The previous year, the mayor of Oka announced plans to extend a golf course and residential development into the ancestral territories of the Mohawk of Kanehsatake, which included a traditional burial ground. The conflict escalated into a 78-day standoff between protesters and the Canadian military that lasted from July 11 to September 26 and dominated the mainstream news media for the duration (Robertson and Anderson 2011, 222). Sophie McCall has described the conflict as a "double-edged event in Canadian history": it catalyzed Indigenous social movements and support for the Mohawk and across the country, yet "the representation of the 'Oka crisis' in the media reinforced Manichean stereotypes of violent Natives versus besieged settlers, while eliding the historical roots of the conflict" (2011, 77). The event spurred widespread debates about the politics of representation and the problem of the appropriation of the Indigenous "voice," a discourse referring to the practice of using and re-presenting elements of Indigenous cultures by dominant settler colonial society and producing knowledge about Indigenous peoples without their involvement or consent, which in effect "silenced" Indigenous peoples and covered over their perspectives (Robertson and Anderson 2011; Todd 1990). "Indigenous sovereignty," a longtime political discourse for Indigenous resistance and social activism, took hold with vigor in Indigenous critical and cultural production, guiding Indigenous cultural activism that has since clearly identified that Indigenous self-determination extends to self-representation, and that Indigenous stewardship in cultural production is an extension of Indigenous rights and title and a crucial precondition to redressing colonial dynamics of settler society shaping art worlds in Canada and North America.

The third social factor contributing to the surge of Indigenous media production in the 1990s was the outrage that met plans to celebrate the 125th anniversary of the Confederation of the Dominion of Canada of 1867, which also happened to fall in 1992, the 500-year anniversary of Christopher Columbus's so-called discovery of North America. During this heightened period of Indigenous-state tensions and greater international awareness of the devastating consequences of colonization, planned celebrations were roundly and widely critiqued by Indigenous people and other minoritized groups across the country, reminding the state and Canadian national public that the anniversary of the creation of a settler state is far from celebratory.

Historic exhibitions were designed to represent Indigenous perspectives and experiences of Canadian history, including *INDIGENA*, a major travelling exhibit consisting of paintings, photographs, video, sculpture, and mixed media work by Indigenous artists that opened at the Canadian Museum of Civilization in Hull, Quebec, in 1992 (McMaster and Martin 1992). *INDIGENA* was the product of Indigenous art-based interventions in the national cultural sphere and in many ways anticipates the energy and strategic institutional engagement undergirding Indigenous media production that emerged over subsequent decades in Canada.

INSTITUTIONAL ANALYSIS: A METHODOLOGY ANALYSIS OF INDIGENOUS MEDIA TEXTS

Through the case studies at the core of each chapter, I model the institutional analysis of Indigenous media, arguing that attention to the institutional dimensions of production is a crucial though underexplored lens for the interpretation of Indigenous screen content. My approach is informed by methods used in studies of production cultures. Production studies is a broad field of study but has in common the understanding that media industries engender production "cultures," that is, communities—composed of workers and institutions—with their own values and identities that are expressed, debated, and affirmed through their meaning-making activities and behaviors: pitch sessions, trade conferences, promotional materials, internal documents, meetings, and so on. Many researchers favor ethnographic methods for studying production cultures, particularly participant-observation and interviews and textual/discourse analysis of institutional materials in complement with industrial/economic analyses (Caldwell 2008, 4). However, not all ethnographic methods are possible when studying historical or contemporary phenomena and sites, which are the focus of the case studies making up this manuscript; consequently, I employ a combination of historical and ethnographic methods, triangulating between institutions, interviews with Indigenous media practitioners and institutional personnel (original and/or published, and where possible and available), and the media texts themselves. Analysis of institutions considers archival research, close reading of their public materials (websites, publicity materials, public reports), and interviews with personnel that ask them about their recollections and experiences of these institutions in order to develop understandings of their institutional discourses, organizational structures, and production practices. Interviews with Indigenous filmmakers, artists, and producers recount their recollections of these experiences, perspectives that often are not captured by institutional materials and records, and which expand on the social and cultural contexts and values infusing their work. Finally, textual analysis combines these registers with relevant theoretical and critical literature from Indigenous media, film, television, video, and digital media studies that elicit the conventions of these forms and technologies to deepen understandings of the representational strategies of the Indigenous media texts that are at the core of each chapter.

It perhaps goes without saying, but this book is not an institutional history of Indigenous media in Canada. As previously discussed, scholarly attention to institutional contexts for Indigenous production has largely focused on the NFB. This book, however, considers a wider field of institutions than have yet been considered in analysis of Indigenous media in order to begin tracing the much larger field involved in Indigenous media history: provincial television (the Saskatchewan Communication Network), the Banff Centre for the Arts (a major and defining arts center in Canada), the Aboriginal Peoples Television Network (Canada's national Indigenous broadcaster), and postsecondary institutions (the University of California, Los Angeles, and the University of British Columbia). This list is far from exhaustive, however, and there remain many more institutional locations that deserve scholarly attention (museums, galleries, art collectives, regional television). I hope that this book contributes to their visibility and the Indigenous artists working with them.

CHAPTER OUTLINES

Each chapter of this book is a case study that demonstrates the applications of institutional analysis to the media output of different figures, organizations, and institutions of the field of Indigenous media in Canada. While emphasizing areas that have had little academic scrutiny, specifically provincial television and academic research institutions, I also examine production emerging from more widely known institutions of media culture, including APTN; though the broadcaster has been a research focus, there has been less attention to Indigenous television programming that it airs. Each chapter therefore places "text in context," a well-established vein of cinema and media studies, but adds institutionality to the cultural context of Indigenous media texts.

Chapter 1, "Prairie Voices: Doug Cuthand, Provincial Television and the National Film Board of Canada" examines the work of Doug Cuthand, a Cree journalist, television producer, and documentary filmmaker who has had a long career that includes over a dozen film and television projects that have yet to receive scholarly attention. This chapter undertakes an author-centered approach in order to make visible underexamined areas of Indigenous cultural production that have contributed to the development of Indigenous media, specifically provincial television and Indigenous news journalism—areas that, as Cuthand's oeuvre demonstrates, intersect with the expansion of Indigenous film and video. While resisting the pull of an exclusively auteurist reading of Cuthand's work and career, this chapter nonetheless proceeds by centering Cuthand's work in order to identify that Indigenous media practitioners tend to, like Cuthand, work across media areas and institutions as a matter of course. Consequently, understanding of their textual strategies and interventions can be enhanced by institutional analysis of specific productions, rather than solely through personal stylistics and cultural aesthetics. This chapter undertakes two case studies to demonstrate this principle, examining one of his educational television productions: *Stay in School* (1995), made for a provincial educational broadcaster, the Saskatchewan Communication Network (provincial broadcasting itself an underexamined area of Indigenous production), and *Donna's Story* (2001), a portrait documentary made with the NFB. Doing so does not simply track stylistic variation between the institutions through which his work was produced but examines the ideological and discursive negotiations he enacts in these productions that cannot be accounted for solely in terms of aesthetics.

Chapter 2, "The Aboriginal Film and Video Art Alliance: Negotiating Indigenous Self-Government in the Arts," is driven by a similar recuperative drive as chapter 1, and examines the history and media politics of the Aboriginal Film and Video Art Alliance (AFVAA), an Indigenous art-based media organization founded in 1991 that emerged in the political ferment of the Indigenous sovereignty movement of the era, designed to explore Indigenous "self-government" in art and media practice. Though Indigenous filmmakers, artists, and organizational personnel frequently identify that the AFVAA played a major role in the history and politics of Indigenous media in Canada, very little scholarship has explored this organization, its values and activities, and its influence on the Indigenous media world. This chapter examines the AFVAA's institutional partnership with the Banff Centre for the Arts, a long-established and world-renowned educational arts institution in Canada. This partnership lasted from 1993 to 1996, during which the AFVAA pursued a model of Indigenous self-government that was intended to be realized through autonomous Indigenous administration and program development at Banff, a model of governance shaped by the prevailing framework for Indigenous self-government that Indigenous advocates lobbied for as a part of the Indigenous social activism of the period. While at the Banff Centre, the AFVAA hosted a nine-week retreat in 1994 that brought together Indigenous artists for training to develop a series of public service announcements (PSAs) on the topic of "self-government" titled *SELF-GOVERNMENT: Talk About It . . . ,* which resulted in seven PSAs that are the case studies for the chapter. The AFVAA operated in a deliberately "experimental" mode as a parallel to debates about the meaning of "self-government" at the time. The eclectic collection of video-based PSAs addresses itself to an Indigenous "public sphere," encouraging Indigenous people to consider and debate what self-government means to them. This chapter argues that AFVAA modeled a form of Indigenous media production that married politics and ideology to form: because Indigenous self-government during this era was being debated and tested in the national sphere, the AFVAA encouraged experimentalism in the development and production of the PSAs.

Chapter 3, "Programming Indigeneity: Indigenous Television Production in the Era of Aboriginal Peoples Television Network," traces the influence of the Aboriginal Peoples Television Network (APTN), Canada's national Indigenous broadcaster, in the field of independent Indigenous television production that has grown since its launch in 1999. With a twenty-four-hour programming schedule to fill, APTN has stimulated the growth of television production that has become, over the past two decades, extraordinarily wide and diverse. In the nonfiction realm, there are hundreds of hours of documentary, public affairs, historical, and reality television series, yet very little of this material is produced in-house; rather, APTN relies on a field of independent television producers for their content, commissioning work from these companies to fill their schedule. Consequently, as this chapter argues, institutional analysis of APTN programming must take into account not only APTN's institutional mandate and programming practices but also the identities, values, and practices of the independent production companies.

Following its launch, nonfiction programming has proliferated, though shifts in programming genres—from documentary and public affairs–style anthologies and series in the early 2000s to more reality-based programming in the later 2010s—are symptomatic of APTN's programming priorities and their effects on independent Indigenous television production. This chapter examines the political, legal, and cultural discourses arising around Indigenous broadcasting during the 1990s that gave rise to APTN's institutional identity as a "cultural bridge" between Indigenous peoples and the rest of Canada, and how independent production responds to this identity in their production strategies. To do so, this chapter examines the shift toward reality television genres that began to populate the APTN schedule in the mid- to late 2000s by focusing on one of these series, *Indians + Aliens* (2013) by Rezolution Pictures. *Indians + Aliens* focuses on unexplained aerial phenomena in the Inuit and Northern Cree communities in Quebec, using the paranormal investigation reality genre. The series places Western scientific interpretations of these phenomena alongside Indigenous interpretations of events, a comparison that enacts a "cultural bridge" along at least two axes: it places Indigenous and Western belief systems on the same field to give them potentially equal epistemological weight, and it shares Indigenous knowledge, histories, and experiences with other Indigenous and non-Indigenous audiences that might otherwise not encounter these communities.

Chapter 4, "Indigenous Documentaries and Academic Research Institutions: *Navajo Talking Picture* and *Cry Rock*," identifies postsecondary and professional training programs as critical but underexamined institutional grounds for Indigenous production. Indigenous filmmakers frequently attend colleges, universities, and postsecondary training programs, undertaking creative work resulting in media-based projects; or their training experiences later inform their media-based projects. In these programs, Indigenous students receive production training and are immersed in the critical and theoretical scholarship that influences their filmmaking decisions and perspectives. This chapter brings together two thematically similar documentaries, *Navajo*

Talking Picture (1984), by Arlene Bowman (Diné) at the University of California, Los Angeles, and *Cry Rock* (2010) by Banchi Hanuse (Nuxalk), developed while a student at the University of British Columbia. Both films deal with issues of generational ruptures in culture and language transmission, and while thematic analyses are well established in Indigenous media studies, this chapter compares these two films in order to examine the very different documentary approaches each filmmaker employs that lead to dramatically different outcomes for each film as a result of taking up prevailing academic methods for Indigenous research at their respective postsecondary institutions. In *Navajo Talking Picture*, Bowman attempts to incite a conflict with her reticent grandmother to produce a "crisis structure" in her film, an established documentary practice in film production at UCLA intended to provoke revelation and understanding between her grandmother and herself. Hanuse, on the other hand, was immersed in curriculum on Indigenous research methods and the ethical implications of filmmaking that characterize contemporary Indigenous studies. *Cry Rock* rhetorically reflects on her reluctance to record her grandmother speaking the Nuxalk language despite its endangered status. The film examines what it means to record Indigenous languages, and what is lost—socially, culturally, and spiritually—when languages and oral narratives are recorded. The film intervenes in popular assumptions that the cinematic apparatus and Indigenous oral traditions can function the same way, and ultimately argues that Indigenous languages are deeply enmeshed in community, territory, and social relations, which filmmaking cannot replicate.

Chapter 5, "Resisting Colonial Relations in Virtual Reality: *Highway of Tears*," demonstrates that institutional analysis holds true for the digital, but requires relevant theoretical literature on specific digital media to unpack the cultural interventions of this work, as demonstrated in analysis of *Highway of Tears* (2016), a four-minute, immersive, 360-degree film produced by Canadian Broadcasting Corporation Radio's current affairs program *The Current* and directed by Anishinaabe filmmaker Lisa Jackson. Though this is the CBC's first VR project, VR development has been made an industry priority in Canada since 2013. The Indigenous media industry has been responsive, leading to a small but significant body of Indigenous VR projects over the past few years. "Highway of Tears" refers to Highway 16, the 724-kilometer stretch between Prince Rupert and Prince George in British Columbia where dozens of Indigenous women have gone missing over at least the past five decades. *Highway of Tears* intercuts images of Highway 16, where dozens of Indigenous women have disappeared and been murdered, with an interview with Matilda Wilson (Gitxsan), the mother of Ramona Wilson, one of the murdered women. Wilson shares her story of grief and loss. The film immerses the viewer in the physical geography that has come to define Canada's failure to address violence against Indigenous women, while also "seating" the viewer in Matilda Wilson's living room to listen to her story. Virtual reality's discourse as a medium encouraging empathy and intimacy frames the project owing to immersive journalism, which has enthusiastically promoted this discourse, yet Jackson's direction deflects and challenges this discourse owing to the anthropological (i.e., colonial) associations of "transparency" and "access" to Indigenous lives and experiences that it invokes. Instead of providing the viewer with the spectacle of Indigenous trauma, she compels the viewer into the position of witness, with the accompanying responsibility and accountability that such a position involves. The issue of murdered and missing Indigenous women is framed as a national issue, not an Indigenous one, and the viewer is guided to affectively acknowledge it as such.

Institutional analysis is relevant across media formats and time periods. While institutions are a major dimension of Indigenous production, their priorities, discourses, and practices do not dictate the meanings and directions of Indigenous media practitioners. Rather, once we understand these contexts, we can further appreciate the critical sophistication and complexity of Indigenous screen strategies. Moreover, institutions of media culture are far from static entities: they shift and change over time with the vagaries of public funding, state priorities, policy developments, and media industry trends. Consequently, any institutional profile would need to be revisited and revised depending on the media text under analysis. Nonetheless, the model of institutional analysis proposed here is meant to provide a template or point of departure for researchers undertaking similar research in the spirit of shining a light on areas of Indigenous media history that have yet to have a spotlight.

1

Prairie Voices

Doug Cuthand (Cree, Little Pine First Nation), is one of the most prolific Indigenous filmmakers and independent television producers in Canada. A journalist by training, Cuthand has had an over forty-year career in both Indigenous and non-Indigenous news media, starting in the 1970s with his work with the Alberta Native Communications Society in Edmonton, where he became editor of the Indigenous news magazine *Native People,* and later *Saskatchewan Magazine,* a publication associated with the Federation of Saskatchewan Indian Nations (now the Federation of Sovereign Indigenous Nations). He has written columns for provincial and regional newspapers that include the *Regina Leader-Post,* the *Saskatoon Star Phoenix,* and the *Winnipeg Free Press* (Cuthand 2005, iii), and has published two books: *Tapwe: Selected Columns of Doug Cuthand* (2005), and *Askiwina: A Cree World* (2007). Over the same period, Cuthand has directed or produced over a dozen documentary films, videos, and television series in addition to narrative short videos, a television miniseries, and an animated series; a body of work comprising over twenty unique productions. Many of these were created through his own production company, Blue Hill Productions, and were also produced in association with institutions that include the National Film Board (NFB), Saskatchewan Communications Network, Vision TV, and Aboriginal Peoples Television Network (APTN). Despite a long and distinguished career, Cuthand has yet to receive close critical or scholarly examination for his media work, a gap that this chapter seeks to redress through analysis of a selection of his film and video productions.

The range and scope of Cuthand's media output reflects the production patterns of many Indigenous media practitioners, who work with different media formats and cultural institutions in order to pursue available media-making opportunities that shift and change as a consequence of the vagaries of public and other funding and other resources for Indigenous artists, circumstances that undergird Indigenous media production historically and contemporaneously. Beginning in the 1970s, policy and legislation took shape with the goal of increasing Indigenous representation in the national cultural sphere by allocating resources and developing programs for Indigenous people in film, video, and communications media. Over the next few decades, these measures engendered a kind of institutional scaffolding across the country that would support the proliferation of Indigenous media nationwide. In the postwar era, Canadian state policy and legislation addressed themselves to a fragmented public sphere under pressure for recognition from social groups, particularly women, immigrants, minorities, and Indigenous groups in the context of then prime minister Pierre Elliot Trudeau's "participatory democracy," a Liberal Party slogan referring to a populist political ideal in which individuals could take part in national politics and effect social change (Litt 2016, 250). In her analysis of the era's communications media and policy, Marian Bredin observes that this ideal was meant to be realized through "community development," which involved the creation of programs and services designed to increase the representation of disenfranchised groups in the national cultural sphere (Bredin 1995, 127). During this era, for instance, the National Film Board of Canada developed *Challenge for Change*, a social activist documentary program that ran from 1967 to 1980 and was conceptualized as a way to bring together "government bureaucrats, documentary filmmakers, community activists, and 'ordinary' citizens" to create documentaries that would not only represent social issues but also support social change (Waugh, Winton, and Baker 2010, 4). State efforts to respond to and manage this variegated social sphere intersected with the patriation of the Canadian Constitution in 1982, an era during which Canada embarked on a process of reimagining its national identity, which took shape in terms of diversity, and culminated in the Multiculturalism Act, 1988, which formally enshrined multiculturalism as Canadian law.

National cultural policy in this era was designed in order to keep pace and boost participation of disenfranchised social groups in Canada, which included Indigenous peoples. Through the 1980s and 1990s, owing in large part to the advocacy efforts of Indigenous artists and activists, state cultural institutions developed programs and established funding envelopes[1] designed to support Indigenous representation; for instance, in 1991, the National Film Board of Canada founded Studio One, the Indigenous studio based in their Edmonton offices; Telefilm Canada created a special funding envelope for Indigenous filmmakers; and the Canada Council for the Arts, Canada's crown corporation for arts funding, established the Aboriginal Arts Office in 1996. While Indigenous cultural politics and national policy cut across cultural institutions and art forms, their applications are far from uniform. The purpose of identifying these common threads is not to identify and extract a unifying cultural politics across institutional contexts of media production, but rather to identify that any discussion of cultural politics must recognize that politics, law, and policy take on meaning as they are interpreted in the context of production, in which institutions of media culture play a pivotal role, particularly in the history of Indigenous media in Canada.

While Cuthand's body of work is wide ranging, his productions are linked by his representational ethic, in which he seeks to adapt filmmaking techniques to better represent Indigenous perspectives, values, and experiences. This claim could be seen as reproducing the analytical approaches seeking evidence of a culturally based aesthetic in Indigenous media, but his various institutional affiliations provide opportunities to read his media ethics and stylistic choices in relation to the conventions of the media formats and institutions through which they were created. To do so, this chapter undertakes two case studies: *Stay in School* (1995), an educational program produced in association with the Saskatchewan Communications Network, which the provincial public broadcaster mandated to support educational programming; and *Donna's Story* (2001), a National Film Board of Canada documentary film focusing on Donna Gamble, a Cree woman working to overcome addiction issues and the colonial legacies that have engendered them. Across media institutions, Cuthand brings a focus on and orientation to Indigenous issues and politics in prairie regions, adapting the codes and conventions of institutional production conventions to integrate documentary ethics he developed through a career that bridges news media, documentary film, and television production. Looking at his documentary work across media institutions makes visible his stylistic consistencies as well as the ideological and discursive negotiations he undertakes that cannot be accounted for in terms of cultural aesthetics alone.

INDIGENOUS NEWS AND COMMUNICATIONS MEDIA

Cuthand's early productions, such as *Healing the Family: The Male Partner* (1994), *Teaching Tolerance* (1994), and *Stay in School* (1995), bridge Indigenous communications media and the history of regional and provincial television by virtue of Cuthand's professional development in both areas. While earning his BA in sociology at Simon Fraser University in British Columbia, Cuthand wrote for *The Peak*, the university's student newspaper (Cuthand 2015). After graduation, he joined the newly launched Alberta Native Communications Society (ANCS) based in Edmonton, and was hired as the editor for *Native People*, its first newspaper. Joel Demay argues that the ANCS emerged from a longer history of Indigenous newspapers that began in Western Canada in the 1960s, and would be a model for Indigenous communications in Canada more broadly (1991, 97–98). ANCS was the result of the pioneering work of Eugene Steinhauer, a Cree entrepreneur and broadcaster, and with financial support from the Canadian Broadcasting Corporation would grow into the largest and most recognized Indigenous communications society in Canada, exploring community radio and news media (Rupert 1983, 53).

While Indigenous newspapers have had a long life in Canada— beginning in the early part of the twentieth century—Indigenous news media surged in the 1970s with lobbying from Indigenous communications societies for increased funds to support their services (Avison 1996, 133). The federal government's support for Indigenous print and radio has two major motivations: the release of the Hawthorn Report of 1963, and attempts to mitigate the backlash from Indigenous groups in response to the "Statement of the Government of Canada on Indian Policy, 1969," better known as "the White Paper," as discussed in the introduction to this book. The White Paper diagnosed the Indian Act as an impediment to Indigenous peoples' ability to participate "equally" in society, and since it was a piece of legislation only applying to Indigenous peoples, the Indian Act was understood to be discriminatory and out of step with the vision of society touted by Trudeau's administration. The White Paper, developed by Minister of Indian Affairs Jean Chrétien, proposed the wholesale repeal of the Indian Act, among other measures (Indigenous Foundations 2009). Not only did the document ignore Indigenous perspectives that were shared during the consultation process, but its rhetoric and proposals were fundamentally assimilationist in their design and implications. The Indian Act was the only piece of federal legislation that formally recognized Canada's unique relationship with and obligations to Indigenous peoples. In the absence of alternatives that would hold the Canadian state to its responsibilities, the White Paper was roundly condemned.

As a result of the outcry, the state backtracked on the policy paper and modified its approach, addressing Indigenous groups in terms of historical and cultural "difference," which resulted in the development of programs and services for Indigenous communities designed to support economic and social parity with the rest of Canada. These federal resources enabled the growth and expansion of Indigenous communications media. Lobbying from Native communications societies in British Columbia, Alberta, and the Northwest Territories led to the Native Communications Program (NCP), which was founded in 1973 to encourage use of communications media among Indigenous people and "to assist native people in defining and participating in the social, political and economic issues affecting their lives in Canada" (Department of the Secretary of State quoted in Avison 1996, 133). The NCP was administered by the Native Citizens' Directorate, a part of the Department of the Secretary of State, which was mandated to ensure that all Canadians have equal opportunity to participate in Canadian society (Avison 1996). If it seems contradictory that the Canadian federal government would fund communications media that would undoubtedly be critical of the state, it can be understood as an exercise of state "governmentality" that seeks to manage social and ideological disruption by appearing to accommodate it, thereby reinforcing the state's authority and validity.

More often than not, federally supported initiatives suffer due to fluctuations in federal funding, as has been the case with Indigenous newspapers. The fifteen southern Indigenous newspapers suffered a serious blow when federal funding for the NCP was cut in 1990; while federal funding has always been based on the vagaries of the federal budget, this funding cut forced some of these newspapers to close, others to convert to a form of "entrepreneurial" self-sufficiency funded by advertising, and yet others to attach to Indigenous political organizations (Demay 1991). The *Saskatchewan Indian,* for which Cuthand was editor since the 1970s, was shuttered for several months before finding support through the Federation of Saskatchewan Indian

Nations (Demay 1991, 103). Thus, while the late 1980s and early 1990s saw significant developments in federal support and resources for Indigenous cultural production, it was a time of instability for Indigenous communications. Nonetheless, Indigenous news and communications media expanded significantly during these decades, helping to foster Cuthand's prolific news and editorial output, and the development of his perspective or "voice" that he has brought to his media production.

THE INDIGENOUS PUBLIC SPHERE: DISCURSIVE STRATEGIES IN INDIGENOUS COMMUNICATIONS

The growth of Indigenous journalism and news media expanded platforms for articulating Indigenous political and social concerns that were addressed to Indigenous and non-Indigenous "publics," employing discursive strategies designed to validate Indigenous perspectives, strategies very much in evidence in Cuthand's print and media work. Shannon Avison argues that the "Indigenous public sphere" should not be considered as a nondominant parallel to that of mainstream Canada; rather, following Nancy Fraser's argument that there are multiple public spheres, she defines the Indigenous public sphere as

> both concrete sites like newspapers and processes of public
> opinion formation at the regional and national levels, as providing
> opportunities for people who are regularly subordinated and ig-
> nored in the mainstream public sphere. It allows them to deliber-
> ate together, develop their own counter discourses and interpret
> their own identities and experiences. (1996, 58)

Avison's definition compliments Michael Warner's concept of "counter-publics," which is useful for understanding Indigenous media and its discursive strategies during this period. Counterpublics produce themselves in conflict with the dominant group and the cultural norms that constitute them "because they differ markedly in one way or another from the premises that allow the dominant culture to understand itself as a public" (2002, 112–13). Counterpublics remain "publics" in the sense that they "work by many of the same circular postulates" (113); that is, a counterpublic does not exist prior to discourse, but is produced by the very discourse that it addresses, creating what Warner describes as a "chicken-and-egg circularity" (67). Nonetheless, the terms by which counterpublics operate help to characterize the nationalist political discourse used to articulate Indigenous sovereignty, employing the terms of the nation-state to assert Indigenous a priori nationalism that is politically and culturally distinct from that of settler Canadian society.

The Indigenous public sphere is not confined to Indigenously controlled forms of communication (that is, those organizations governed or directed by Indigenous people). Avison explains that Indigenous public spheres

> are also constituted in some measure through the mainstream media. At the national level, the public sphere is a range of phenomena substantive in every discursive interaction in face-to-face situations and representation in the mass media, where the topics of discussion are of concern to Aboriginal people, and especially their relationship to the Canadian state. (1996, 58)

This "site" is not an information silo for Indigenous peoples alone; rather, the Indigenous public sphere "engages in inter-public interaction in which the cultural values, political aspirations and social concerns of its participants are introduced into the larger public spheres where they can have an influence on the discussions that take place there" (60). Indigenous public spheres interact with other public spheres while in tension with dominant ones. The counterpublic stance of the Indigenous public sphere can therefore find its expression within sites of dominant public spheres, which provides a framework for analysis of the politics and rhetorical strategies of Cuthand's articles and editorials in provincial newspapers.

Beginning in the 1970s, Cuthand wrote for the *Saskatchewan Indian,* and in the 1990s was published frequently in regional and provincial newspapers, most often in the Saskatchewan *Star Phoenix* where he had a regular column and the Regina *Leader-Post,* as well as in the *Toronto Star* and the *Vancouver Province.* His editorials and articles that were published in Indigenous newspapers employ what Steffi Retzlaff has described as a "Native discourse," which "refers to a distinct discursive practice, i.e., a distinct way of speaking and writing and thus thinking employed and circulated by First Nations in Canada" (2006, 27). Retzlaff notes that this discourse should not imply a monolithic Indigenous identity, but rather that a shared experience of colonial history has engendered a "collective memory which is reflected in the discursive practice of Aboriginal people today" (27). Among these different discourse strategies, Retzlaff identifies the use of words and phrases from a "semantic field" that exert a "cohesive force within texts" (29). Cuthand's articles published in the *Saskatchewan Indian* employ lexical strategies that produce such cohesiveness between himself and a projected Indigenous public, employing "our" and "we" in an editorial discussing treaty rights and Indigenous governance (1982, 46), and using personal anecdotes to make broader political observations and arguments (1999, 1997). Cuthand also, however, uses these same semantic strategies, such as "our" and "we," in his articles written for and published in mainstream regional and provincial newspapers, embedding the Indigenous public sphere within dominant ones. Cuthand explains his rationale for his shift to writing for mainstream newspapers:

> So I can reach a large audience of both First Nations people and non-First Nations people, simply because so many people are reading the newspaper now. I've always had the belief that information is power and you should share it with as many people as you can, so they can make some of the right decisions, because right now people in Saskatchewan have to do some serious thinking about Aboriginal issues and address them. (Cuthand quoted in Foster 2008, 36)

By anticipating Indigenous and non-Indigenous audiences, Cuthand's use of "we" and "our" in mainstream newspapers enacts the Indigenous public sphere within a dominant public. The personal pronoun and possessive determiner interpellate an Indigenous public and index the Indigenous public for non-Indigenous readers. These lexical strategies link Cuthand directly with the Indigenous public; he has been described as "an important voice for the Aboriginal community" (Orthner 2009), which semantically links him to an Indigenous public and body politic.

While the Indigenous public sphere can employ the communicative styles of the dominant sphere, Avison argues, "its raison d'être are understood to be [Indigenous] cultural preservation, self-determination and integration with the wider society" (1996, 59).

"Integration" is a fraught term given its assimilationist implications; however, Avison here brings attention to the cultural politics of the Indigenous public sphere through which difference is expressed. Cuthand's writing speaks to these cultural politics in the terms recognizable to the dominant public, a strategy that carries over to his film and television production. In an editorial published in the *Toronto Star* in 1999 titled "Remembering Dief the Man from Prince Albert," for instance, Cuthand commemorates John Diefenbaker, the thirteenth prime minister of Canada, on the twentieth anniversary of his death, as a means to raise questions about his socially progressive legacy for Indigenous peoples. Diefenbaker, a leader of the Progressive Conservative Party, is popularly known in Canada for his social reforms that included granting First Nations and Inuit people the right to vote in 1960. Cuthand's reflections on well-known aspects of Diefenbaker's persona—his magnanimity, friendly relations with Indigenous people and immigrants, skills in debate and oratory—create a discursive "common ground" for an Indigenous and non-Indigenous readership, as these are generally "agreed-upon" characteristics of the former PM. Doing so allows Cuthand to develop an "Indigenous perspective" on Diefenbaker and his legacy by relating an anecdote in which he and other members of the Federation of Saskatchewan Indians visited him as a part of their lobby work:

> We headed into his spacious office. He greeted us and we proceeded to make our pitch to him. To this day, I can't remember what it was because he didn't have the slightest interest. He took over the meeting and gave us a tour of his office. The tour included a small closet which, Dief said, Mackenzie King used for meditation and séances. (Cuthand 1999, para. 10)

Cuthand's recollections are a departure from popular perceptions of Diefenbaker, suggesting that his gregariousness toward Indigenous peoples was perhaps more a performance of office than a closely held personal commitment. Mention of Mackenzie King, the tenth prime minister of Canada, is telling, as King had long been a Spiritualist during much of his time as prime minister, which was unknown to the Canadian public and "caused Canadians to question the purpose of this activity, the extent of it, and its effect on King's public policy"

(Government of Canada 2002). By referencing King's somewhat unconventional spiritual practices, and their possible impact on his decision-making while in office, Cuthand raises doubts, even skepticism, about Diefenbaker's administration. Relating that Diefenbaker had been made an honorary chief of the Blood nation in southern Alberta, Cuthand states:

> And after he was inducted into the Kainai chieftainship, he stood up and announced that, as long as he was prime minister, our treaty rights would be recognized. I don't know if he meant it, or if he knew what treaty rights were, but it was a memorable declaration which struck a chord with Indian people that day. (1999, para. 16)

Cuthand here describes to Diefenbaker's somewhat "ceremonial" role for Indigenous peoples in Canada: he was perhaps an inspirational and meaningful political figurehead, but one who was not necessarily equipped to represent Indigenous interests. Cuthand provides an "Indigenous perspective" on Diefenbaker that is diplomatic, but gives the former prime minister a dimensionality that overturns mainstream tendencies to venerate, even glorify, former heads of state. Cuthand produces a discursive common ground by commemorating a historical national leader, shaping commemoration with his perspective and lived experience, which allows him to bracket the authority of Canadian state leadership and the extent to which it is prepared to meaningfully engage with Indigenous concerns, instead offering critical perspectives of the Canadian state from an Indigenous standpoint. Cuthand's news and editorial publications demonstrate his strategy of creating discursive common ground in order to present and validate Indigenous perspectives, a practice that he extends into his film and television production.

THE CANADIAN DOCUMENTARY TRADITION ACROSS FILM AND TELEVISION

Cuthand's work in provincial educational television and at the NFB reflect documentary opportunities available to Indigenous producers at the time he produced them, and are enmeshed with documentary traditions in Canada: the pervasiveness of documentary forms across media formats affirms the documentary as a defining modality of Canadian national film and television production. Like law and policy, cultural forms can and do have traditions within geopolitical contexts and cut across media—producing institutions, as is the case in Canada with the documentary mode. Cuthand situates his nonfiction work within this tradition, noting that "the documentary is a Canadian invention . . . it's been a standard in the film, television industry here" (Cuthand 2015). The documentary form was institutionalized in Canada in large part owing to Scottish documentary filmmaker John Grierson, Canada's first film commissioner and a major architect of the NFB (Gittings 2002, 76–102). Documentary genres have expanded significantly across formats, genres, and sites of production, crossing film, television, video, and digital media. In *Documentary Television in Canada: From National Public Service to Global Marketplace*, for instance, David Hogarth traces the history of documentary public television in Canada from the 1950s, examining how its public service mandate was realized via its aesthetic of social realism which sought to "faithfully and creatively [represent] Canadians and the real conditions in which they live, while formally empowering them by engaging the civic and aesthetic skills they need to participate in cultural affairs" (2002, 6). By situating his work within the spectrum of documentary media in Canada, Cuthand also implicitly positions his representational politics and strategies within the conventions of institutionally situated documentary forms.

Canada's "documentary culture" has played a key role in debates around provincial and national sovereignties: the provinces vis-à-vis the nation, and Canada vis-à-vis the United States. The proximity of the United States to Canada, and the pervasiveness of Hollywood film and television on Canadian screens, has long been perceived as a threat to a Canadian national culture; in relation to Canadian movie theatres, Charles Acland states that "the U.S. economic command over Canadian movie theatres circulates as a symptom of the overall 'americanization' of Canadian culture" (2003, 168). Though Canada's regulatory agency for broadcast and telecommunications, the Canadian Radio-Television and Telecommunications Commission (CRTC), places Canadian content requirements on cable companies, Canadian television producers are unable to compete with American counterparts, who have greater resources available; in addition, Canadian television screens are dominated by American content owing to the inroads that subscription-based television (i.e., cable television) made in the 1980s. As Marc Raboy explains, pay television gained traction through the debates in the 1970s and 1980s concerning the role of public broadcasting in Canada. The cable industry played a major role in these debates, lobbying for the introduction of pay television following the U.S. model, while its supporters pointed to the potential revenues generated by subscription service, all the while couching their arguments in nationalist rhetoric that pay television could represent all public interests—broadcasters, cable operators, producers, and the public (1990, 272–279). Their position was that "commercial success was the path to achieving what fifty years of public and private broadcasting had failed" (275), arguing that privatization and commercialization could be used to achieve national goals. This rhetoric was intended to position pay television within Canadian national broadcasting policies, and provide it with the rationale to support the private sector. This argument was ultimately successful when pay television went on air on February 1, 1983, and was "another boon to the American export market" that made Canadian subscription television an extension of the American distribution system into Canada (276–277).

Canadian content requirements have taken shape in part in relation to the pervasiveness of American programming: it was to be what American commercial entertainment programming was not, codifying national film and media traditions in which documentary played a central role, while reflecting the realities of funding limitations for Canadian production. As Cuthand states: "Documentary is quite popular in Canada because it's low-cost television compared to [fiction], and that sort of thing. It's quite a bit cheaper to produce, and we have a very small market up here" (2015). Documentary is therefore an appealing format, both ideologically and economically. Canada's "documentary culture" has taken shape in response to geopolitical relations (in particular to the United States), television technologies and infrastructure, and the economics of Canadian screens, but was articulated in the terms of Canadian nationalist discourses, illustrating the imbrication of economics, politics, and culture in Canadian television that shaped the documentary opportunities available to Indigenous and non-Indigenous media practitioners.

EDUCATIONAL PROVINCIAL TELEVISION: THE SASKATCHEWAN COMMUNICATIONS NETWORK

Cuthand's early television productions were created for Saskatchewan's public broadcaster, the Saskatchewan Communications Network (SCN), which itself emerged from an educational provincial broadcasting model that developed in the 1970s onward. Given the specificities of provincial educational broadcasting policy, funding structures, and modes of address, some historical and industrial detail is needed to contextualize Cuthand's work, while attention to his television work for SCN illuminates an area of television production that was available to Indigenous producers in southern Canada prior to the founding of the national Aboriginal Peoples Television Network in 1999.

Provincial broadcasting emerged in what Marc Raboy has characterized as "a period of intense transformation in the social context of broadcasting in Canada" (1990, 226). With the fragmentation of a unified national identity flowing from the ideology of a "participatory democracy," a centralized state fell out of favor ideologically; furthermore, other provinces echoed Québec's assertions of sovereignty, seeking their own "state" authority at the provincial level (226–228). In this context, provinces gained jurisdiction over public broadcasting in the form of educational broadcasting. Dorothy Zolf (1986) traces the roots of provincial broadcasting's educational mandate to the Canadian Constitution Act, 1867, which granted provinces exclusive jurisdiction over education. Through the 1960s and 1970s, provinces increasingly sought control over broadcasting, which would culminate in the federal "Direction" issued by the CRTC in 1973 which gave the provinces control over programming on educational television stations (Zolf 1986, 22). Since what constitutes "educational programming" has been a matter of debate and interpretation, the Direction included the following definition:

(a) programming designed to be presented in such a context as to provide a continuity of learning opportunity aimed at the acquisition or improvement of knowledge or at the enlargement of understanding of members of the audience to whom such programming is directed and under such circumstances such that the acquisition or improvement of such knowledge or the

> enlargement of such understanding is subject to supervision or assessment by a provincial authority by any appropriate means; and
>
> (b) programming providing information on the available courses of instruction or including the broadcasting of special education events within the educational system, which programming, taken as a whole, shall be designed to furnish educational opportunities, and shall be distinctly different from general broadcasting available on the national broadcasting service or on privately owned broadcasting undertakings. (quoted in Zolf 1986, 33–4)

From the 1970s to the early 1980s, Quebec, Ontario, Alberta, and British Columbia established provincial broadcasters, with Saskatchewan eventually founding its own broadcaster, the SCN, in 1991.

The SCN was established under Saskatchewan's Communications Network Corporation Act, 1990–1991, as the designated provincial authority for the act. As a provincial broadcaster, SCN's educational mandate is bound up in the province's efforts to link a geographically dispersed population via its telecommunications infrastructure while also supporting independent production, as identified in its 2006–2007 Annual Report:

> SCN's public broadcast network creates opportunities for independent filmmakers to share Saskatchewan stories and culture. SCN's broadcast signal reaches 90% of Saskatchewan households, and satellite subscribers across Canada. (Saskatchewan Communications Network 2007, 8)

Whether or not the broadcaster has been able to realize the kind of infrastructural integration claimed here, SCN nonetheless grafts its educational mission to its broadcasting system and the field of independent film and television. This framework guides its criteria for regional programs that it selects for broadcast, which it defines as the following:

> Mandate: Programs must meet the SCN mandate of delivering cultural educational TV while supporting the work of independent producers.

Public Priorities: Programs are also chosen to meet public priorities, like literacy, substance abuse, and energy and environmental issues. (SCN 2007, 9)

Cuthand explains that SCN commissioned low-budget documentaries (by his estimate, approximately C$20,000 per documentary) that would air on the educational channel, or be held in libraries. This form of television production is indicative of broader trends in Canadian television, in which television is dominated by American programming, with Canadian content—in the form of educational and documentary programming—primarily reserved for public and regional broadcasters.

EDUCATIONAL PROGRAMMING AND INDIGENOUS POLITICS: *STAY IN SCHOOL* (1995)

The historical and ideological dynamics of public television intersect with Indigenous political platforms in Cuthand's early production for SCN, which this chapter examines in relation to his thirty-minute documentary, *Stay in School* (1995). This program brings together the pedagogical design and intent of educational programming with Indigenous educational advocacy, in which Cuthand participated as a politician and journalist. *Stay in School* examines secondary schools and school programs administered by Indigenous staff and communities in Saskatchewan that have been designed to support Indigenous students by incorporating Indigenous cultural practices and services designed to meet their specific needs. The film is focused on two such schools: the Peepeekisis Pesakastew School, a school on the Peepeekisis First Nation in Saskatchewan, and the Joe Duquette High School[2] in Saskatoon. Modest in terms of style and budget, *Stay in School* is largely composed of individual and group interviews with Indigenous students, as well as interviews with both Indigenous and non-Indigenous staff. All of those interviewed speak to the importance of education for Indigenous peoples, but specifically advocate for educational institutions and programs shaped by Indigenous priorities and traditional approaches to learning. As Emile Bell (Cree), identified as a member of the Parents' Counsel for Joe Duquette High School, states, "we're not trying to fit the kid into an institution, we're trying to fit an institution into the kid."

FIGURE 1. Opening titles for *Stay in School* (Doug Cuthand, 1995). Image courtesy of Doug Cuthand.

The immediate context for the program is "Indian Control of Indian Education," a political platform that dates to the 1970s, driven by Indigenous political organizations in Saskatchewan. In the early 1970s, the Education Task Force of the Federation of Saskatchewan Indians produced a report on the state of Indigenous education in the province in response to the ongoing imposition of a federal and provincial education system, extending from the history and legacy of residential schools. Based on the report, the National Indian Brotherhood[3] developed a policy paper entitled "Indian Control of Indian Education" that called for Indigenous peoples' control of the direction and design of educational programs and schools that served Indigenous peoples, which would involve parents and be managed locally, rather than provincially or federally (Taner 1999, 293). The policy paper was eventually adopted by Minister of Native Affairs Jean Chrétien in 1974, paving the way for educational institutions and programs designed and operated by local Indigenous groups in the provinces. The focus for *Stay in School* is shaped by Cuthand's participation in this political project. From 1977 to 1982, Cuthand was vice-chief of the Executive of the Federation of Saskatchewan Indian Nations, and during his tenure participated in founding provincial Indigenous postsecond-ary institutions. He continued to advocate for and bring visibility to Indigenous education as a journalist, later publishing a column in the Indigenous newspaper, the *Saskatchewan Indian,* in 1988 that traced the then ongoing negotiations between the Federation of Saskatche-wan Indians and the federal government over educational issues and legislation (Cuthand 1988). Cuthand's political work extends from the politics of Native nationalism, seeking Indigenous autonomy into educational and political systems.

Stay in School's textual features bring together the conventions of educational programming with aesthetic strategies to support Indige-nous self-representation. Elements of the segment appear "boiler-plate," which Cuthand explained came from a required template for educational programming to be shown in classrooms and for broad-cast: canned music and titles, and a woman's voice-over using the kind of nonregional English heard on news programs. These didactic com-ponents contrast with Cuthand's techniques that seek to diminish his presence in order to foreground the perspectives of those interviewed. Cuthand explained that he developed this approach in discussion with

FIGURE 2. Interviews with students and family members frame *Stay in School* (Doug Cuthand, 1995). Image courtesy of Doug Cuthand.

Indigenous artists concerned with formulating principles and ethics of representing Indigenous peoples in visual culture in the early 1990s:

> How could we shoot and be different? What were we doing that was different? I'd have to examine my work and say, "This is different from the way a white producer or director would have shot the same thing." What I did, I used very, very little narration. In fact, you could watch some of my productions all the way through and not hear narration. Television stations want a star out front . . . taking you every step of the way. To me, it was always important that the people themselves tell their stories. Sometimes that wouldn't be my story, and I wouldn't force my story on them. . . . You have to be honest and truthful. It's the old Indian way of doing storytelling. It's the oral tradition, you have to maintain the truth. (2015)

In *Stay in School,* a negotiation takes place between the imperative of educational programming to guide the "story" per Western pedagogical models, and Cuthand's efforts to minimize his presence and voice, which at times renders the screen content unwieldy. The didacticism

Colin Head
Student, Joe Duquette School

FIGURE 3. *Stay in School* features lengthy, uninterrupted comments and reflections from interview participants, illustrating Cuthand's filmmaking ethic that foregrounds Indigenous voices (Cuthand, 1995). Image courtesy of Doug Cuthand.

of the voice-over contrasts sharply with interview segments that involve very little by way of editing or camera movement, and in which Cuthand does not appear, either on camera or in voice-over. Shots of interview participants are remarkably long from an editing standpoint, and intended, in Cuthand's terms, to give participants room to tell their story. As a result, there are abrupt tonal shifts throughout that can be quite jarring, because the program brings them—somewhat irresolvably—together. The competing representational strategies speak to the politics shaping the program. The film emerges from a politics of advocacy, which seeks political reform through educational law and policy. This program does not call for wholesale dismantling of the educational system, but rather argues that the education system can be reformed under the direction and stewardship of Indigenous people. Thus, *Stay in School* is instructive, showing how the educational system can be negotiated to benefit Indigenous students and communities, paralleling the screen content's negotiation with the representational conventions of provincial educational television.

DONNA'S STORY (2001): DOCUMENTARY EMPATHY AT THE NATIONAL FILM BOARD

Cuthand referred to his early television programming as practice for later documentary work with the NFB in the late 1990s and early 2000s. Cuthand relates that he approached the NFB after having developed experience and expertise in provincial television: "I had to build up a certain amount of credibility and experience before I went to the [NFB]" (2015), speaking to both his increasingly specific focus on media and expectations of experience and quality associated with the NFB. If the NFB was increasingly subject to budget reductions through the 1980s onward, Cuthand indicates that it nonetheless has sustained its historical and cultural prestige and is an advantageous platform for Indigenous stories and perspectives. Here, Cuthand continued his practice of overturning institutional documentary conventions, adapting NFB textual strategies to represent Indigenous interests. *Donna's Story* is a fifty-minute portrait documentary of Donna Gamble, a thirty-four-year-old Cree woman from Saskatchewan and a recovering addict and former sex worker. Consistent with the personal portrait documentary genre, *Donna's Story* focuses on the individual in order to illuminate the link between the personal and political, the particular and the social (Nichols 2010, 244). The personal is a window onto broader social issues that shape an individual's experience; in *Donna's Story*, Donna's life provides a window onto the context for addiction in Indigenous communities, specifically for Indigenous women.

As is characteristic of Cuthand's work, his presence is minimized throughout the film, privileging the voices of those interviewed, especially Donna's. In talking head interviews, Donna reflects on the sexual, physical, and emotional abuse she experienced as a child and adult, and how they have shaped her addiction issues and previous work in the sex trade as well as her determination to continue working on life in recovery, which involves raising two of her six children at home, conducting community outreach and counseling, and participating in cultural activities such as powwows and beading. The documentary follows Donna through several pivotal life moments, including marriage to a fellow recovering addict that ends soon thereafter, and the birth of one of her grandchildren. Her counseling and community work is woven throughout, in which her mother, Sylvia, also participates: in one scene at a workshop, Sylvia recounts her own childhood of horrific sexual abuse and exploitation, which led to sex work and her eventual decision to place her children, including Donna, into foster care. Sylvia's story closely parallels Donna's, as four of Donna's own six children are in the foster care system, foregrounding key themes of the film: addiction must be understood in relation to intergenerational trauma and abuse that have fragmented Indigenous families and communities. In order to create a portrait of Donna's life, the film necessarily examines the historical and social conditions that have contributed to her life circumstances, as well as those in her family and community.

The portrait documentary is well established at the NFB, which has a body of such work that stems from its socially engaged documentary tradition. Zoë Druick has characterized this tradition as "government realism," which

> reflected the technologies of the liberal democracy that it was developed to support. Not only was documentary intimately bound up with the democratizing projects of mass and adult education, but it also embodied social scientific techniques, such as the interview and the representative sample, which were foundational

to the development of new techniques of governance such as the opinion poll. (2007, 23)

Druick argues that the scopic and positivist dimensions of this practice shifted in the 1950s onward as multiculturalism and diversity became the state's modus operandi and as nondominant groups demanded control of the filmic apparatus as a part of redressing social power imbalances. Over the next several decades and into the 1990s, the NFB developed programs for disenfranchised social groups, including the poor, women, minorities, and Indigenous peoples. While seeking to "empower" these social groups, these programs nonetheless produced films in terms of the NFB's discourse of government realism; in terms of Indigenous production, Druick argues these films "tacitly become a part of the national dialogue about the place of aboriginal communities in Canadian society" and "contribute to a larger government dialogue about the meaning and organization of a federal system" (174).

Indigenous production at the NFB therefore exhibits interactions of political discourses of different stakeholders: those of the NFB, as a public film agency, seeking to adapt to and reflect a shifting social and political landscape through its programs, documentary genres, and production practices; and those of Indigenous producers who engage with these institutional practices to create space to represent Indigenous social realities and priorities. *Donna's Story* emerges from this discursive context, harnessing the social realist discourse of the NFB documentary tradition to make visible social issues affecting Indigenous women and the colonial legacies underpinning them. The film was, however, produced after the NFB terminated its formal programs for Indigenous production, namely, Studio One, the Indigenous studio, which launched in 1990 in Edmonton and was shuttered in 1995. Its subsequent iteration, the Aboriginal Filmmaking Program (AFP), converted resources for Indigenous production training and development to a funding envelope, an annual allocation to which Indigenous producers were directed for their project proposals to the NFB (Cardinal, n.d.). Nonetheless, the NFB still upholds its mission to represent Canadian national culture and its constituencies, and the ongoing promotion of Indigenous representation as a part of the NFB's institutional culture made Cuthand's project all the more viable.

Cuthand explains that he was interested in Donna's story because she and her family had experienced endemic sexual abuse and subsequent addiction issues:

> They were all in the process of recovery. It was a story of a family that had gone off the rails, all generations were going back on. . . . Things were improving. It was an interesting story from that point of view. It was more the strength of the human spirit. . . . The family story was what was interesting, and that's what I focused on. (2015)

He further described the film's development in terms of the grant-giving model that the NFB had adopted through the 1990s: he created a proposal, produced a twenty-minute interview with Donna, and submitted them to the NFB. He relates that the NFB was "very cooperative" (2015), likely because the film resonated with NFB production models and thematic concerns. The NFB regionalized in the 1970s in the same historical and ideological context as the decentralization of national television, establishing satellite studios in each province headed by an executive producer who would coordinate regional proposal processes and productions (McSorley 2006, 273). This institutional restructuring parallels the transfer of educational television production to the provinces with the goal of expanding regional representation, and ultimately supports the rationale for the local focus of Cuthand's film.

Donna's Story retains some of the features of Cuthand's television production: its structure is similar to that of the "human interest" approach of his earlier work; it is local to Saskatchewan; it emphasizes the personal dimension through talking-head interviews intercut with footage of Gamble's home, work, and social life; and it deemphasizes voice-over narration. In fact, there is no voice-over narration at all. Instead, Gamble's interviews are the main structuring device, and interstitial footage illustrates topics or issues she raises in her interviews. The lack of voice-over narration for Indigenous documentaries was not new to the NFB: in her NFB-produced films of the 1990s to the early 2000s, Loretta Todd, for instance, brought an experimental documentary approach that, among other things, conscientiously minimized her use of voice-overs to decenter the authority of the filmmaker as the "voice of God" and give primacy to Indigenous voices.

Jennifer Gauthier, describing Todd's style as "postmodern," argues that "her films rely on multiple voices rather than a single narrator, celebrating polyphony and calling into question the act of representation" (2010, 33). Though Cuthand is not necessarily experimental in conventional terms, his stylistic choice to eliminate voice-over coincides with contemporaneous documentary practices.

Gamble's life is shaped by the devastating social and historical conditions afflicting Indigenous people, and women specifically, across the country. Having grown up in a family and community that suffered generations of sexual and physical abuse, which she also suffered, Gamble worked in the sex trade and abused drugs for years before entering recovery. Gamble's story, while her own, manifests broader social issues affecting Indigenous women in Canada that see them disproportionately overrepresented in the sex trade and subjected to higher incidences of physical and sexual violence (Royal Canadian Mounted Police 2014, 3). While these issues are, as the film goes on to explore, generations old, they began to receive greater public attention in the late 1990s as rumors of a serial killer in Vancouver, British Columbia, began to appear in the national media (Vancouver Police Department, Sisterwatch Project, and Women's Memorial March Committee 2011, 10).[4] As a journalist, Cuthand has been at the forefront of responding to Indigenous issues, and *Donna's Story* closely coincides with renewed focus on the issue of systemic violence experienced by Indigenous women. The film, however, works against victim narratives through which Indigenous women are typically represented by mainstream media sources. The film opens with Gamble, in voice-over, explaining that "when most people see a prostitute on the street, they see a prostitute, they don't see beyond that. I see the other things: addictions, abuse issues. . . . I see the hurt. That was my life, you know. It's something so hard to get away from. I got away from it." The narration plays over footage of Indigenous women attending a vigil for victims of violence, visually reinforcing the human dimension of the tragedy. The film then cuts to a scene of a bustling highway, while Gamble's narration is heard: "It's got to get better. It certainly couldn't get any worse than it has been." Gamble is then shown driving on her way to a speaking engagement at a local high school, where she speaks to an assembly of students in a gymnasium about her background as a former sex worker before turning to discussion of sex education. Throughout this scene, she is shown to be lively and funny, and engages giggling high school students in discussion of safe sex practices. Another scene shortly thereafter shows Gamble's nervous and thrilled preparation for her wedding to a fellow recovering addict and the wedding itself, well attended by joyful family and friends. The structure of this sequence of scenes moves from death, implied by the vigil, to life, conveyed by Gamble's movement through traffic, the vigor of her work as an outreach worker, and her family life. Cuthand states that his intent with the film was to represent the "strength of the human spirit" (2015), a theme familiar to broad audiences that serves the film's overarching ethic, which is to show that Gamble is far more than is implied by the designation of "prostitute," a term that is often used to dehumanize women by conflating them with the work they do. The film seeks to restore their basic humanity, which Gamble voices by repeatedly telling the story of the catalyst for leaving life on the streets: "This woman walked up to me and she said, 'Can I give you a hug?' All of a sudden I thought, you know, if she could hug me, you know, maybe other people will talk to me, want to talk to me and want to hear me out." This opening sequence undoes the representational problem surrounding Indigenous women in sex work, giving Gamble a complex human dimension. Her previous life on the streets shapes her work and recovery, but does not define the scope of her reality and ambitions. The film enacts as a counternarrative to historical trends in Canadian mainstream media, which has either ignored Indigenous women who work in the sex trade or represented them in ways that naturalize the violence they often experience.

Donna links her recovery to her connections to her family and community, and thereby to culture, which the film frames as a part of her healing and recovery process. In one of the opening scenes of the film, Donna states, "All my life, all I wanted to do was be a part of the community. Now I am. I'm a working part of the community. And there's a lot of addicts who want to be that." For Donna, being a "working part" of her community is focused on counseling, diversion programs, and youth education, contributing to the health and well-being of its members and, in so doing, her own. A part of her well-being, she explains, has to do with participating in family and community through cultural activities. In a scene following her wedding, Gamble is shown in full regalia dancing the round dance at a pow-wow. Her

FIGURE 4. Donna Gamble speaks to high school students (*Donna's Story*, 2001). Image courtesy of Doug Cuthand and the National Film Board of Canada.

voice-over explains the connection between family, community, and cultural practices:

> My auntie took me out dancing. And I did. I remember I cried when I first went around, 'cause it was really overwhelming. Probably the greatest high I ever had without chemicals. Dancing has helped me to focus somewhere, and a lot of people, when they get straight—Aboriginal people especially—figure that life ends when the party stops. And it doesn't. Like I have a whole new party going on here. . . . It's a family. Like, I had a street family. I had a street family for years, and that'd probably be the biggest reason why I wouldn't leave the street. Now I have a pow-wow family, a round dance family, and they're the most support to me and they're the reason I keep coming back.

The return to traditional cultural practices is a well-established discourse in Indigenous cultural politics, but *Donna's Story* does not pivot around a cultural triumphalist narrative of linear progress through recovery and reconnection. Gamble must daily face the challenging and often devastating realities of her addictions as a part of the recovery process. In an interview that is a part of a sequence where she makes breakfast for her two children at home, she explains that they are "recovery babies," as she was taking substances while she was pregnant, and that she believes that it may have affected her son. She states that her work is to learn to be patient with him, before the film cuts to a shot of Gamble burning sage and she and her son smudging. The scene does not resolve the conflict that Donna clearly has with herself about the effects of her addictions on her children, but does position cultural practices as a means to build healthier relationships with her family and community. Nor does the film argue that cultural traditions and practices are a panacea for recovery. Toward the end of the film, Gamble appears in an interview in which she explains that she has recently admitted to her mother that she has started drinking. She has shaved her head, explaining that she did so because she "had to start somewhere," that some people go to treatment or therapy, but

FIGURE 5. Donna participating in a round dance as a part of developing family and community connections (*Donna's Story*, 2001). Image courtesy of Doug Cuthand and the National Film Board of Canada.

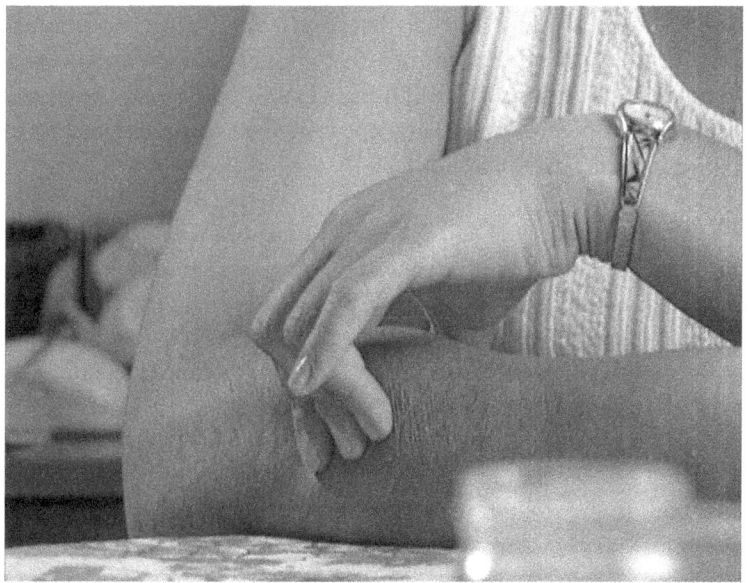

FIGURE 6. Donna reflects on her relapse and the recovery process (*Donna's Story*, 2001). Images courtesy of Doug Cuthand and the National Film Board of Canada.

she cuts her hair, and had done it once before. Gamble is at a point of transition: she is not mired in relapse, but rather moving herself into a process of recovery. Gamble's experience is characteristic of addiction, where "falling off the wagon" is a part of recovery and an opportunity to understand why the relapse occurred. As Gamble states, "*Today* I didn't drink," identifying the ambivalence of addiction: the success of one day counterbalanced with the uncertainty of the future. The film structure echoes this dynamic: the opening scene of the vigil also closes the film, not to position Gamble within a cycle of abuse, but rather to visually convey the cyclical nature of recovery. Gamble's closing voice-over reinforces this message: "You know the calm before the storm? Well, I'm in the storm. And after the storm there's always beautiful skies. I'm sure that's what's going to come. I hope I get there soon." The viewer is left with the impression that Gamble's tenacity and her ability to both survive and thrive through adversity will carry her through, despite the uncertainties of the future.

The film's resolution, or lack thereof, was an issue of debate and tension between Cuthand and NFB producers. He related that producers wanted a "clean ending" (2015); that is, an ending with a resolution of some kind. Cuthand explains that the film did not have a resolution because "it's a person's life" and human lives do not resolve into such endings; however, he reportedly encountered some resistance from NFB producers over this choice:

> The story doesn't end. It isn't all wrapped up in a nice little ball. Some of the problems continue, the struggle continues, life continues, and we left it like that. [NFB producers] wanted to wrap it up. And I said, well, you really can't, it's a person's life, everybody's on their journey, we've been lucky enough to capture a piece of that journey. (2015)

Cuthand's statement links to his journalistic ethic in that he is being "truthful" to the realities with which he was faced, and would not impose "his story" or anyone else's on Gamble's. A more pat conclusion would conflict with Cuthand's more "humanist" approach located in Indigenous representational politics and journalistic ethics. This tension is instructive, as it points to the intersection of competing institutional, ideological, and political frameworks in the creation of Indigenous production, as well as the traces of a regional television model in its textual features and lineage via Cuthand's production experience.

CONCLUSION: NEGOTIATING MEDIA AUTHORSHIP IN INSTITUTIONAL CONTEXTS

Part of the challenge, and value, of taking an institutional and historical approach to analysis of Cuthand's production is that his diverse portfolio invites consideration of multiple and overlapping areas of influence that undergird it—institutional, political, and technological. The length and breadth of his career—bridging journalism, television production, and documentary film—invites attention both to the specificities of the modes and institutional contexts of his work, but equally invites consideration of the thematic focuses and ethics-informed aesthetic decisions he brings to all of his productions. Without losing the filmmaker's "signature," which is shaped and refined over years of practice, bringing institutional context to bear on understandings of the screen texts enriches understandings of how Indigenous filmmakers recode and repurpose established practice to make them "mean" differently, and meaningful for Indigenous representation.

Placing the filmmaker at the center of analysis makes visible the historical conditions that engendered the kind of mobility and responsiveness to the media landscape that his work represents. Cuthand's media trajectory is not outside the norm for Indigenous practitioners, but rather characteristic of those pursuing opportunities in a field of increasingly defunded public media and cultural institutions. As a case in point, in the early 2000s, Cuthand directed episodes of television series by independent production companies for broadcast on the Aboriginal Peoples Television Network, explaining that the Indigenous documentary market has now shifted toward APTN (2015). In this arrangement, APTN acquires programming it requires while producers have the benefit of a longer production schedule and therefore greater financial stability in a field of piecemeal contract work. This model can be very tenuous in Canada, however, as Cuthand's experience illustrates. A major support for film and video production in Canada is tax credits, which allow a corporation to claim a percentage of labor costs for a production, reducing the amount of tax a corporation is required to pay (Government of Canada 2022), which provides incentive for corporations to film in Canada and particular provinces. In 2012, however, the Saskatchewan provincial government eliminated the Saskatchewan tax credit on which provincial film and television production relied; consequently, at that time almost every Saskatchewan production company had to shut down, including Cuthand's Blue Hill Productions. Such turns of events are indicative of the contraction of public funding for media that has increasingly taken place across Canada, which subsequent chapters trace via their effects on the Indigenous production landscape, particularly chapter 3's examination of the field of independent Indigenous television production in Canada.

2

The Aboriginal Film and Video Art Alliance

NEGOTIATING INDIGENOUS SELF-GOVERNMENT
IN THE ARTS

In 2014, the imagineNATIVE Film + Media Arts Festival hosted "indigiTALKS: Following That Moment," a panel featuring a set of videos curated by Lisa Myers (Anishinaabe) that focused on the experimental, often radical projects of Indigenous video artists in Canada in the early 1990s. Their work was framed as an origin point for the ideological and formal strategies developed by subsequent generations of Indigenous artists who challenge not only colonial representations of Indigenous people but the medium itself (film, television, video, digital platforms) and the role of the apparatus in these meaning-making activities (Myers 2014). The historiographic work of the panel in particular emphasized the role of the Aboriginal Film and Video Art Alliance (AFVAA) in this era and thus to the development of Indigenous film, television, and digital media vernaculars over the past three decades, a role reinforced at the 2018 festival via a retrospective of work by Métis artist, activist, and educator Marjorie Beaucage, one of its founders and organizers (Myers 2018). Myers is not alone in identifying the AFVAA's historical significance: others have similarly remarked on its influence on the development of Indigenous media in Canada (de Rosa 2002; L'Hirondelle 2016; Ginsburg 2003; Crey 2021). Despite these acknowledgements, and though its membership included some of the most prominent Indigenous filmmakers in Canadian history (Beaucage and Delegates 1993), there has been a dearth of scholarship on the organization. While this chapter is far from a comprehensive history of the AFVAA, it seeks to contribute to the historical record by examining its institutional interventions and media-based creative production.

The AFVAA was founded in April 1991 at a gathering in Edmonton,

Alberta, called together to create an organization that would promote and practice "Aboriginal self-government" in the arts (Beaucage 1991). This meeting brought together approximately fifty Indigenous filmmakers, performers, artists, and journalists, a gathering through which the AFVAA subsequently emerged as a group consisting of a Steering Committee made up of representatives from regions across Canada, with four well-established media practitioners as advisors: Alanis Obomsawin (Abenaki), Wil Campbell (Cree-Métis), Bernelda Wheeler (Cree, Assiniboine, Salteaux), and Maria Campbell (Métis) (Beaucage 1991). The AFVAA's goals were to "promote and encourage the interdisciplinary art form of film and video production, and [to create] new cultural storytelling forms within the principles, values and traditions of Aboriginal Self Government" (Beaucage 1991), and "to create space, access programs and resources and include Aboriginal values and self-government principles in the production/ process of culture" (Aboriginal Film and Video Art Alliance Steering Committee 1993, 2). These statements articulate the framework for the AFVAA's art-based activism, which sought to bring together Indigenous cultural traditions with creative technology-based production, developed through training programs "by and for Aboriginal people" (Aboriginal Film and Video Art Alliance Steering Committee 1993, 2). Oriented by a commitment to Indigenous self-government," AFVAA organizers sought to advance Indigenous stewardship in the arts both creatively and operationally, advocating for Indigenous self-representation in the arts, and for Indigenous leadership in the development of Indigenous programs and resources within Canadian arts institutions and funding agencies, which ultimately led to their three-year partnership with Banff Centre, one of Canada's most prominent arts centers.

The Banff Centre for Arts and Creativity,[1] located in the Rocky Mountains of Banff, Alberta, is one of Canada's oldest and most influential art institutions. Founded in 1933, the Banff Centre was envisioned as a "world centre for art and culture in the Canadian Rockies" (Reichwein and Wall 2020, 4), and in subsequent decades has acquired a prestigious reputation nationally and internationally that has made it a worldwide destination for professional arts training and development (8). The Banff Centre is affiliated with Alberta's postsecondary system and offers non-degree-based professionalization programs for artists in all disciplines. It is known for creating the "Banff Method," a residency program designed to immerse participants for several weeks in a creative and natural environment to spur innovation (Cook and Diamond 2012, 23). With the Banff Centre, the AFVAA created an institutional model of Indigenous governance that would form the basis for exploring self-government across the creative arts. AFVAA documents and records consistently frame Indigenous organizational stewardship as the precondition for Indigenous creative practice, refusing to separate questions of governance from cultural production. In so doing, the AFVAA played a key role in contributing to a highly influential discourse of Indigenous media that has been theorized since in terms of "visual sovereignty," a concept "whereby Indigenous filmmakers take a holistic approach to the process of creating moving images" that "connects film production to larger aesthetic practices that work toward strengthening treaty claims and more traditional . . . modes of cultural understanding" (Raheja 2013, 19).

At the Banff Centre, the AFVAA developed self-government in media production through a video-based project that brought together a cohort of six Indigenous artists for a nine-week residency to develop and produce a series of seven, 30- to 60-second public service announcements (PSA) called SELF-GOVERNMENT: Talk About It. . . . (1994). The PSA project was an experiment in self-government as institutional and aesthetic principle, first, by adapting the Banff Centre's long-established residency model under the direction of AFVAA organizers, and second, by bringing together a group of artists to collaborate in creating PSAs to express what "self-government" means to them. This political discourse forms the context for the AFVAA's organizational and advocacy work. In its relationship with the Banff Centre, the AFVAA modeled self-government within an institution seeking to develop capacity and spaces within the broader institution to experiment with Indigenous cultural values in cultural production. The PSA project thereby emerged at the intersection of a consolidation of an influential discourse of Indigenous media arts, and the Banff Centre's institutional frameworks and media production capacities. Moreover, by strategically partnering with an institution with such extraordinary reach and influence in Canadian and international art worlds, this model could have profound and far-reaching influences on state and mainstream approaches to Indigenous engagement, and understandings and interpretations of Indigenous cultural production.

INDIGENOUS SELF-GOVERNMENT: POLITICS AND CULTURAL PRODUCTION

The model for the AFVAA's institutional partnership with Banff emerges in the context of the cultural politics of the art world in Canada in the 1980s and 1990s, which was a period of heightened activism critiquing systemic issues of racism and equity within Canadian national institutions. Multiculturalism, which had been official policy since 1971 and passed into law in 1988, had given rise to an ideal of a pluralistic Canadian national identity epitomized by the term "cultural mosaic" that came into common use. The adoption of multiculturalism ignited debates around its definition and scope, which presumes an "Anglo-Canadian core culture" against which other cultures are defined as "multicultural" (Mackey 1999, 15). Critics identified it as a form of liberal pluralism that created a hierarchy of social difference that ultimately stabilized hegemonic social and racial orders, and pointed out the obvious contradictions between this national ethos in light of the deplorable underrepresentation of marginalized groups, particularly Indigenous people and people of color, in cultural institutions across the country. In the arts, organizing driven by Indigenous artists and artists of color sought ways to address systemic and institutional racism and discrimination in Canadian arts-based institutions, employing a politics of recognition—"the demand of minorities to be recognized" (Saha 2018, 89)—to compel institutions to address structural issues of equity and racism. In "Building Blocks: Anti-Racist Initiatives in the Arts," Monika Kin Gagnon identifies that much of this arts-based activism was led by racialized and Indigenous artists within alternative cultural networks who had historically been excluded from dominant cultural institutions. These groups, Gagnon explains, organized through a strategy of "identity politics": artists who "self-identified as First Nations or of colour, who challenged white-dominated cultural organizations" (1999, 52).

The distinction between "First Nations" and artists of color that Gagnon makes is critical, one that Beaucage elaborates on when discussing this era where it proved to be problematic for Indigenous people to be grouped into a broader cultural category of "people of color" given Indigenous peoples' specific cultural and political histories within Canada:

There was always "people of color *and* First Nations." . . . They didn't have access either. We did collaborate together on some things. But there was big cultural differences between us too. They didn't get that we were First Nations. It was still "people of color and . . . oh yeah, First Nations." And I always tried to help them understand that this is the only place we have, that we've never been anywhere else. This is our home, and you're our guests. (2014a)

As Beaucage states here, though Indigenous people share experiences of systemic discrimination and institutional exclusion with other marginalized social groups, their concerns and position vis-à-vis the state are not commensurate with those of other groups. As First Peoples, Indigenous peoples have collective identities, rights and title, and unique relationships with Canada enshrined in law and policy, which, it has been argued, reflects their status as "a third participant, a separate founding nation" of Canada (Erasmus 1989, 2–3). Consequently, Indigenous engagement with the state has been based on demands that Canada abide by its commitments and acknowledge Indigenous peoples as Original Peoples, and by extension, Indigenous nationhood and attendant rights and title. As discussed in this book's introduction, cultural production is coextensive with Indigenous rights, a relationship that Dene scholar Glen Coulthard defines in terms of a "mode of life," which describes a social totality of "the resources, technologies, and labor that a people deploy to produce what they need to materially sustain themselves over time, and the forms of thought, behavior, and social relationships that *both condition and are themselves conditioned by these productive forces*" (2014, 65; emphasis in original). Political economy and culture are not separable in Indigenous traditions, context that is crucial for understanding Indigenous arts-based advocacy during this period, which engages in recognition politics like other socially marginalized groups but is oriented by the context of Indigenous self-determination and efforts to extended self-determination into art and culture.

Arts-based activism during this period took place through antiracist and coalitional cultural politics. A series of conferences and meetings were organized in the 1980s and 1990s by artists' groups who sought intergroup affiliations to address systemic and institutional racism and discrimination in Canadian arts institutions, including "In Visible Colours" (1989); "About Face, About Frame" (1992); "It's a Cultural Thing: Individual Expression, Collective Inspiration" (1993); and "Writing Thru Race" (1994). Notably, "It's a Cultural Thing" was organized by Minquon Panchayat,[2] a group of Indigenous and artists of color that formed a caucus within the Association of National Non-Profit Artist Run Centres (ANNPAC) at its 1992 national annual general meeting. The seven-member group took shape as a response to the low numbers of Indigenous artists and artists of color within the organization, and sought to advance equity within ANNPAC through structural change, including changes to its governance and decision-making; adding artist's groups of Indigenous people and people of color to its membership; and supporting the development of a national network for Indigenous artists and artists of color (Cronin and Robertson 2011, 143).

While these efforts were widespread and characteristic of broader social shifts, they were not without resistance and conflict. "It's a Cultural Thing," organized by the Minquon Panchayat caucus, featured work from forty Indigenous artists and artists of color and was designed as a lead-in to the 1993 ANNPAC annual general meeting (Gagnon 1999, 65). However, tensions erupted at the meeting as a result of what has been referred to as ANNPAC's failure to honor its commitments to antiracist initiatives. Gagnon, herself originally a caucus member, relates that conflict arose in relation to Miquon Panchayat's operations from 1992 to 1993, "through a form of resistance that can only be considered covertly racist," in which meeting and organizational procedure was used to delegitimize caucus activities and members and maintain the status quo (Gagnon 1999, 65). As a result, many artists' groups withdrew from ANNPAC, which led to its eventual dissolution by 1995 (Robertson 2006, 39–40).[3] In 1994, "Writing Thru Race: A Conference for First Nations Writers and Writers of Colour" was held with the sponsorship of the Writers' Union of Canada. The conference asked only Indigenous writers and writers of color to attend to "ensure a milieu in which writers directly affected by racism [could] engage in candid and personal discussions" ("Call for Participation" quoted in Gagnon 1999, 67). This participation policy was met with accusations of "reverse racism" by politicians and the media, resulting in key conference funding being rescinded by then minister of Canadian heritage Michel Dupuy (Gagnon 1999, 68).

These grassroots antiracist efforts, and the controversies and conflicts arising in response, illustrate the broader context of ideological struggle taking place in the cultural sphere through which the AFVAA emerged. There are significant overlaps between the discourses of self-representation and access employed by marginalized artists and others to call for institutional reform, and articulations of Indigenous self-government and cultural sovereignty. As Beaucage (2014a) points out, however, Indigenous artists and activists maintained the specificity of Indigenous concerns and issues, which were based on distinct and continuous histories and cultures, and a specific legal and political relationship with the state. Thus, even as Indigenous advocates developed intergroup partnerships and alliances to realize shared goals, much of their work was oriented by a commitment to Indigenous self-determination driving their grassroots approaches to institutional change.

INSTITUTIONAL INTERVENTIONS

One of the AFVAA's first initiatives was to take over the Pincher Creek Film Festival in Edmonton, Alberta (First Nations Filmmakers Alliance 1992). At the time, the Alberta government looked to transfer management of the festival to a film-based organization, to which the AFVAA responded, arguing the festival should serve Indigenous interests (d'Auray 1991). Beaucage explained that some features of the festival deterred Indigenous participation, such as submission fees that Indigenous filmmakers could not always afford, and screening films by non-Indigenous filmmakers that featured colonial depictions of Indigenous people (2014a). When the AFVAA took over the film festival, they renamed it the Dreamspeakers Film Festival and removed many of the impediments to Indigenous participation by, for instance, dispensing with submission fees for Indigenous filmmakers (Beaucage 2014a). This was the implementation of one of the founding principles of the AFVAA, which was to remove systemic barriers to Indigenous participation in the arts, and they forged relationships with sympathetic or related organizations and institutions in order to do so. Beaucage explains: "We tried to do things in partnerships or alliances. We went to the public library, the community friendship centers and asked them to host when we had events so that we were self-governing" (2014a). Such affiliations, according to Beaucage, are an extension of Indigenous values that emphasize cultivating and sustaining community relations. In this model, the festival would have an open submission policy welcoming any Indigenous-produced film and video work without requiring submission fees. Their work would be screened under the principle of "giving back," in which Indigenous filmmakers would receive feedback on their work within the participation of community members:

> The first [Dreamspeakers] festival was free, and the first festival was in the community, the principles of giving back, right? When you do work, you give it back, and you talk to each other about what you made and why you made it. And you let people decide for themselves what it is for them. (Beaucage 2014a)

The Dreamspeakers Film Festival can be seen as an early test of Indigenous governance in the cultural sphere, which the AFVAA then explored in its interactions with mainstream cultural institutions in Canada, and ultimately the Banff Centre with its three-year partnership.

The AFVAA envisioned itself as having national scope operating on self-government principles (Beaucage 1991), with regional representatives constituting the Steering Committee, and goals acting as a hub for the collection and distribution of information and resources relating to Indigenous artists and filmmakers and regional offices across the country (Beaucage and Delegates 1993, 4). Its aspirations suggest that it would structurally operate parallel to national institutions, but within terms determined by Indigenous leadership. Commenting on the founding of the AFVAA, Loretta Todd (Cree/Métis), one of its co-organizers, stated: "We hold as a philosophy the practice of self-government and the exercise of Aboriginal rights in the building of our own cinema and television industry/community" (1994, 7). Todd's framework for self-determination is grounded in self-representation, though not necessarily in isolation from other institutions or industries. Rather, Todd asserts that "we want to work with other film and video industries and communities, but we want to do so from a site of power, and not as part of someone else's power, always on the margins" (1994, 7), making clear that while Indigenous media necessitates Indigenous people's access to and autonomy over media resources, Indigenous production does not occur in isolation from other arenas of cultural production. The AFVAA's organization reflects these principles: the role of the "runner" was created as a cultural ambassador, acting as an interface between mainstream cultural institutions and the Indigenous programs and artists working with them:

> As tradition has it, the "runners" were the ones who went ahead to prepare the place and the people for what was to come. At the Banff Centre, these ambassadors would "go ahead" and create cultural space for the artists, storytellers, communities who would come to the Centre as residents, associates, for gatherings, symposia, residencies, etc. (First Nations Film and Video Art Alliance 1993)

Marjorie Beaucage served as this runner in the AFVAA dealings with mainstream cultural institutions. In order to develop its organizational capacity, the AFVAA sought partnerships with these institutions, where spaces for Indigenous participation would be supported. Such spaces would be dedicated to Indigenous programs and services and would have Indigenous administration, working as an extension of self-government by actualizing it through Indigenous governance within a larger institutional body. As a part of this mission, AFVAA representatives reached out to federal cultural institutions and funding bodies, including among others the Canada Council for the Arts (CCF). Beaucage recounts having worked with the CCF as an effort to build institutional representation of Indigenous people, who would steer decision-making and resource allocation for Indigenous artists. As Beaucage explains, this institutional restructuring would be an exercise of Indigenous self-government because it would transfer control over Indigenous affairs and resources to Indigenous people, and involve Indigenous people in mainstream operations and decision making:

> None of us had ever been invited to sit on media arts juries, we weren't a part of any of that mainstream process, or eligible as independent artists. The other disciplines only had the superstars of visual arts. Now every single department at the Canada Council has an Aboriginal arts component. (2014a)

The CCF was responsive, and founded the Aboriginal Arts Secretariat in 1994, which oversees grants to support Aboriginal artists (Research Office of the Canada Council for the Arts 2008, 7), and also later supported AFVAA initiatives (Maskegon-Iskwew 1994, 26).[4]

INSTITUTIONAL PARTNERSHIPS AS INTERVENTION: THE BANFF CENTRE

Ultimately, the AFVAA's search for an institutional space was success-fully negotiated with the Banff Centre for the Arts. In 1992, Loretta Todd was approached by Sara Diamond, then director of the Banff Centre's Television and Video Program, with an invitation to partici-pate in one of the Banff Centre's artist residencies (Todd 2014). Todd recalled that she guided Banff Centre away from residencies, which modeled individual creativity, and toward a framework of "commu-nity" that the AFVAA sought to embody, and encouraged Diamond to invite the AFVAA to meet with them and explore the possibilities of a partnership:

> I said that it's not about me, it's about the community, and really, we need to have a conversation with the Banff Centre because it shouldn't be just about individual artists coming here—certainly, individual artists can come here anytime they want, you guys should be more open and embracing of Aboriginal artists—but really we need to have a discussion with the institution, and we need to talk about systemic barriers, we need to find out about having that sovereign space within this institution. . . . I said why don't we have a meeting with community, with people involved in the Alliance, we can come together and we can start to formulate some formal relationship with the Banff Centre, some formal arts space within the Banff Centre that we would control and be our sovereign space. (Todd 2014)

Todd and Beaucage reported that the AFVAA envisioned an egalitar-ian partnership in which the AFVAA would create space and capacity for experimentation in self-government across art forms, a partnership that was formalized with the Banff Centre in 1993 (Century 1993a).

Diamond's invitation to the AFVAA Steering Committee to partici-pate in a meeting to "discuss workshops and residency programs on the national regional level, outreach and coordination" outlines the Banff Centre's goals of finding approaches to "cross-cultural practice and inclusion" (Diamond 1992). References to "cross-culturalism" and "inclusion" here are linked to internal discussions occurring at the Banff Centre during this period that responded to prevailing debates about systemic racism in Canadian art worlds, and from the state's adoption of multiculturalism as law, revealing an instance of an institution of media culture in Canada "making sense" of social, legal, and political shifts in terms of its own identity and operations. Institutional records from the early 1990s, including internal communications and reports, reveal that Banff Centre was undergoing a process of institutional reflexivity, developing principles and practices by which it could increase the representation of minoritized groups in its staff and in the artists and faculty participating in its programs and services. In a memo dated September 2, 1992, Carol Phillips, then director of the Banff Centre for the Arts, asked Michael Century, director of program development, to research and develop cultural policy for the Banff Centre. The itemized memo states:

> 1. Research and development of policy for the CFA [Centre for the Arts] addressing transcultural programs. (I would not choose the word, [sic] "multicultural [sic] to define our activities; but there may be a term preferable to the above). (Phillips 1992, 1; underline in original).

Phillips's suggestion of the term *transcultural* and guidance to avoid using the term *multicultural* in his proposal illustrates the unwieldiness of terminology surrounding social and cultural "difference" during this period, as well as institutional skepticism and criticism of official multiculturalism. Century's April 1993 report, entitled *A Policy Framework for Intercultural Programming*, explicitly examines the aversion to the term *multiculturalism*, stating that the "traditional 'multicultural paradigm' damages the development of artists by defining their practices in ways that exclude them from support schemes available to mainstream artists" (1993b, 8–9). Century argues that "multiculturalism" is an inadequate or even failed policy for dealing with cultural and social difference, "perpetuating systemic racism" by segregating minority artists from the mainstream (8). Century's critique of multiculturalism has been well established in debates about cultural difference in Canadian culture, which Ric Knowles has described as "its links to government policy and tendency to ghettoize" (2009, 3).

Century's report instead argues for a policy of "interculturalism" defined as "transformative personal growth through the expansion of the individual's horizons of cultural significance" (1993b, 15).

Though this definition is somewhat abstract, Canadian cultural critics and academics have debated interculturalism as an alternative to multiculturalism: on the negative end of the spectrum, critics have questioned "whether interculturalism is a form of homogenizing globalization that 'threatens the diversity of cultures and tends to level everything by reducing the different to the identical,'" while others have seen it as a productive antidote to the cultural balkanization associated with state-sanctioned multiculturalism, a "dialogic" process in which "the representation of a cultural 'self' is articulated in response but not necessarily in opposition to the 'other'" (Nothof 2012, 97). Century's report is inclined toward the latter interpretation, contrasting interculturalism with multiculturalism by arguing that interculturalism moves beyond multiculturalism's "ghettoizing" identity categories and social barriers, to a "dialogic identity" through which to develop "mutual cultural understanding" (1993b, 10–11) that emerges from contemporary global realities. The report states that

> When an Afro-Caribbean director stages *Oedipus Rex* from the standpoint of Yoruban conception of fate, or a Japanese director places *Macbeth* in the historical context of samurai warriors, the works are allowed to speak with new urgency, new complexity, new resonance. (10)

These examples draw from international contexts that cast interculturalism in terms of a global cosmopolitanism, which seems to be an institutional priority: Phillips's memo to Century identifies that "detailed attention should be given to the Pacific Rim, aboriginal nations in North America, people of colour in North America, Latin and South American peoples" (1992, 1) and the report asserts that interculturalism is the means by which Banff would be able "to re-align itself as an innovative new breed of intercultural global arts centre" (Century 1993b, 15). In this way, the Banff Centre leverages the federal party line of "multiculturalism" (sanctioned by Conservative prime minister Brian Mulroney, no less) in order to position itself within leading debates in the Canadian arts world, but at the same time distinguish itself from the political theatre of the state.

At the proposal stage, the AFVAA's agenda and the Banff Centre's appeared to mesh around the concept of "access" for Indigenous artists and filmmakers. The AFVAA sought an institutional partner for both a physical space and resources to support the skills development for Indigenous trainees and artists, which aligned with the Banff Centre goals to increase the representation of minorities in its existing training programs to fulfill their interculturalism mandate. The emergent formation of the AFVAA provided an immediate response to an institutional equity issue that was complex, systemic, and had an institutional scale far beyond Banff Centre. Carol Phillips touts the partnership project in a memo to the president and CEO of the Banff Centre, stating that, "it really could create a new model for institutions like ours to work bilaterally with First Nations" (1993). In terms of social relevance and reach, the partnership between the AFVAA and Banff Centre provided a mutually beneficial relationship.

PRODUCING SELF-GOVERNMENT: THE PSA PROJECT

Once situated at the Banff Centre, the AFVAA initiated experiments in Indigenous representation using the Banff Centre's existing program infrastructure. Though its scope became interdisciplinary, Beaucage relates that the AFVAA maintained an emphasis on film and video because it was an area to which Indigenous artists did not have widespread access.[5] The PSA project grew out of one of the AFVAA's first initiatives, which was to create an Indigenous residency program analogous to the Banff Centre's existing residency program, which would operate in the winter months for five to ten weeks. Their first residency program invited six Indigenous artists for nine weeks to work together to produce a series of seven public service announcements exploring the topic of self-government.

Following the national scope on which the AFVAA was premised, the PSA participants were drawn from regions across Canada: Joane Cardinal-Schubert (Kainai), Gary Farmer (Cayuga), Ruby-Marie Dennis (Tl'azt'en Nation), Isabelle Knockwood (Mi'kmaq), Crissy Red (Blackfoot),[6] and Angie Campbell (Dene/Cree), several of whom had not previously worked with media but who received production training in preparation for their projects. Organizers were careful not to conflate national scope with national representation:

> The AFVAA makes no claim to represent all Native Indian film and video makers, writers, producers, and technicians. Rather the AFVAA consists of those who would like to make film and video

> products part of the collective reality of being an Aboriginal artist and storyteller. (Todd 1994, 7)

The qualification Todd makes here is crucial to Indigenous nationalism, which is premised on understanding that Indigenous Peoples comprise many groups and nations with distinct social forms, cultures, and traditions, thereby voicing how the AFVAA and the PSA project embedded self-government principles within their organizational practices.

Collaboration was fundamental to the development and production processes, with all participants taking part in each other's projects. As Cardinal-Schubert discusses, collaboration involved in-depth group discussions that shaped their productions, even those with ideas already formulated: "Those people who arrived with scripts and concrete ideas began to adjust them and those who had never thought about . . . scripts began to get ideas" (1994, 12). Thus, the AFVAA modeled a form of collaborative creativity generating interpretations of self-government that shaped the PSAs themselves. In this case, the process by which the project came about is at least as significant as the product itself because through discussion and collaboration, the artists developed their interpretation of "self-government" that then shaped their individual productions. Angie Campbell, one of the participants, explains the relationship between the collaborative and individual dimensions of the PSAs. Maintaining the individual "vision" of each participant's PSA, Campbell explains, arose in recognition of the specificity of each person's Indigenous heritage and experiences:

> Everybody that came to the training at Banff Centre for the Arts on this project came from different places across Canada, they all had different issues from their lands from where they came from and their whole experience of life living at that place and time period of events that occurred there. It was about how that combination of events and growing up there, the contrast, the ideas, the politics and everything there was to talk about—that's what we talked about. We talked about ourselves and it gave us all a broader image of where we were [as Indigenous people]. (2016)

The group's exploration of the concept of self-government echoes the premises of Indigenous cultural nationalism, which does not seek to homogenize Indigenous groups, but rather insists that they be understood in their tribal or national specificities, demonstrating that Indigenous nationalist principles cut through the structure and production process of the PSA project.

PSAs as a genre have historically lent themselves to television as a broadcast medium. George Dessart identifies that public service announcements, particularly in the United States, came into being during World War II and are currently defined by the FCC as

> any announcement (including network) for which no charge is made and which promotes programs, activities, or services of federal, state, or local governments (e.g., recruiting, sale of bonds, etc.) or the programs, activities or services of non-profit organizations (e.g., United Way, Red Cross blood donations, etc.) and other announcements regarded as serving community interests, excluding time signals, routine weather announcements and promotional announcements. (Dessart n.d.)

PSAs are therefore directly linked to social reality, as messages from an authority or expert entity intended to serve the interests of a community by generating awareness of a problem or change public opinion about a social issue. PSAs intend to rally support behind particular campaigns of immediate social imperative. This form of televisual address lends itself to the AFVAA's creative activity and the urgency of social issues to which they were addressed.

Materially, however, this kind of televisual genre aligns with Banff media production capacities and culture in the early 1990s that supported television and video in particular. Since 1979, the Banff Centre had been the site of the Banff Television Festival (Humphreys 1999), possessed video production facilities (Williams 1997), and as indicated by Sara Diamond's position title—director of the Television and Video Program at Banff Centre—cultivated creative video and television production. The PSA project is therefore in part oriented by institutional media culture and technological capacities. At the same time, the project retained its support for creative experimentation. Angie Campbell explains that they did not follow broadcast quality or standards in the creation of their PSAs; there were "no restrictions" (2016). The PSAs' experimental approach echoed the experimental nature of the AFVAA's negotiation of a form of "self-government" in their relationship with

Banff administration, and in the broader social and political sphere as Indigenous groups and organizations tested Indigenous sovereignty in the court system and their own communities.

AFVAA organizers did explore the possibility of broadcasting the PSAs, as Beaucage explains, with the goal of intervening in the federal government's framework for Indigenous self-government, which was functionally an extension of assimilation (2014b). As a part of then prime minister Brian Mulroney's neoconservative agenda, the federal government increasingly decentralized federal institutions and re-sources, and transferred responsibility for local services and programs to provincial and regional governing bodies in the name of economic efficiency. Mulroney's approach to Indigenous policy sought to dis-mantle the Department of Indian Affairs and Northern Development, the federal agency responsible for Indigenous programs and services, and transfer responsibility for these programs to reserves, an approach that conflicted with Indigenous goals of self-government by forcing them to operate as administrators of state programs (Cosentino and Chartrand 2007, 308–9). As Beaucage explains, this model of local governance would effectively convert reserves to municipalities, a community and land tenure model alien to Indigenous approaches to land stewardship. Moreover, it would mean acquiescing to a political and social system imposed by the state, in which Indigenous people would become administrators of their own oppression: "[It was] their idea of a real estate deal. . . . you can buy/sell your land . . . make your rez into a municipality, collect taxes . . . and when you can't pay them . . . we'll take the land . . . no more treaties. That was Mulroney's plan . . . [which] didn't work" (2014b). State models for Indigenous governance conflicted with Indigenous concepts of self-government, and these contemporary iterations of colonial politics and assimila-tion added urgency and immediacy to the rationale for developing the public service announcements.

While generically PSAs as a televisual genre construct and address broad publics per their public service function, the self-government PSAs formally and didactically address themselves to an Indigenous counterpublic, modeling different visions of self-government by sus-taining the distinct perspectives and styles of each artist. To summa-rize Michael Warner as discussed in chapter 1, publics are produced through the circulation of discourse; that is, through a speech act that "is addressed to indefinite others, that in singling us out it does so not on the basis of our concrete identity but by virtue of our participation in the discourse alone and therefore in common with strangers" (2002, 77–78). Counterpublics are similarly produced through the circulation of discourse; however, these acts produce "a scene where a dominated group aspires to re-create itself as a public and in doing so finds itself in conflict not only with the dominant social group but with the norms that constitute the dominant culture as a public" (112). A counterpublic, Warner elaborates, is not simply "subaltern," but maintains awareness of its subordinate status in relation to a dominant public (119). The PSAs, as productions intended for circulation via television, are such speech acts and construct a specifically Indigenous public that sets this audience against the dominant, colonial public sphere.

VISIONING SELF-GOVERNMENT: YOUTH, SPECULATIVE FUTURES, AND INDIGENOUS RESURGENCE

The seven PSAs focus on the theme of self-government, all incorporating the statement "Self-Government: Talk About It" as their address to Indigenous viewers. Despite these consistencies, each PSA is stylistically unique, modeling self-government as a concept involving a range of viewpoints.

Hip Hop, directed by Ruby-Marie Dennis and written by Crissy Red, is stylized like a music video, with rapid-fire editing cuts to the rhythm of the music. It opens with a close-up of a striking Indigenous woman saying, "What is your destiny?" and cuts to a sequence of shots of Indigenous youth dancing, laughing, and talking, at work and school, and gathered with an elder, intercut with shots of graffiti, historical photographs of Indigenous lives, and close-up shots of individual youth. Multiple voices are heard in voice-over making statements such as "Learn about your heritage," "Learn your language," "Get an education," "Follow your traditions" before ending with another close-up on the woman who states, "It is the destiny of our nations. Talk about it."

Future Child, written and directed by Angie Campbell, was produced in two versions, one in English and one in Cree. It takes place in an apocalyptic future, in which a young Indigenous boy wanders a desert wasteland before encountering a portal through which he sees a lush, natural landscape. A man's voice in voice-over states, "The destiny of our land is pitiful. If we do not respect and take care of our land today, our grandchildren will suffer." Text appears over images of the

FIGURE 7. *Hip Hop* (Ruby-Marie Dennis and Crissy Red, 1994). The Aboriginal Film and Video Art Alliance. Image courtesy of the artists and VTape.

FIGURE 8. *Future Child* (Angie Campbell, 1994). The Aboriginal Film and Video Art Alliance. Image courtesy of Marjorie Beaucage and VTape.

boy wandering the wasteland, reading, "Self-Government, Talk About It . . . For the future of the next seven generations."

Too Many Chiefs, Not Enough Indians, written and directed by Ruby-Marie Dennis, presents a screen displaying the "Indian Head" test pattern, on which is draped a white headdress. The voice-over says "self-government," as the image display changes to a sequence of talking heads, in which each person makes an individual statement about the meaning of self-government to them. An animated graphic of a bison emerges from the "screen" and travels out of frame, suggesting the meaning of "self-government" exists outside the confines of the screen in the real world.

Timeline, directed by Gary Farmer and Angie Campbell and written by Isabelle Knockwood, is very dense visually and symbolically, overlaying graphics on videorecorded images throughout. Knockwood narrates in voice-over that "First Nations governed themselves twenty thousand years before the Europeans came to Turtle Island five hundred years ago. Self-governance is our legacy." The visuals seek to represent Indigenous historical continuity in North America as the

FIGURE 9. *Too Many Chiefs, Not Enough Indians* (Ruby-Marie Dennis, 1994). The Aboriginal Film and Video Art Alliance. Image courtesy of the artist and VTape.

FIGURE 10. *Timeline* (Isabelle Knockwood, Gary Farmer, Angie Campbell, 1994). The Aboriginal Film and Video Art Alliance. Image courtesy of the estate of Isabelle Knockwood and VTape.

basis for assertions of sovereignty: a landscape of glaciers is overlaid with graphics of petroglyphs, which crossfades to a shot of drumming near a fire with graphics of historical, archival images of Indigenous people and activities layered overtop. An image of Turtle Island appears, and Knockwood appears on screen toward the end of the voice-over. Audio of traditional singing and drumming is heard over images of a contemporary round dance, firmly situating Indigenous peoples in the present.

Turtle Island . . . Take 'Em All is written and directed by renowned visual artist Joane Cardinal Schubert, and is stylistically highly reminiscent of her visual artworks; in fact, the images are stop-motion animation of her paintings. The PSA is a collage of images and sound. Sounds of gunshots are heard over images of a map of Turtle Island, with a legend layered over the map marking out five hundred years. A beaded strand is looped and laid over a map of Blackfoot territory. The sound of traditional singing is heard and cuts to a rooster crowing, layered over an image of a gold crown moving across the screen to an imperial horn flourish. The crown collides with a turtle to the sound of

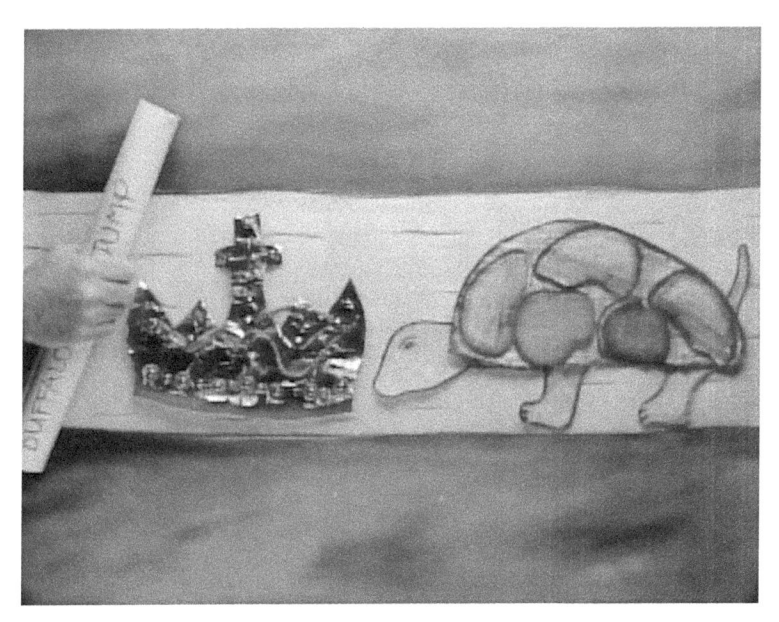

FIGURE 11. *Turtle Island . . . Take 'Em All* (Joane Cardinal Schubert, 1994). The Aboriginal Film and Video Art Alliance. Image courtesy of the artist's estate and VTape.

church bells tolling. The crown then consumes the turtle, to the sound of a shout of dismay. A piece of paper with "Indian Act" written on it is then swallowed by the crown. The turtle extricates itself from the crown, and kicks it away, to a shout of "No!" A piece of paper appears reading, "Self Determination. It's History in the Making."

The final PSA, *Indian Life with TV,* is written and directed by Gary Farmer, and is the longest PSA at sixty seconds. A satire of a family sitcom, the PSA depicts an Indigenous father, mother, and young daughter watching television in a highly staged kitchen on a theater stage. While the father excitedly watches a horse race, the mother, dressed to the nines in chic blouse and slacks with elaborate hair and makeup, changes the channel to the anger and dismay of the father. As the daughter looks on warily, the mother shouts at him that she wants all that television has to offer and wants to "watch the lives of the rich and famous!" When the parents start fighting over the remote, the daughter shouts "No!" and walks off the set and out of frame, grabbing her winter jacket as she leaves. The scene cuts to an exterior winter scene, the daughter seated in the lap of an elder woman. The camera zooms

FIGURE 12. *Indian Life with TV* (Gary Farmer, 1994). The Aboriginal Film and Video Art Alliance. Image courtesy of the artist and VTape.

back as the elder speaks, her words translated in subtitles. She explains that Indigenous people will take the "talking box of space" (television) to help themselves. As camera continues to zoom out, the parents and others walk over to join them.

As a part of conveying these messages, Beaucage relates that the PSAs had to contend with and challenge prevailing colonial discourses of Indigenous peoples that consign them to the past, which she identified as "the New Age notion of 'empowerment' current at the time" (Beaucage 2014b). Philip Deloria's analysis of New Ageism locates its roots in the counterculture movements of the 1960s and 1970s, and by the 1980s it had gained visibility and traction in popular culture (1998, 170). New Ageism draws on romanticized versions of non-Western cultural traditions, and particularly North American Indigenous cultures, fetishizing cultural traditional practices for the purposes of individualized spiritual growth. As Deloria argues, New Ageism both appropriates from and depoliticizes Indigenous peoples:

> When non-Indian New Age followers appropriated and altered a
> cosmopolitan understanding of Indianness, they laid bare a slow

rebalancing away from the collective concerns with social justice that had emerged in the 1960s and towards the renewed focus on individual freedom that has characterized America since the 1980s. (173)

New Ageism's romanticization of Indigenous cultures reinforced associations between Indigenous peoples and the past, which conflicted with efforts to make it clear that Indigenous self-determination is far from settled, and moreover, that Indigenous cultures are part and parcel of Indigenous sovereignty. The PSA works against New Ageism using several strategies, including critique of screen space, and their emphasis on resurgence, futurity, and Indigenous social and political contemporaneity.

The shared messaging of the PSAs in the collaborative production context resulted in thematic consistencies across the PSAs, even as it supported the unique aesthetic of each PSA. The PSAs are very self-reflexive, using a repeated motif of screens and foregrounding their textual construction to emphasize the historically real world outside of the screen where Indigenous communities live, and where debates about self-government must take place. The formal features of production and manipulation of images are made visible and amplified across PSAs. Images of screens recur: a portal to another future (*Future Child*) and television screens (*Too Many Chiefs, Not Enough Indians; Indian Life with TV*). The materiality and construction of screen texts are emphasized by indexing the production process (a theater stage in *Indian Life with TV*), while the textuality of screen content is foregrounded through heavy use of video graphics (*Too Many Chiefs, Not Enough Indians; Timeline*) and stop-motion animation (*Turtle Island . . . Take 'Em All*). Reflexivity makes visible the parameters of the screen, illustrating that self-government is not screen content, but a political principle enacted by Indigenous communities outside the screen space. Moreover, the unique style of each PSA was the outcome of a production process that sought to support the specific vision of the artists creating them, a process paralleling Indigenous discourses of self-government, which recognizes that there is no one form of Indigenous governance but rather a multitude determined by distinct collectivities and political affiliations.

In addition to their formal reflexivity, the PSAs have in common an emphasis on Indigenous youth, which are the focus for four of the seven PSAs: *Hip-Hop, Future Child (English and Cree versions)*, and *Indian Life with TV.* In each of these cases, youth are positioned to realize possible futures in which self-government is a reality: as a generation directly addressed by the PSA's messaging (*Hip-Hop*); as the inevitable inheritors of the future, whether it be apocalyptic or redeemed through Indigenous intervention in the present (*Future Child*); and as leaders steering Indigenous Peoples to a future grounded in and shaped by traditional values and relationships (*Indian Life with TV*). Moreover, in their orientation to possible futures, these PSAs incorporate elements of Indigenous futurisms, a term coined by Grace Dillon (Anishinaabe) (2012) that, as Danika Medak-Saltzman (Turtle Mountain Chippewa) elaborates,

> provide authors, readers, filmmakers, audiences, and our communities with opportunities to explore beyond what is and what has been and moves us toward imagining, creating, and manifesting a variety of possibilities that better represent our understandings of, our place in, and our responsibilities to this world and to those yet to come. (2017, 144)

Indigenous youth are central to possible futures as the generation that will inherit and inhabit them, and are thereby closely associated with the resurgence of ways of being in the world that hold promise and regeneration. In *Future Child,* a young boy (Campbell's son) in a plastic jacket and metallic boots stands at the edge of a dry and decimated land lit with a burning orange-red light; his face is dirty and his hair disheveled, indicative of the apocalyptic conditions he has endured. The scene cuts to the landscape and its burning orange sun, which dissolves to a "portal" through which are seen images of a green landscape, a healthy body of water, and animals grazing and swimming. It is suggested that the portal is the product of the child's vision, and implies that given the right conditions, the child would be the source of the land's redemption, saving it from its fate. Moreover, the reference to "the next seven generations" invokes prophecy to link the possibility of a redeemed future to Indigenous traditional knowledge. As Gail Guthrie Valaskakis (Chippewa) explains:

> In Indian Country, some Native people speak about the prophecy of the Seventh Fire, predicting a time when we will return to tra-

ditional ways, relationships, and responsibilities. Some Elders say that this prophesy decrees that only Native people will be among the "New People," the Seventh Generation, who will return to the cultural teachings of Indian traditions. Other Elders say that non-Natives, too, are among those who will recognize the cultural ways that honour the earth and its people. For both, there is the promise that the Seventh Generation will lead us to the Eighth Fire, which embodies an eternal era of peace and kinship built upon the shared ideology of renewed wisdom and a new relationship among Indians and Others. (2005, 257–58)

The Seventh Fire prophecy is an Anishinaabeg prophecy, and as Valaskakis describes, it has been taken up in pan-Indigenous mobilizations to unify the political vision of self-determination movements across the continent. Here, an Indigenous worldview is positioned as the path through which the world may be saved from settler colonial society, the source of its suffering.

Campbell drew on her community's experiences of unchecked resource extraction in the production of *Future Child*. She links her approach to understandings of the cultural background that each participant brought to the table for their group discussions, explaining:

Everybody that came to the training at Banff Centre for the Arts on this project came from different places across Canada; they all had different issues from their lands from where they came from and their whole experience of life living at that place and time period of events that occurred there. It was about how that combination of events and growing up there, the contrast, the ideas, the politics, and everything there was to talk about—that's what we talked about. We talked about ourselves and it gave us all a broader image of where we were [as Indigenous people]. (2016)

Thus, Campbell drew on her community of origin for her individual creative vision, which reflects the political vision through which the PSA artists were brought together at Banff Centre. *Future Child* uses genre markers of science fiction to depict a dystopia for Indigenous peoples without self-government. William Lempert argues that Indigenous speculative fiction and futurism is distinguished by dystopian narratives, stating:

> Unlike Hollywood sci-fi films that project Western desires and anxieties regarding colonization, self-destruction, and Euro-typical utopia–dystopias, Native counterparts explore categorically different subjects, including noncolonial encounters of the third kind, utopian sovereignty, and dystopian assimilation. (2014, 165)

The "future" projected by *Future Child* is one of dystopian assimilation, should Western development continue unchecked. Campbell elaborates on this scenario, linking it to exploitative forestry practices in her community:

> If our people don't take a stand on the oppressors that continue to destroy our homelands and our way of life, which includes our forests and water, that's how it's going to look. It's not science fiction. That's reality. That's how it's starting to look in my home community when they're cutting the trees. (2016)

Campbell's comments align with those of Mi'kMaq filmmaker Jeff Barnaby, who has stated that "Native America *is*, by any measure, a post apocalyptic [*sic*] culture" (Barnaby quoted in Lempert 2014, 172). These comments make clear that for Indigenous peoples, the apocalypse is not a potential scenario, but has already happened. Campbell's use of science fiction tropes is therefore not so much "speculative" as a symbolic representation of the present.

Like Future Child, *Hip-Hop* (Ruby-Marie Dennis and Crissy Red) is shaped by elements of Indigenous futurisms in linking youth to possible futures shaped by self-government. Indigenous hip-hop insists upon Indigenous cultural persistence, challenging essentialist discourses of Indigenous cultures linked to "past-ness." Instead, Craig Proulx employs theoretical frameworks of hybridity and cosmopolitanism to characterize it as a form of self-expression grounded in contemporary Indigenous social realities of Indigenous identities. In his analysis of Indigenous hip-hop, Proulx employs the concept of "rooted cosmopolitanisms" to describe the simultaneous local and global dimensions of social relations that shape Indigenous identity and examines "how roots and routes are creatively reconfigured in emerging social, oppositional, and self-determinative projects of Aboriginal hip hoppers" (2010, 42). Indigenous "rooted cosmopolitanism," Proulx argues, is "premodern"; that is, it existed prior to contact, as Indigenous groups maintained trading and social relations across broad geographical and cultural regions while sustaining their own distinct tribal and cultural identities (43). Marianne Ignace employs a similar spatial, social, and cultural framework of the global/local, examining "how artists weave the functions and messages of hip-hop music as art of resistance into very localized messages shaped by their particular histories, meanings, languages and experiences" (2011, 204). The work of Indigenous hip-hop artists is therefore "intertextual messages . . . of dialogue between the artists' own lived experiences of the rez and the city, between Aboriginal culture and globalized pop culture, marginalization, and race, and with the images of Aboriginality out there" (204–5). Just as Proulx locates Indigenous cosmopolitanism on a continuum of Indigenous history, as a part of a longer, precolonial practice movement and exchange, Ignace argues that Indigenous hip-hop is a form of "storytelling": "where stories creatively employ images of the past, interwoven with commentary on the present and intertextual messages from other contexts, to engage in moral commentary" (205). Therefore, Indigenous hip-hop is not surface consumption of popular culture or the dilution of Indigenous cultures, but a contemporary iteration of Indigenous cultural traditions.

At the same time, hip-hop undeniably has a popular appeal, a dimension of the genre that Crissy Red states that she drew on as a part of her strategy for her messaging around self-government. In keeping with the AFVAA's emphasis on realizing an individual's creative vision, Red drew on her own familiarity with hip-hop in order to create an accessible message that encouraged youth to engage with the concept of self-government. She explains that as a participant in the PSA project:

> I was young at the time, I was in my early twenties. That was the music that was there, that was the big thing at the time, hip-hop and graffiti. I was young, I think I was one of the younger ones there at the time as far as the students. And I think that made sense too: do what you know as well. Incorporate what you're familiar with, and I think that was the thing. The music was familiar to me. (2016)

In addition to drawing on familiar cultural forms, Red explains that hip-hop's popular appeal connected youth to this political project, who she perceived as self-government's greatest stakeholders:

> It just makes sense that if we're going to talk about stuff like self-government, that we have to bring in the youth. And at the time, I thought this is what would make it interesting for me. If I'm going to do this, it has to be interesting to me, and then it has to incorporate self-government, and logically for me it was having young people involved. And also bringing in hip-hop music because it's attractive to them. (2016)

In order to engage youth with the concept, Red reasons that messaging that is more popular had a greater chance at being received by a youth audience, which she weighed against her anxieties about more "radical" interpretations of and approaches to self-government:

> If you look at it in the extreme, Native people no longer have anything to do with Canada. We make our own rules, our own laws. We take back huge sections of the land to control. That for me was very scary, because that's when people start getting hurt, when the radicalness of it comes out. That scared me. I didn't like that whole aspect of it. In my mind, trying to convey my opinions on it with them . . . I want to do something that shows we want to work together with the rest of Canada, and come to a certain respect. (2016)

Having just witnessed the violence inflicted on the Mohawk and their supporters during the Oka Crisis, as well as other standoffs, Red here reflects on the possibility of potential tensions and conflicts arising from different political approaches to self-government struggles, a consciousness that shapes the aesthetic strategies of her PSA. Form is therefore linked to cultural politics, as Red's individual vision did not seek to represent a tribal- or community-specific issue or priority, but rather is guided by her personal experiences and politics.

In *Hip-Hop*, Red employs familiar markers of youth to speak to Indigenous youth and encourage youth to "talk about" self-government, a refrain that occurs at the beginning and end of the PSA. Red explains:

> My whole idea was, let's all work together to convey this message in a way that is not threatening, and involves youth, and makes younger people think about this stuff. About their culture, and

where you want it to go. Do you want to not be a part of huge government, or do you want to run your own laws? I wasn't coming from the aspect of "I have this message," but like, "This is the subject, what do you think about it? What do you think? Talk about it." That's the whole thing about my video, "Talk about it." (2016)

The PSA is structured around a hip-hop track composed by Russell Wallace, which combines beats with Indigenous singing. The rhythm sets the tempo of the editing, with quick clips of Indigenous youth break-dancing, hanging out together, and sitting together with an elder. The voice-over is composed of different voices stating, "Learn your language," "Know about your heritage," "Get your education," "Follow your traditions," and "Listen to your elder." These statements evoke Indigeneity broadly, containing identifiers that cut across specific Indigenous cultures, and as "instructions" point to the kinds of social and cultural relations that would form the basis for debates and discussions over self-government. Thus, the PSA is concerned less with expressing a vision of self-government tied to a specific cultural context and more in the social and cultural conditions that would support its development.

CONCLUSION: TAKING THE AFVAA NATIONAL

Crissy Red's reflections on the meaning of self-government reveal the variability of how the concept was being theorized as a political platform by the PSA participants. Her reflection on the range of possible forms of political engagement—and possible conflict—gave shape to messaging aimed to appeal to Indigenous youth and encourage discussion and debate. Angie Campbell drew on her community's experiences of resource exploitation, aligning her creative vision with community concerns. Their different ideological and political approaches to the topic of self-government are revealing of the fundamental nature of how Indigenous artists and activists approached "self-government": not as a one-size-fits-all model, but as one being actively debated and shaped during this crucial period of Indigenous political consciousness and mobilization.

Ultimately, the AFVAA's partnership with the Banff Centre was short lived, lasting from 1993 to 1996, when AFVAA members determined that a more functional and productive arrangement would be for members to return to their respective regions to continue their work on self-government locally, as Beaucage explains:

> The AFVAA council made a decision to . . . pull out of Banff. And we still continued to work locally in our respective areas, like Saskatchewan, Ontario, BC. . . . Everyone worked wherever they were to continue to work against appropriation of our stories, and work towards telling our own, and having our workshops in different areas with gatherings of our own on a smaller scale . . . to try to continue that vision in other ways. (2014a)

AFVAA member Cynthia Lickers (now Lickers-Sage) (Mohawk), for instance, returned to Ontario and was instrumental in founding the imagineNATIVE Film + Media Arts Festival in Toronto. As recounted by Adrian Foster, imagineNATIVE in its early years "was merely a catalogue and resource guide, with Lickers conducting outreach into Aboriginal communities 'to increase the profile of Aboriginally produced works'" (2012, 37), but which has since grown to be the largest Indigenous media arts festival in the world. As Beaucage suggests, the AFVAA's reach and agenda has legacies across a broader cultural field than a single-site analysis can account for. At the same time, however, given the Banff Centre's influence and reputation in media arts production in Canada and worldwide, this single-site focus provides perspective on the reach of the AFVAA's influence within media arts worlds, and the discourse of Indigenous media it advanced to actualize the link between Indigenous sovereignty and cultural production in order to meaningfully reflect Indigenous worldviews and modes of life.

3

Programming Indigeneity

INDIGENOUS TELEVISION PRODUCTION IN THE ERA OF
THE ABORIGINAL PEOPLES TELEVISION NETWORK

The Aboriginal Peoples Television Network (APTN) began broadcasting on September 1, 1999, and is celebrated as the first national Indigenous broadcaster in the world.[1] Since then it has made an indelible mark on the field of Indigenous media in Canada. APTN airs both first- and second-window programming that include feature and documentary films, drama and comedy series, news magazines and current events programs, documentary series, children's series, music and variety, lifestyle programs, and reality television. However, the network has limited in-house production capacity[2] and instead relies on the independent production sector in Canada for original content,[3] acquiring and commissioning dozens of nonfiction programs and series, many of which are multiyear productions and/or are rebroadcast each year. In the 2018 fiscal year alone APTN reported it had committed to 38 television productions and 24 "digital media components," or 307 hours of original programming from independent producers (APTN 2018, 11), and boasted that of the 86 percent of Canadian content it aired, 98.9 percent was independently produced (APTN 2018, 5). Though a comprehensive number of Indigenous independent television production companies is not completely certain, some estimate there are around eighty Indigenous independent companies in Canada involved in producing television (AAMP Board of Directors 2013, 2), many of which have worked with APTN.

The mark that APTN has left on the Canadian and Indigenous media industries is well recognized in Canada and around the world. This might appear to contravene the goals of this book to attend to media-producing institutions in Canada that have had less scholarly attention; however, this chapter approaches APTN via the independent production companies that supply the lion's share of its original programming. Given APTN's round-the-clock programming schedule, there is much to be said about what it airs and why, though such critical attention is a relatively recent undertaking (Bredin 2010; Knopf 2010). More specifically, given the television production the broadcaster has stimulated from the independent production sector in Canada, attention is needed to how independent producers and their programming are responsive to APTN's programming priorities, mandate, and institutional identity. These companies have their own identities, values, and content priorities that intersect with APTN's mission and programming criteria in the development of original content for the network. In other words, the institutional context for APTN's content is "unwieldy" in the sense that analysis of one institution is not sufficient for understanding the textual features and strategies of this programming; instead, such analyses must bring together multiple "sites" that shape screen content. APTN programming, then, is positioned at the intersection of network priorities and the Indigenous independent producers that create them, and represent the mutualism of the network and the independent Indigenous television industry in Canada.

Nonfiction television genres have tended to be strongly represented on the APTN schedule since the broadcaster's early days, including documentaries, current affairs, news magazines, and reality television. The pervasiveness of nonfiction programs makes it possible to trace programming trends over time, which have shifted from largely educational and informational documentary series in the early 2000s to more popular, reality-TV-based models in the 2010s. This shift aligns with broader cultural trends in television programming in North America as reality television took hold as a major commercial genre in the mid-2000s; it also intersects with APTN's shifting audience priorities emphasizing youth audiences most likely to be drawn to American-style reality programming. Audience considerations position the network's cultural concerns of "sharing our Peoples' journey, celebrate our cultures, inspiring our children, and honouring the wisdom of our Elders" (APTN 2016a) in relation to popular culture and are innately tied to APTN revenue streams: audiences represent markets for advertisers, and audience demographics are used by federal funding sources to justify allocations for Indigenous television broadcasting.

Despite their commercial origins, reality TV series' appeal does not preclude their critical capacities for representing Indigenous concerns and perspectives. The Indigenous media world has historically been ambivalent about mainstream and commercial media industries, which bear much responsibility for the proliferation of Indigenous stereotypes in popular culture. Moreover, some arenas of Indigenous media theory have been interested in tracing distinct cultural aesthetics and politics in Indigenous production as the basis for defining Indigenous media, which has emphasized formal innovation and cultural politics associated with formats that typically fall outside of mainstream or commercial fare (for instance, experimental film and video; see the AFVAA's organizational mission in chapter 2). At the same time, Indigenous artists and filmmakers have always engaged with contemporaneous and popular forms that comprise their everyday experiences, for which there are countless examples, though one could easily point to Dane-Zaa artist Brian Jungen's restructuring of Nike sneakers to create masks resembling those of Northwest Coast Indigenous peoples; Ligwilda'xw Kwakwaka'wakw artist Sonny Assu's satirical appropriation of Disney and Coca-Cola images and motifs; and the authors and artists included in *This Place: 150 Years Retold* (2019), a recent anthology of Indigenous comics. Artists, critics, and scholars have discussed the significance of their work with popular culture (and that of many others) on its own merits, but have also considered the broader ideological interventions that it embodies as unmistakably contemporary. In *Indians in Unexpected Places* (2004), Philip J. Deloria (Dakota) reflects on instances where Indigenous peoples have appeared in historical and cultural contexts as "anomalies;" that is, where their presence disrupts cultural expectations of where (and when) Indigenous peoples are "supposed" to appear. These instances are almost invariably when Indigenous people are participating in modernity, whether they go to the hair salon, take part in sports, or are members of early twentieth-century jazz bands. He argues that the expectations that render these appearances as anomalous are derived from colonial ideologies in which, among other things, "the Indian" is consigned to a "pastness" that is incommensurable with modernity, despite these so-called anomalies in and of themselves being clear evidence of Indigenous contemporaneity and participation in contemporary and popular environments and activities. Artists, critics, and scholars remind us that Indigenous people are not just a part of popular culture (in the sense of being a product of the settler colonial imaginary) but play an active role in it, and more to the point, their engagement with it is hardly passive: Indigenous artists, filmmakers, and producers are in critical conversations with popular cultural forms and genres, adapting them to Indigenous concerns and lived experiences.

This chapter examines the political economy and theoretical capacities of reality television on APTN. Traditionally, nonfiction genres—particularly documentary—have been linked to historical reality, involving questions of ethics, power, and accountability. Reality television, on the other hand, has decidedly *not* been afforded such gravitas, and has instead been considered largely entertainment and/or exploitation (usually both). By recognizing the theoretical potential of reality television, this chapter seeks to level the analytical playing field and give equal critical weight to APTN's reality television series, looking at one of APTN's reality television programs *Indians + Aliens* (2013–2014). *Indians + Aliens* examines Indigenous experiences of unexplained aerial phenomena, comparing Indigenous interpretations of the events with those of Western scientists in order to guide viewers to consider the validity of Indigenous understandings of these events, an ethic that aligns with APTN's mandate to be a "cultural bridge" between Indigenous and non-Indigenous audiences (Hafsteinsson 2010, 55). The "cultural bridge" is an institutional discourse that forms the backdrop to APTN's programming priorities and commissions, a metaphor that describes the broadcaster's role as a mediator for increasing "understanding and community" between Indigenous and non-Indigenous communities (APTN 2014, 3). The ideological alignment of *Indians + Aliens* with this discourse is not meant to argue that APTN dictates independent television production "top-down," but rather to elicit APTN's influence in shaping the field of Indigenous independent production in terms of patterns of television production, genres, and ideological frameworks. This chapter first traces a history of APTN's founding to map the development of the cultural bridge discourse that guides its programming priorities and commissions. I then examine how *Indians + Aliens* intersects with APTN's mandate and advances understandings of Indigenous traditions, narratives, and epistemological frameworks required to understand the phenomena it investigates.

A BRIEF HISTORY OF THE ABORIGINAL PEOPLES TELEVISION NETWORK

The history of APTN has been traced in detail by Valerie Alia (1999), Lorna Roth (2005), Michael Evans (2008), Marian Bredin (2012), and Jennifer David (2012), who locate the network's origins in the longer history of northern Indigenous broadcasting and pressures from southern Indigenous producers and professional organizations for access to television. These accounts overlap in their emphasis on the role of the Northern Native Broadcast Access Program (NNBAP), a program of thirteen regional northern Indigenous communication societies that since 1984 had, with federal support, produced radio and television content relevant and meaningful to northern Indigenous communities. These groups did not have the means to distribute their own content, but instead formed distribution arrangements with regional, provincial, and national radio and television broadcasters, arrangements that were, Bredin explains, "notoriously unstable and did not provide optimal scheduling for Aboriginal content" 2012, 76). The NNBAP societies lobbied the federal government for a dedicated northern channel to distribute their content, and were granted a license for the Television Northern Canada (TVNC) satellite channel in 1992. TVNC operated primarily as a distribution mechanism for existing content by federally funded groups and did not have resources to produce its own content, circumstances that left TVNC, as Bredin describes, as "a 'parallel' Aboriginal system, marginal to the new kind of broadcaster incentives and production funds being developed for the larger Canadian television industry" (2012, 76).

Developments in northern broadcasting intersected with shifts in legislation and broadcast policy that ultimately supported the creation of APTN. Section 35 of the amended Canadian Constitution, 1982, which recognized and affirmed existing Indigenous rights and treaty rights, gave Indigenous–state relations a national scope. Following the repatriation of the Canadian Constitution in 1982, Canada underwent a period of law and policy reform meant to bring the state into alignment with the prevailing social and political climate in the 1980s. "Multiculturalism," which had been Canadian cultural policy since 1971, was made law under the Multiculturalism Act, 1988. Subsequently, cultural policy through the 1980s was articulated in reference to "diversity" in which women and minorities were prioritized as social groups (Druick 2007, 168). Indigenous peoples' unique relationship with the state was formalized within Canadian broadcasting via the 1991 Broadcasting Act, Section 3, which states that the Canadian broadcast system should reflect "the special place of aboriginal peoples within that [Canadian] society," and identified a need for Indigenous programming within Canadian broadcasting.[4]

Within a social and political climate in which Indigenous peoples and issues had unprecedented visibility, TVNC was able to successfully argue for a national Indigenous broadcaster. This was first proposed by TVNC in 1993, but gained momentum following the Royal Commission on Aboriginal Peoples (RCAP) in 1996, a federal inquiry into the relationship between Indigenous peoples and the Canadian state following numerous conflicts between Indigenous communities and regional, provincial, and federal governments, the most visible of which was the seventy-eight-day standoff between the Mohawk of Kanehsatake and the Canadian military that became known as the Oka Crisis of 1990. The final report argued that the Canadian media, and mainstream visual culture more broadly, are saturated by Indigenous stereotypes that contribute to tensions between Indigenous and non-Indigenous groups. Citing media coverage of the conflict at Oka, the report states:

> The events at Oka are remembered for startling media images of rock-throwing residents and scuffling Indians, staring soldiers and crying children. But in all the television, radio and newspaper coverage, one image was repeated again and again: that of the "warriors"—bandanna-masked, khaki-clad, gun-toting Indians. . . . The image bore a remarkable resemblance to the war-bonneted warrior—the dominant film and media image of Aboriginal men in the last century. (Dussault and Erasmus 1996, 582)

The report goes on to cite northern broadcasting controlled by Inuit peoples as a model for Indigenous self-representation, which supports greater understanding between Indigenous and non-Indigenous groups by more meaningfully representing Indigenous cultural values and traditions in broadcasting: "The potential of Aboriginal media to reinforce identity and community while providing a bridge to participating in the larger society is demonstrated in the history of broadcasting in the north" (Dussault and Erasmus 1996, 584). This statement brings together the politics of Indigenous cultural autonomy with the technological and discursive apparatus of the state, a dominant paradigm guiding Indigenous media engagement during this era. Assisted by calls from southern Indigenous producers for access to television broadcasting, TVNC partnered with southern Indigenous producers to submit an application to the Canadian Radio-Television and Telecommunications Commission (CRTC) for a national Indigenous broadcast network, the Aboriginal Peoples Television Network, which was approved in February 1999 (Bredin 2012, 76).

CANADIAN CULTURAL POLICY, INDIGENOUS PEOPLES, AND NATIONAL BROADCASTING

APTN took shape as a national broadcaster reconciling the specificities of Indigenous cultural nationalism, organized around Indigenous cultural continuity and Indigenous peoples' unique relationship with the Crown, and the legal and national discourse of multiculturalism undergirding Canadian national broadcasting. In the social and political climate of the late 1980s and early 1990s, the Canadian public sphere was framed in terms of "multiculturalism" as the Canadian state attempted to manage minority demands for social and political representation, in which national broadcasting and communications policy became deeply implicated. In Canada, the inception of multiculturalism as state policy in 1971 marks a reconfiguration of discourses of "national unity" from integration and assimilation to the "ethnic mosaic" attending multiculturalism. Sarah Wayland explains that this policy was introduced to ameliorate the social unrest from ethnic groups that followed the 1963 Royal Commission on Bilingualism and Biculturalism (RCBB), which was established to recommend steps to

> develop the Canadian Confederation on the basis of equal partnership between the two founding races [sic], taking into account the contribution made by other ethnic groups to the cultural enrichment of Canada and the measures that should be taken to safeguard that contribution. (RCBB quoted in Wayland 1997, 46)

These groups expressed concerns that their history and contributions to the nation were being ignored (47). Along with the widespread protests accompanying the White Paper of 1969, which represented an updated version of Canada's assimilation policies toward Indigenous peoples, Trudeau's liberal government quickly abandoned (French and English) biculturalism and instead sought a "multicultural society within a bilingual framework," attempting to balance Quebec's interests with ethnic collectives that represented important votes to the Liberal Party (47). Critics of multiculturalism, Wayland notes, have argued that it celebrates cultural and ethnic difference at the expense of addressing the economic and social needs of minorities: "The ethnic groups which originally fought for a multiculturalism policy were mainly white, European, and had resided in Canada for some time. Their needs were principally expressive, namely cultural promotion and language retention" (48). Will Kymlicka has argued that this form of multiculturalism effectively results in social balkanization, maintaining "a wealthy, educated white majority and impoverished, unskilled racialized minorities" (2010, 21). These criticisms emerge from the recognition that multiculturalism does not necessarily represent a shift in the status quo, but rather converts the terms of state management from policies based on assimilation to "management" via the maintenance of cultural or ethnic difference.

Legislation surrounding national communications participated in this political shift. Following the passage of the Multiculturalism Act, 1988, the Canadian Broadcasting Corporation (CBC), Canada's public broadcaster, had its mandate reaffirmed by the 1991 Broadcasting Act, which stated that it was to "contribute to shared national consciousness and identity . . . (and) reflect the multicultural and multiracial nature of Canada."[5] Lorna Roth explains that as a part of Canada's cultural development strategy, minority and Indigenous broadcasting would help to "inscribe . . . cultural pluralism as a prime characteristic of the democratic state" (2005, 10). However, Indigenous peoples refused to be subsumed within multiculturalism as another constituency group, and instead argued that they "merit a special status because of their exceptional positioning within Canada's history as a subjugated people in a settler society" (13). This position has been echoed in Canadian liberal political philosophy, particularly work by Kymlicka, which concerns the minority groups' collective rights. When discussing patterns of "cultural diversity," Kymlicka differentiates between diversity arising from immigrant "ethnic groups" and that arising from "the incorporation of previously self-governing territorially concentrated cultures into a larger state," which he terms "minority nations" (1995, 10). In Canada, Kymlicka asserts, Indigenous peoples and the Quebecois constitute minority nations and possess collective rights apart from those of the state owing to their unique histories preceding the formation of the contemporary state. Given Quebec's colonial origins and its displacements of Indigenous peoples, it is highly problematic to equate them, let alone frame Indigenous nations as "nested" within the state; however, Kymlicka speaks to the ideological roots for a category of "Indigenous rights" that functions within the liberal pluralist state.

Roth points to such roots in perceptions that Indigenous television has fostered "acceptance" of Indigenous peoples "as integral participants in the developing fabric of a pluralistic community of communities" (2005, 11). Indigenous recognition in Canadian federal law and policy implicitly positions Indigenous peoples within the Canadian pluralist public sphere. As argued in chapter 1, however, when speaking of the pluralist liberal state, it is more useful to think of multiple and overlapping public spheres as the context for Indigenous broadcasting (Avison 1996; Meadows 2005). This is relevant to APTN in particular as it constructs and addresses an Indigenous public sphere in terms of "counterpublics" that, as discussed in detail in chapter 1, describes how nondominant groups employ the discursive norms of the dominant group in order to produce themselves in conflict with it, a framework useful for understanding how Indigenous social movements have deployed "nationhood" to mark out a terrain of Indigenous historical and cultural difference as the basis for claims to political and social autonomy. APTN, as a minority yet national broadcaster, retains the cultural politics of an Indigenous counterpublic even as it seeks to resolve them within the discursive and institutional demands of national broadcasting.

APTN emerged from this organizational, economic, and discursive field as a national broadcaster that seeks to reconcile Indigenous cultural nationalism with the multicultural discourse of national broadcasting. Like the CBC, APTN operates in "the public interest" as determined in the CRTC's 1999 decision granting APTN's broadcast license (CRTC 1999), which the regulator justified citing Section 3 of the 1991 Broadcasting Act that affirmed Indigenous peoples' special place in Canadian society and the importance of Indigenous programming. The CRTC decision therefore uses the law to rationalize policy by defining Indigenous broadcasting as integral to the Canadian public sphere:

> APTN will offer new, diverse programming with a high level of Canadian content that reflects the culture, history and concerns of Aboriginal peoples. Through this programming, APTN will provide social benefits by strengthening the cultural identity

of Aboriginal peoples and offering a cultural bridge between Aboriginal and non-Aboriginal Canadians. The Commission has, therefore, determined that national distribution of APTN is in the public interest. (CRTC 1999)

The metaphorical language of a "cultural bridge" links national identity to the public sphere via communications policy and broadcast technologies. Thus, in terms of policy, APTN is positioned as a mechanism for bringing Indigenous people into the national public sphere while sustaining Indigenous cultural, historical, and political specificity. The discursive context for APTN, then, supports key premises of Indigenous cultural nationalism that assert Indigenous cultural and political continuity. The discourse of "cultural bridge" also invokes the RCAP report's characterization of Indigenous broadcasting, as it implies communication and mutual understanding between Indigenous and non-Indigenous Canadian society.

APTN IN THE FIELD OF CANADIAN NATIONAL BROADCASTING

APTN has emerged in the context of Canadian national television, which must be understood in terms of its internal industrial structure and its relationship to the global television market that undergirds APTN's shift to more commercially successful programming formats. Marc Raboy describes the domestic television industry as a hybrid system or semiprivate system owing to the mutual imbrication of public broadcasting and private production sectors that definitively took shape in the 1980s (1990, 178). Canada's national broadcaster, the CBC, had not been an exclusively public enterprise since the postwar period, when it began to derive a portion of its funding from advertising, though its relationship to the private sector developed further when it was positioned an "alternative" to private broadcasters, which the CRTC licensed throughout the 1960s and 1970s. In the 1980s, the private sector was nested within Canadian national broadcasting when in-house production was contracted out to private producers, who received subsidies from the newly created Broadcast Program Development Fund that was administered by Telefilm Canada (187). The CBC's new role was to be a "provider" of Canadian programming created by private producers—in other words, a significant portion of the CBC had now been privatized, with the private sector receiving public funds (187), leading to its current semiprivate state.

The particularities of the "internal" industrial makeup of Canadian public television, and the programming that it airs, take shape within the broader global television market. Serra Tinic argues that Canadian productions negotiate between domestic and international markets via a process of "mediation," in which they "reproduce recognizable Hollywood genres but tend to speak to a broader range of social, political, and cultural discourses. This particularly enhances their value to media buyers in countries with similar histories of public broadcasting" (2009, 171). Tinic invokes the external, market-based logic of Canadian television production, and by doing so complicates cultural nationalist analyses of Canadian television that seek out the expression of Canadian "identity" or "sensibility" in its screen content. Mediation is less concerned with making claims to a coherent national identity than in the ways in which this content appeals to and negotiates different international markets.

Tinic's concept of mediation is useful for examining how APTN attempts to reconcile Indigenous cultural nationalism with the national and transnational dimensions of Canadian television. Like the CBC, APTN is a hybrid public-private system. While it is regulated by the CRTC, it does not receive federal funding and instead generates revenue largely through subscriber fees and advertising revenue, which in 2013 came to just under C$38.5 million and C$2.4 million respectively,[6] of which about two-thirds goes toward costs associated with network programming (KPMG LLP 2014, 5). It is governed by a board of directors "from all regions of Canada" (APTN 2016b), seeking representation with national scope. Its programming policies demonstrate how "Indigenous control" is implemented in institutional policy and practice. APTN relies on content commissioned from private production companies, and as a part of its eligibility criteria, requires that these be "Aboriginal Production Companies" in which "Aboriginal Persons" or "Aboriginal Businesses" have at least 51 percent ownership and control (APTN 2016c), attempting to facilitate the growth of the independent Indigenous television sector through institutional policy. In his ethnography of APTN's head office and national news division, Sigurjón Baldur Hafsteinsson describes APTN's journalistic practice as an exercise of "deep democracy," as theorized by Arjun Appadurai (2002), which "endeavor[s] to introduce or revive deep democratic principles among Aboriginal peoples and others in a way that 'suggest roots, anchors, intimacy, proximity, and locality'" (Hafsteinsson 2008, 5). Through interviews with APTN personnel and analysis of their journalistic practices, Hafsteinsson argues that APTN exhibits sensitivity to Indigenous ceremonies, national differences, and "foreground[s] . . . narrative, feeling and intimacy" (2010, 60), techniques that are not frequently seen in mainstream media practices, which align with practices of an Indigenous counterpublic, as evoked by his claim that "APTN suggests an institutional model for the representation of difference that rejects mainstream news-media practices fraught with sensationalism and stereotyping" (Hafsteinsson 2010, 53).

BALANCING ACTS: THE LIMITS OF APTN'S MANDATE

While APTN seeks to reconcile Indigenous cultural nationalism with Canadian broadcasting, as discussed in the previous section, the critiques the broadcaster has received from Indigenous groups, particularly around APTN's support for Indigenous languages, reveals the material and discursive limitations of the broadcaster's mandate. During the CRTC's license renewal hearings for APTN in 2005, the Independent Aboriginal Screen Producers Association (IASPA) submitted an intervention that critiqued APTN for, among other things, what it perceived to be the limited representation of Indigenous languages on the network, arguing that

> our languages hang precariously perched on the edge of survival. Without our language we lose our distinctiveness as first nations and aboriginal people. Some languages are stronger than others. We need to develop a system where we can address both the educational and entertainment needs of the Canadian audience while placing emphasis on the need for a more effective and diverse language programming strategy. (APTN Conditional Support 2005)

IASPA's emphasis on the importance of languages to Indigenous cultural survival, and the role of broadcasting in sustaining Indigenous languages, echoes the findings of the 1996 RCAP, which throughout its four thousand pages emphasized the centrality of languages to Indigenous cultures:

Language is the principal instrument by which culture is transmitted from one generation to another, by which members of a culture communicate meaning and make sense of their shared experience. Because language defines the world and experience in cultural terms, it literally shapes our way of perceiving—our world view. (Dussault and Erasmus 1996, 563)

In the commission's recommendations, it positions broadcasting as a means to enable cultural revitalization via language programming:

By increasing the presence and legitimacy of Aboriginal languages, broadcasting reinforces the interest and language competence of younger Aboriginal community members and helps slow the growing linguistic and generation gap between them and older unilingual members. (Dussault and Erasmus 1996, 588)

The view of RCAP, echoed in IASPA's intervention, is that Indigenous broadcasting would serve a direct educational function; in addition, it identifies that language programming will immediately affect and benefit Indigenous audiences, which Chon Noriega has described as the "hypodermic needle" model of media reception frequently employed by minoritized groups, a discursive strategy that allows minority interests to argue for the need for minority programming (2000, 170). In this case, RCAP and IASPA argue that resources for Indigenous television and language broadcasting can directly facilitate language competency and intergenerational and community relations.

In his response to IASPA's intervention, Jean La Rose (Abenaki), then CEO of APTN, reinforces APTN's role as a means for enabling Indigenous cultural revitalization, but qualifies his claims by citing the material, industrial limitations of a national broadcaster. La Rose identifies that while APTN has a "role to play in revitalizing Aboriginal languages," that role must be weighed in relation to "other aspects of [their] mandate," and that IASPA's recommendations for prioritizing Indigenous language programming would actually "disadvantage" Indigenous peoples who do not speak an Indigenous language, which were about 75 percent in 2005. Further he states:

APTN must ensure that the balance that is struck in providing Aboriginal language programming, on the one hand, and programming in English and/or French on the other, be reflective of APTN's mandate in this regard, but also very mindful of the audience reality and the expectations of that audience that they can also "share in the stories" by understanding them. (CMF 2013b)

La Rose here makes an argument about language programming based in proportional representation in order to foreground APTN as first and foremost a broadcaster subject to the parameters of institutional and broadcast policy and resource limitations to fund program development. La Rose is grappling with the complexities of APTN as a broadcaster established through the politics of Indigenous cultural nationalism that is premised on Indigenous cultural resurgence, yet within the political economy of Canadian broadcasting. He therefore seeks to resolve the issue within this political economy, specifically the field of independent television production, identifying growth in Indigenous language programming that he attributes to "the growing diversity among Aboriginal producers of applications to the Aborignal language fund administered by the Canadian Television Fund" (CMF 2013b). By identifying alternative sources for funding for Indigenous programming, as well as a diversified field of Indigenous broadcasters, La Rose locates the potential for Indigenous language programming in the private sector of the Indigenous production industry, rather than solely within APTN's resources. Thus, IASPA's intervention and APTN's response makes visible the political economy of Indigenous television industry and APTN's symbiotic if not always harmonious relationship to it.

APPROACHES TO TEXTUAL ANALYSIS OF INDIGENOUS TELEVISION

Literature testing analytical approaches to the interpretation of Indigenous television programming in Canada is a developing area of study. Hafsteinsson's ethnography of APTN's journalism division links institutional discourses to APTN's journalistic practice, though he does not undertake content analysis; rather, he focuses on "the fluid ideas and practices that are essential in producing the network and its diverse programming" (2008, 48–49). Bredin's political economy of the Indigenous television industry includes two case studies of drama series that link the social position of the production companies (Indigenous and non-Indigenous) to ideological differences in the series, where the series by Indigenous producers links contemporary social issues with the legacy of colonialism, while the other elides colonial history, locating social issues in the realm of the personal (2012). Bredin argues that APTN's programming is not ideologically consistent, linking these differences to identities of the producers themselves. Similarly, Kerstin Knopf identifies ideological contradictions between APTN's mission and some of its content, arguing that non-Indigenously produced children's series and feature films by non-Indigenous filmmakers that the network has licensed because they have Indigenous themes or performers complicate what Knopf characterizes as APTN's decolonial mission (2010).

These authors make an invaluable contribution to analytical approaches to APTN's programming by addressing its diversity in terms of mode and genre, and by tracing the ideological inconsistencies of the program day, revealing just how much pressure the cultural bridge discourse can sustain. My intent is to contribute to theoretical questions we can ask of APTN's content by bringing together analysis of audience construction and genre with APTN's institutional discourse to discuss *Indians + Aliens*. The broadcaster's audience construction is key context for the series, as *Indians + Aliens* airs in APTN's prime-time slot, which is largely dedicated to "entertainment" content—mainly variety programming and dramas—aimed at general adult audiences and increasingly to young adult and teenage audiences in the latter 2000s. Audience *construction* is key here since, as Marian Bredin argues, research on APTN's actual audience is difficult to obtain; moreover, there isn't a mechanism by which to consistently and reliably measure Indigenous vs. non-Indigenous audiences over time (Bredin 2010). Bredin identifies that some research is proprietary and therefore not readily available, but draws together several quantitative sources to develop a picture of APTN's actual audience in the early 2000s, including the Bureau of Broadcast Measurement, Neilsen measures, a focus-group study commissioned by APTN in 2002, a Print Measurement Bureau (PMB) study from 2004 of urban Indigenous media use, surveys commissioned by APTN in communities north of the sixtieth parallel, and an Indian and Northern Affairs Canada (INAC) study from 2003 of on-reserve residents' responses to APTN (82). Bredin identifies that the INAC study, for instance, identified that nearly half of on-reserve residents watched APTN some of the time (82), and that the PMB study reported that southern, urban APTN audiences were "75 percent white, 7.4 percent Aboriginal people, 5 percent black, and 12.6% from 'other ethnic backgrounds,'" and that of these audiences, APTN reaches 46 percent of southern urban and Indigenous audiences in the eighteen- to twenty-four-year-old age bracket, concluding that available quantitative data indicates that APTN reaches a broad audience and was drawing young Indigenous viewers (83).

Bredin's research on audience demographics from the early 2000s suggests that APTN would have been aware of the coveted older youth demographic that was a key constituent of its audience from the mid-2000s and therefore an important market to court in its programming decision-making. APTN's audience priorities were further refined over the 2000s to young adult and teenage audiences; at the same time, reality television was gaining traction in North America as a popular television genre. While the origin of the genre has been dated to 1992 with MTV's *The Real World,* Leigh H. Edwards points to the remarkable success of *Survivor* (CBS, 2000) as the starting point for the reality television "boom" that definitively took hold by the mid-2000s (2013, 4). Dominated as it is by American television programming, Canadian television would have been a built-in audience for reality television. The point at which reality television gained a foothold in the domestic Canadian television industry deserves more detailed attention; however, as is discussed in relation to *Indians + Aliens,* it is possible to identify a trend toward reality television on APTN in the later 2000s. Bringing together APTN's audience priorities with broader cultural trends in television programming, and within the political economy of the Canadian television industry, suggests that this programming strategy was designed to boost primetime audiences overall, which would appeal to APTN advertisers while also triggering more funding for independent Indigenous television producers, where funding bodies use audience metrics to determine annual allocations for production. In other words, the larger the audiences, the greater the allocation, making more programming available for broadcast on the network.

APTN AND POPULAR U.S. TELEVISION GENRES

Rezolution Pictures was one of the first independent production companies to be recognized for borrowing from reality television formats

(Bredin 2012, 80), and its institutional profile has positioned it in the vanguard in Indigenous media, both economically and creatively. Rezolution Pictures was cofounded by husband and wife Ernest Webb (Cree) and Catherine Bainbridge in 2001. The company's website outlines a diverse production history that includes dramatic and documentary feature-length films and television series, claiming that "since 2001, Rezolution Pictures has been at the forefront of Canada's cultural landscape, having attracted over $25 million to develop and produce award-winning projects" (Rezolution Pictures, Inc. 2016). The company has produced several dramatic and documentary-based series for APTN, including *Rez Rides* (2004–2005), *Indians + Aliens* (2013–2014), *Working It Out Together* (2010–2015), *Mohawk Girls* (2012–2017), and *Moose TV* (2011). These series draw on popular U.S. television formats or recognizable Indigenous personalities,[7] which are designed for widespread appeal and which capitalize on contemporary popular figures and genres.[8] Press coverage contributes to Rezolution Pictures' aura of innovation, characterizing its production as "edgy" (Broadcaster Magazine 2014) and "eye opening" (Dunlevy 2011), and includes quotes from the executive producers stating that they are "breaking new ground" and that their comedy series are "a refreshing change" (Guelph Mercury 2006, F12).

Their company profile is consistent with their production strategy and output, which aligns with APTN's audience priorities and programming trends that cater to older youth audiences. Marian Bredin notes that as of at least 2005, the network sought programming targeted at "Aboriginal Youth" that included not only youth-oriented programs but also content that was more "broadly appealing and accessible" for "a diverse audience, including urban and rural, Aboriginal and non-Aboriginal, and speakers of English, French, and Aboriginal languages" (2012, 80). In the latter 2010s, however, APTN made a more definitive shift in audience priorities, stating that "young adults and teenagers have been identified as the primary demographic and mature adults and younger children are the secondary demographic" (APTN 2011a), and announced on the "Milestones" page on its corporate website that in June 2011, "APTN approves a new business plan developed and focused on youth as a primary target audience" (APTN 2011b), linking this audience demographic to market considerations. While the network does not provide an explicit rationale for this shift, there are industrial considerations influencing the network's direction.

APTN does not provide funding for the majority of the programming it airs; rather, independent producers rely on both private and public funding to develop their work. The Canada Media Fund (CMF) is particularly significant: it is a public/private entity created by the Department of Canadian Heritage and the Canadian cable industry, which delivers significant financial support in the form of allocations referred to as "performance envelopes"—totaling some C$1.4 billion—to Canadian television and digital media content (CMF 2016c). The CMF has an Indigenous "performance envelope" called the Aboriginal Program, which delivers development and production funding for Indigenous television programming, approximately C$10 million in 2012. APTN therefore depends on the CMF to support programming it airs. However, the annual allocation is not stable, but rather based on a set of criteria, or "performance factors," that the CMF uses to determine each year's allocation: audience success—total hours tuned (to CMF-funded programs); audience success—Original First Run (total hours tuned to new CMF-funded content); historic performance (the broadcaster's previous success in securing CMF funding); regional production licenses (an incentive to develop regional production); and digital media investment (an incentive for broadcasters to develop digital media content to augment broadcast programming) (CMF 2016a). Audience success factors are the most heavily weighted, and with the historic performance factor, total approximately 70 percent of the weight (CMF 2013a).

Thus, there is an industrial incentive for broadcasters to support popular programming that would encourage a broad audience, either via new content or through programs that can encourage greater return viewership. APTN suggests that Indigenous youth represent a potentially large and growing audience: "With the growing population of Aboriginal Peoples in Canada, especially the rising proportion of youth, it is more important than ever that Aboriginal Peoples see themselves and their experiences and aspirations reflected in mainstream media" (CMF 2013b). Cultivating this audience with youth-oriented programming—particularly those based on U.S. popular genres such as reality-based television—would potentially encourage youth audiences (who may develop network loyalty over time), as well as a larger general audience drawn to such formats. Larger audiences are attractive to advertisers, of course; therefore, popular formats attracting larger audiences represent a promise of greater revenue for APTN. Indeed, reality-style programs had already begun to appear on APTN's schedule by 2007, the first among them being *Rez Rides* (2007–2009) that its producer, Rezolution Pictures, describes as "in the spirit of *Pimp My Ride, American Chopper* and *Monster Garage, Rez Rides* is a documentary series about two very different custom car shops" (n.d.b).[9] While nonfiction series tended to be confined to the afternoon timeslots that APTN dedicated to lifestyle, educational, and cultural programming, by 2013 a substantial number of entertainment-based documentary series were represented across the schedule. "Lifestyle" programs include the long-running kitchen series, *Cooking with the Wolfman* (2002–present), as well as more recent series that include *Chefs Run Wild* (2014), *Native Planet* (2014), *Moosemeat & Marmalade* (2013–present), *Akiboyz* (2016), *Face the Music* (2016), *Fit First* (2011–present), and *Fish Out of Water* (2007–present). Lifestyle and cultural programming still largely remains associated with older adult audiences in the afternoons; however, entertainment-based nonfiction and reality formats are increasingly represented in prime time, including the long-running true crime series *Exhibit A* (1997–present), *Rez Rides,* the front-lines emergency services series *Chaos and Courage* (2013–2014), the paranormal reality series *The Other Side* (2014–2014), and *Indians + Aliens* (2013–2014). Prime time continues to be associated with a "general adult" audience (APTN 2004), but the greater representation of series based on popular U.S. formats speaks to an effort to appeal to youth audiences and a broad Indigenous and non-Indigenous audience as well.[10]

INDIANS + ALIENS: INDIGENOUS EPISTEMOLOGIES MEET REALITY TV

Rezolution Pictures describes *Indians + Aliens* as being "about encounters with unidentified flying objects in the Cree territories of northern Quebec. From the unexplained to the all-too-explainable: it is a slice of truly contemporary Native mythology, now taking shape in the Canadian North" (Rezolution Pictures, Inc., n.d.a). The series consists of nineteen 22-minute episodes over two seasons hosted by Ernest Webb, who is himself a member of the Cree community of Chisasibi in northern Quebec. Each episode investigates an Indigenous witness's first-hand account of their experience with unexplained phenomena and explores possible explanations for these sightings from scientific

FIGURE 13. A title screen from *Indians + Aliens,* (Season 1, 2013). Image courtesy of Rezolution Pictures.

and traditional Cree perspectives. The co-presentation of these perspectives anticipates both Indigenous and non-Indigenous audiences, doing ideological double duty by providing a platform for Cree perspectives and belief systems, and giving them weight and credibility associated with scientific explanations, which can, as represented in the series, at times supersede scientific perspectives.[11]

The first episode sets up the narrative structure and presentation of "evidence" that each subsequent episode generally follows. Webb acts as narrator, describing the history of unexplained sightings by Indigenous people from the northern region, then introduces the witness whose account will be investigated in that episode. The witness's sighting is then re-created, followed by Indigenous and scientific interpretations of the event. The first episode focuses on a sighting by Matthew Mukash, a former Cree political leader who went through a period of illness and participated in a traditional ceremony to help treat it. His interview, which takes place in his home, is intercut with a dramatic re-creation of the encounter. He relates that following the ceremony, he and a friend were walking down a forest trail and were approached by a set of lights that emerged from the forest. His friend gave the lights an offering (in his recollection, either candy or tobacco), and then returned to the lodge to get the elders to witness and explain the event while Mukash remained with the lights. Mukash recounts that he prayed to Creator, saying that he needed healing, and as he stood there, the symptoms of his illness abated. The elders, upon witnessing the lights, were very moved, and explained that traditional oral narratives contain accounts of such sightings, but that this was the first time they had seen them. In the re-creation, the camera assumes Mukash's perspective, observing renderings of the lights floating gently through the dark forest and hovering in front of him. The music for the sequence conveys the benevolence and spiritual reverence of the encounter, which Mukash echoes in his interview, describing the moment as "very emotional," his hand held to his chest. He relates that his friend told the lights that they could go, and they disappeared into the west, which is depicted in the re-creation as a shot in which the lights gather together and arc away above the tree line.

The story and Mukash's subsequent recovery from his illness are spectacular events, and to guide the audience to consider the veracity of his perspective, the episode methodically establishes Mukash's credibility as a witness, a strategy characteristic of the paranormal reality genre. In his analysis of a UK-based paranormal reality television, *Most Haunted,* Mikel J. Koven argues that the show, which investigates legend-based paranormal experiences in different regional locales, "recognises the ambivalence of the legend genre itself, which encourages neither belief nor disbelief, as essentialist categories, but a metatextual debate about whether or not such events are *possible*"

FIGURE 14. Matthew Mukash's encounter with unexplained orbs of light is the focus for the series' first episode. *Indians + Aliens,* 2013. Image courtesy of Rezolution Pictures.

FIGURE 15. A re-creation of Mukash's encounter with the lights. Episode 1, *Indians + Aliens*, 2013. Image courtesy of Rezolution Pictures.

(2007, 187). As such, *Most Haunted* employs a range of techniques designed to encourage the audience to consider the possibility of supernatural interpretation, which in part relies on the credibility of the parapsychologists who investigate these events (192–93). Similarly, *Indians + Aliens* sets out to convince the audience of the witnesses' credibility in order to support the possibility of interpreting these events through Cree epistemologies. The first ten minutes of this twenty-two-minute episode are a portrait of Mukash, who is at the time of production in his early sixties and a longtime political representative of his community. He is grounded by his professional experience, age, and commitment to the Cree people. In his interviews, he is soft spoken, clear, and humble. His character lends credibility to the experiences he describes, which is then reinforced by an interview with Harry Snowboy (Cree) that follows Mukash's account. Snowboy is introduced as a former police officer who is currently a traditional healer and who, as Webb states in voice-over, is "familiar with Cree legends and our view of the universe" (Webb 2013). The development of Snowboy's credibility parallels Mukash's, but also contextualizes and bolsters Mukash's first-hand experience. Snowboy explains that "legends" encode historical experiences, saying that they are "passed on from generation to another, and these stories are very, very old." By way of illustration, he explains that "there are stories that talk about the time when there was no summer. So that would be the Ice Age. And there are stories that are about certain creatures that existed during this time that are now extinct. So you can tell how old these stories are." Having asserted the historicity of Cree oral narratives, Snowboy describes Cree stories that refer to "other worlds than this one that we live in now, and there are other beings that inhabit that world." Between Mukash's experience and Snowboy's expert knowledge, the episode builds the case for the plausibility of otherworld encounters as understood in terms of Cree oral narratives.

At the same time, Snowboy's comparison between Cree oral narratives and scientifically verified historical events like the Ice Age enact a comparison between Indigenous and Western epistemologies that acts as a motif for the series as a whole. The series places oral histories and scientific interpretation side-by-side, often tipping interpretation toward Cree perspectives. The sequence with Mukash and Snowboy cuts to Webb's voice-over, where he states, "So if our legends talk about other worlds that are inhabited, what's really out there? What if Matthew [Mukash] encountered intelligent beings from another planet? ... I want to know what people are saying from the scientific perspective." The sequence then cuts to an interview with Chris Rutowski, introduced as a science writer, who describes a history of unexplained aerial phenomena in Canada. Like Mukash, Rutkowski is represented via a talking head interview, though while Mukash is interviewed in his home among familiar belongings, Rutkowski is recorded in front of a less-personal green screen onto which are displayed images thematically related to the phenomena he discusses. The intimacy given to Mukash's account contrasts with the more abstracted scientific knowledge that frames Rutkowski. This effect is enhanced by other contexts in which he is depicted: his interview is intercut with shots of him in his office, its shelves bursting with books mixed with stuffed toys of aliens and other alien-related paraphernalia. Mukash and Snowboy's gravitas contrasts with Rutkowski's enthusiasm for the topic, their culturally grounded reflections with his scholarly and popular fascination.

Indians + Aliens stages comparison between Cree and scientific perspectives in order to provide a platform for understanding Cree epistemology, histories, and traditional knowledge that are shared by Cree witnesses and experts in their interpretations of these events, which are given equal if not more weight than scientific explanations. The first episode sets up an Indigenous interpretive framework through Mukash, who says that when it comes to spiritual events, "you don't

FIGURE 16. An interview with Chris Rutkowski conducted against green screen background images. Episode 1, *Indians + Aliens*, 2013. Image courtesy of Rezolution Pictures.

FIGURE 17. Chris Rutkowski and Ernest Webb in Rutkowski's office. Episode 1, *Indians + Aliens*, 2013. Image courtesy of Rezolution Pictures.

try to figure out how things work." Instead, a person must accept what they see as an encounter with another world or dimension of reality, which can be understood as a "gift." This orientation is set alongside scientific perspectives that examine physical, evidence-based understandings, comparing their merits. In each episode, Webb and representatives of the scientific perspective speculate and experiment with possible explanations for unexplained phenomena, but these invariably result in uncertainty. Unexplained aerial phenomena *could* be early experimental military aircraft that looked like flying saucers, though these aircraft could only hover a few feet off the ground; or a burning object in the sky falling on an erratic path could be a crashing plane or meteorite, though no reports exist of any such accidents, and meteorites only fall in straight lines. This rhetorical structure highlights the potential limitations of scientific explanations, as the cycle of questioning and testing only generates more questions and more ambiguity. The Indigenous perspective—here, Cree specifically—accommodates the ambiguity and unknown because it acknowledges the autonomy of other "worlds" or dimensions of reality that cannot readily be known or observed directly.

At the same time, however, the comparison between Cree and scientific perspectives is neither absolute nor constant in the series. In fact, the series weighs them alongside each other to illustrate the significant overlaps between these systems of knowledge. Toward the end of episode 3, Webb reflects in voice-over that Cree theories of a multilayered world or multiple dimensions resonates with contemporary scientific knowledge, saying "apparently this stuff is the latest thing in theoretical physics and it's an idea the Cree have been on to for thousands of years." Ideas of multiple dimensions, the stuff of quantum mechanics, is found within Cree traditional knowledge and has existed for millennia. Further, the potential existence of other, nonhuman beings in other worlds is also found within both Cree and scientific belief systems. In episode 1, Harry Snowboy states, "Our stories say there's other worlds than this world that we live in. And there's other beings that inhabit that world. It was just a normal part of who we are as a people, our belief system." Later in the episode, Webb interviews Professor Robert Lamontagne, an astrophysicist at the University of Montreal, who explains how astronomers deduce the existence of planets orbiting other stars by observing their gravitational effects on the stars, and by detecting the dimming effect on the star's brightness when a planet's orbit brings the planet in front of it. Both Rutkowski and Lamontagne assert that such empirically derived evidence of other planets implies the possibility of life elsewhere in the universe; Lamontagne states explicitly: "I believe that there is life out there. Even though we cannot communicate with it, I believe there is life out there." Inferential evidence here complements and even supports

Cree traditional narratives, bringing the two knowledge systems into alignment.

Though the series is structured to compare Cree and scientific perspectives, it does so in order to also illustrate profound connections between Cree and scientific perspectives, suggesting that they have much in common that closer and meaningful attention can uncover. Webb's investigations, which structure each episode, effectively model a journey into knowledge that other inquiring minds might wish to follow in order to discover more about this world and the many others that comprise it. In so doing, the series echoes the cross-cultural work of Indigenous television on APTN: it represents an "Indigenous perspective" as a condition of the industrial and discursive context for Indigenous television in Canada and APTN specifically, but also speaks and appeals to a broader, non-Indigenous audience. In part, this may be ideological and industrial strategy: where an Indigenous audience might be more likely to be receptive to oral histories as explanation for these phenomena, the inclusion of the scientific perspective appeals to skeptics; that is, those unfamiliar with Indigenous belief systems who are likely to be non-Indigenous viewers. Yet, through the process of comparison, the series illustrates the compatibilities between knowledge systems that enact the "cultural bridge" function of APTN's mission, utilizing the popularity of the reality genre in order to draw youth audiences as a part of APTN's programming priorities.

CONCLUSION: BUILDING BRIDGES WITH *INDIANS + ALIENS*

Approaching Indigenous television programming using institutional analysis makes visible the relationship between the independent Indigenous production sector and APTN, which, while not integrated, are mutually implicated in one another. An institutional approach also makes it possible to trace discursive and industrial trends in Indigenous television production, and the shift toward reality-based television in the mid- to late 2000s, through which *Indians + Aliens* emerges. It bears the ethics of Indigenous cultural nationalism, particularly the personal relationship that the producers have to the specific Indigenous communities and nations that are their focus. Furthermore, the series is a platform for building and communicating Indigenous cultures' epistemological systems to a broad audience, further underlining Indigenous cultural specificity and historical continuity while enacting the "cultural bridge," in line with APTN's dominant institutional discourse.

At the same time, *Indians + Aliens* cannot be separated from commercial considerations. APTN's series are tied to particular audiences, and therefore represent markets for advertisers. Shifts in programming priorities and genres are linked to APTN revenue streams: for independent producers developing programming that APTN relies on for its broadcasting schedule, and for advertisers seeking network audiences. Thus, the terms of "cultural autonomy" are tied up with the industrial structure of Canadian television, using templates from U.S. commercial television to navigate them.

4

Indigenous Documentaries and Academic Research Institutions

NAVAJO TALKING PICTURE AND *CRY ROCK*

Both *Navajo Talking Picture* (1986) by Arlene Bowman (Diné) and *Cry Rock* (2010) by Banchi Hanuse (Nuxalk) exhibit striking thematic similarities that prompt comparison: they are documentaries made by Indigenous women emerging from university contexts who seek closer contact with their Indigenous cultural heritage, which they explore through their relationships with their grandmothers. Their relationships manifest a profound cultural disconnect, as neither filmmaker can speak their traditional languages, though their grandmothers are fluent. The gap in language ability points to a rupture that has taken place in the interceding generation. The cultural ruptures inflicted on Indigenous peoples by colonial systems are well known: efforts to eradicate traditional social organization through reservation/reserve systems and residential/boarding schools—among other legal, institutional, and physical means—were designed to eradicate Indigenous cultures and impose settler colonial norms. The residential and boarding school systems targeted Indigenous languages to this end, frequently using corporal punishment to punish students when they did not speak English.[1] As a result, a generation suffered massive cultural and social disruption, which is illustrated by the generation gap between Indigenous language speakers.

The topic of generational disruption and "reaching across generations" to forge family and cultural connections is a familiar one in Indigenous documentary history, also seen in Gil Cardinal's (Métis), *Foster Child* (1987) and Tasha Hubbard's (Cree) *Birth of a Family* (2017). Well-established analytical approaches to Indigenous media might undertake thematic analysis, comparing these films and eliciting a "narrative arc of enlightenment," wherein the filmmakers deepen their understandings of their family members, family histories, and themselves, and develop meaningful relationships with far-flung relatives. In such an analysis, *Navajo Talking Picture* would immediately stand out as a failure to connect, as Arlene Bowman's repeated and frustrated attempts to film and communicate with her grandmother, Ann Biah, culminate in a notorious scene in which Bowman and her film crew pursue a fleeing Biah through her home in an attempt to have her explain on camera why she no longer wants to participate in the film. As the earliest of films dealing with these themes, *Navajo Talking Picture* would mark the beginning of the evolution of the enlightenment narrative, in which subsequent films dealing with the similar themes "do better" ethically than Bowman's film. Such an evolutionary trajectory is, of course, artificial: it focuses on the films' themes and motifs evacuated of their material and historical contexts, and therefore cannot substantiate any presumed conversations or development between them.

Examining their contexts of production, however, reveals material elements that make more than thematic comparison possible: both films were produced in relation to postsecondary training programs, and in association with Indigenous studies programs at the filmmakers' respective institutions. Bowman produced *Navajo Talking Picture* in the early 1980s through the University of California, Los Angeles (UCLA) film production program in association with the American Indian Studies Center (AISC), and *Cry Rock* was deeply informed by Hanuse's experience in the First Nations Studies Program (FNSP) at the University of British Columbia in the mid-2000s, and her experience in media-based project development at the National Film Board of Canada (NFB).[2] For *Navajo Talking Picture*, the reinvention of film-based anthropology that began in the 1960s intersected with developments in Indigenous studies during the same era to engender a research environment in which it was understood that Indigenous people are best equipped to undertake research on Indigenous people and topics, a frame of reference that the film examines and complicates via Bowman's interactions with her grandmother, Ann Biah. Made twenty years later, *Cry Rock* engages with debates in Indigenous studies about the relationship between oral narrative traditions and the media used to record them, questioning the impact that recording technologies have on oral narratives and their survival. By doing so, the film intervenes in assumptions that the cinematic apparatus can function as an extension of oral traditions, a discourse promoted by the NFB, raising the possibility that recording technologies actually hasten their erosion. *Cry Rock* ultimately explores oral narratives as a mode of understanding that is intrinsically tied to specific geographical places and relies on a direct relationship between storyteller and listener, which media technologies cannot replicate.

As a study of Indigenous filmmakers and their film production education, this chapter is preceded by Sol Worth and John Adair's research with the Diné people,[3] *Through Navajo Eyes: An Exploration in Film Communication and Anthropology* (1972). This study is often positioned within a historical trajectory of ethnographic research and cited as an example of the reflexive turn that took place in the discipline in the 1960s, which sought to cultivate participatory research methods between researchers and their "subjects" in order to redress the inherent power imbalances between those who produce knowledge and those who are the object of it (Ginsburg 1991). Worth, a professor of communications, and Adair, an anthropologist, designed the project as an attempt to determine if a Diné "film language" could be determined if the film apparatus were put in the hands of Diné participants, who received minimal training or intervention from the researchers in order to derive an "authentic" Diné visual communicative structure (1972, 28). Despite its efforts to develop a collaborative approach to film and research production, the project has been critiqued for its essentialist assumptions that cultural identity can be directly expressed and interpreted through cultural production (Pack 2000, 274), and for focusing on the films as "texts" requiring expert interpretation by the researchers while neglecting the Diné participants' own interpretation of their experiences or of the films, thereby reinforcing power dynamics their methods were meant to ameliorate while reifying the film text as the source of cultural meaning (Bredin 1993; Ginsburg 1991). Nonetheless, this project has been acknowledged as the start of "Indigenous media" as an area of academic study (Deger 2006, 38), which coincided with one of the first instances of "film education" for Indigenous filmmakers as a part of the academic record, despite the process receiving very little examination.

This chapter focuses on questions of Indigenous filmmakers' "education" by virtue of their postsecondary training, which raises questions about the ways in which these contexts informed their theoretical and representational approaches. Indigenous media practitioners have availed themselves of media training programs for decades, both within and outside of formal educational institutions. In Canada, there are approximately fifty professional training programs, many of which have existed for decades and are associated with postsecondary institutions. Indigenous-specific programs date to 1968 with the Indian Film Crew at the NFB, while Indigenous training programs affiliated with postsecondary institutions are a more recent phenomenon that began in the early 1990s, including the Banff Centre for the Arts (discussed in chapter 2), the Indigenous Independent Digital Filmmaking program at Capilano University (British Columbia), Indigenous Visual Culture at the Ontario College of Art and Design (Ontario), and the Mohawk College broadcasting programs (Ontario), to name only a few (Film Studies Association of Canada. n.d). Beverly Singer (Tewa/Diné) identifies the beginnings of Indigenous film training education in the United States to *Navajo Film Themselves* (1966), and traces the diverse landscape of media training programs from which Indigenous filmmakers have emerged, a small handful of which are or are associated with postsecondary institutions, such as the Institute of American Indian Art (Santa Fe, New Mexico) and the Center for Media, Culture and History at New York University (2001, 33–44). These are fruitful areas for future research, and mentioned here in order to contribute to scholarship in this arena. Institutional analysis of *Navajo Talking Picture* and *Cry Rock*, however, requires a somewhat broader framework of institutionality, as these films did not emerge from Indigenous-focused media training programs, but rather through academic research institutions in association with Indigenous studies. Nonetheless, institutional analysis of these documentaries benefits from scholarship on practice-based film education that offers analytics through which to understand their complex institutionality.

PRACTICE-BASED FILM EDUCATION AND INDIGENOUS STUDIES

By attending to debates in Indigenous studies and their effects on film production, this chapter engages somewhat elliptically but productively with scholarship from film schools studies or "practice-based film education," which as a field seeks to understand "how filmmakers become filmmakers" (Hjort 2013, 1). Scholarship in his area has historically tended to consider a filmmaker's education in terms of two institutional models as described by Duncan Petrie (2010): the "national conservatoire" that emerged in continental Europe in the early twentieth century to benefit national film industries and cinema cultures, which received state support; and university film schools, which expanded in the United States during the postwar period to examine the theory and practice of film linked to a "larger educational establishment and therefore constrained and guided by the academic policies and practices of that institution" (34). At the same time, Duncan Petrie and Rod Stoneman (2014) argue, the postwar period saw an increased demarcation between the theory and practice of filmmaking owing to two major factors: the first being the emergence and dominance of neoliberalism, through which the economy became the mediator of social relations, cultural activity, and education, steering film school education toward technical competency and professionalization rather than critical thinking and theory; the second was the proliferation of film and screen studies at universities in the 1950s onward, which encouraged a broader intellectual engagement with theoretical areas germane to the study of the moving image, but at the same time engendered a division between programs focused on the study of film and those that taught creative practice (5–7).

The legacy of the theory/practice divide continues to be experienced in the contemporary postsecondary institutions, yet is hardly absolute (nor does it claim to be). Students, faculty, and administrators bring their experiences and critical perspectives from different social and educational arenas into creative production, contributing to the development and evolution of film education, conditions that Mette Hjort outlines in her introduction to *The Education of the Filmmaker in Africa, the Middle East, and the Americas*:

> There can be no one-to-one correspondence between the profile of a given film school on the one hand, and the priorities and values of its graduates on the other. After all, film schools are subject to the full range of complexities that characterize institutional life. . . . If being a filmmaker is the outcome of a process of becoming, factors shaping that process are not merely to be sought in the institutional landscape of film schools and practice-based training programs. (2013, 4)

Being attentive to the social experiences and institutional contexts that filmmakers traverse brings to light the history, theory, and criticism outside of production programs that nonetheless come to bear on their work. This complicated "ecology" (11) of practice-based film education is important for contextualizing Bowman and Hanuse's films, which engage with intellectual frameworks from other disciplinary areas of universities and other media-producing institutions. In doing so, their work countervails the theory/practice divide of creative production, showing instead how media production and theory and methods from Indigenous studies are intertwined. Furthermore, their institutional "unwieldiness" is generative, as it makes visible the ways in which theory and practice from academic research institutions intersect with and place pressure on discourses and practices from other institutions of media culture.

NAVAJO TALKING PICTURE (1986)

Navajo Talking Picture is perhaps best known in Indigenous cinema history for its controversial depiction of its filmmaker's interactions with her grandmother, Ann Biah. The documentary was Bowman's thesis film for her master of fine arts degree in film production at UCLA. Bowman, a Diné woman, was raised away from her family's Diné community, and set out to create an ethnographic film of the daily life of her grandmother, who speaks only the Diné language and largely eschews a Western lifestyle and conveniences. In the film's voice-over, Bowman explains that she intended to create a portrait of her grandmother and her lifestyle, but that after several days of filming, her grandmother stopped cooperating with the film crew and asked them to leave. Bowman, unable to speak the Diné language, did not understand her grandmother's objections, and returned to the reservation several times to continue filming. The film is reflexive about her efforts and frustrations: she narrates her confusion with her grandmother's behavior, and attributes her hostility to being misperceived as a "big shot" from Los Angeles who is bent on exploiting her.

For Bowman, the film's central conflict emerged from cultural differences between herself and her traditional grandmother. The film portrays Bowman as very much urban and cosmopolitan: she lives in Los Angeles, wears youthful and stylish clothing, and attends UCLA.

FIGURE 18. Arlene Bowman at UCLA in *Navajo Talking Picture* (1986).

FIGURE 19. Ann Biah in her kitchen in *Navajo Talking Picture* (1986).

Her grandmother, meanwhile, is shown living in a small hogan without plumbing or electricity, weaving wool rugs, and periodically traveling to the local store for provisions. Their cultural divide is compounded by their inability to speak the same language, which, Bowman explains in the film, exacerbated tensions between them. Ultimately, Bowman incites a confrontation with her grandmother in the climactic moment of the film where she ambushes her in her home, accompanied by the film crew and translator. Through the translator, Bowman tries to explain her intentions to her grandmother and find out why she is so resistant, while Biah tries to evade them, telling them to leave. The scene is extremely charged and, as Randolph Lewis has detailed, the focus for much debate and criticism. In *Navajo Talking Picture: Cinema on Native Ground* (2012), Lewis identifies that critiques of the film largely focus on the filmmaker's "ethical lapses" (79) owing to her persistence in filming her grandmother despite her clearly stated refusal to participate. Such critiques, he argues, overlook how Bowman's techniques are typical of prevailing filmmaking practices, and cover over its interventions in critical paradigms attending Indigenous identity and cultural production. Lewis discusses, for instance, the film's relationship to family portrait films in which intergenerational conflict is a central feature that is often thematized by tensions between the filmmaker and their family members' reluctance to engage with the camera (114–15). By showing that such techniques are characteristic of the genre, Lewis seeks to reveal the film's complex textuality, "bracketing" criticism in order to make visible the film's contributions to understandings of Indigenous identity, art, and ethics. He argues *Navajo Talking Picture* intervenes in major critical paradigms in Indigenous studies that he critiques for making essentialist claims about Indigenous identity and art, "tribalcentric criticism" and "Indigenous aesthetics." Both paradigms, Lewis argues, are premised on "authenticity" as a means to recognize and legitimize Indigenous artists and their work. In his view, tribal-centric criticism, which emerged from Indigenous literary nationalism, is "a sort of aesthetic nationalism in which tribal citizens, or at least those fluent with the culture's history and language, are ideally positioned to appreciate a work of art that originates among its ranks" (133) and risks "granting critical authority solely by virtue of biography" (136). Indigenous aesthetics, he states, is a concept that has been enigmatically described as an underlying "logic" to Indigenous cultural production, or as a set of characteristics appearing in this work, including intergenerational continuity, respect for elders, and a sense of community (140). Looking at Bowman and *Navajo Talking Picture* through these critical lenses makes visible their limitations, as they cannot accommodate her "liminality" as an Indigenous person, nor account for the film's problematic representation of Bowman's grandmother. Doing so, Lewis argues, allows him to produce an "anti-essentialist" reading of the film that defines its major contribution to understandings of Indigenous identity and art:

> Indigenous filmmakers face the same hazards as any other documentarians working in the field, and that to assign them special representational powers (or a unique aesthetic) is as misguided as the limiting notions that portray them as spiritual, wise, or close to nature. Unless they choose otherwise, Native filmmakers have no special purchase on accountability to their subjects but instead operate like artists anywhere, able to persist long into the night with ill-advised plans for wrong-headed projects just like anyone else. (142)

Lewis's intent is to make visible Bowman's complicated identity as a Diné person, and thereby recover her from criticism emerging from essentialist assumptions about what an Indigenous filmmaker is "supposed to be." Doing so makes it possible to appreciate the human dimensions of her flawed endeavor, and the way the film raises important questions about the applications and limitations of critical paradigms in Indigenous studies.

Lewis centers *Navajo Talking Picture* an Indigenous film "outlier" to demonstrate the pressure that the film and Bowman herself place on critical frameworks in Indigenous studies, providing a compelling analytical model that I build upon by bringing institutional analysis into the interpretive fold. As a film emerging from an academic research institution, it speaks to beliefs and practices for undertaking Indigenous research contemporaneous with its production circulating in Indigenous studies, anthropology, and ethnographic film at UCLA. Lewis touches on ethnography in his analysis of *Navajo Talking Picture*, acknowledging the film's original intent to be an "ethnographic film," but more so as a means of attenuating criticism of the film's ethics by arguing that such critiques are anachronistic when considering the film in light of documentary trends of the era (i.e., family portrait films). Thus, Lewis's analysis shifts away from ethnography and attendant questions of ethics in order to contextualize the film and examine its textual plurality. Institutional analysis, however, recenters questions of ethics by examining the film's contributions to understandings about research and knowledge production of Indigenous peoples. Examining the intersections of ethnography and documentary film at UCLA, in complement with Bowman's training in still photography, contribute to understandings of the film's representational strategies for depicting cross-cultural conflict between Indigenous people.

THE REINVENTION OF ANTHROPOLOGY AND COLONIAL LEGACIES OF INDIGENOUS IMAGES

Bowman describes the rationale for the film in annual progress reports submitted to the UCLA AISC, a research unit that provided funding to assist her project from 1982 to 1986, and in interviews conducted in 2015 reflecting on these reports and her experience making the film. The reports detail Bowman's progress, difficulties encountered in the filming process, and her reasons for employing particular approaches to address them. Though these challenges are documented within the film itself, the reports are revealing of the ethnographic and documentary discourses through which the project was designed and to which it was responsive. In interviews, Bowman also describes the influence of still photography on the film, substantiating the confluence of photography-based and ethnographic practice that Lewis examines.

The first annual report from 1982/3 indicates that the project was intended to be a portrait of her grandmother, Ann Biah, but explains that her grandmother's lack of cooperation and interaction motivated her decision to include herself in the film because "in an ethnographic, direct cinematic film, if the film depiction of a person's daily life does not interact with other people a lot, the film looks less interesting" (Bowman 1983, 68). Moreover, the choice to include herself in the film was a reflexive move intended to "make the connection between both our worlds," indicating that the film shifted from an "ethnographic, direct cinematic film" (Bowman 1983, 68) to, as Bowman describes in an interview, a "personal documentary" (2015b). For Bowman, the "personal documentary" dispenses with objectivity and is instead defined by her point of view (2015b), which was enacted by reflexively inserting herself into the film in order to focus on issues affecting the progress of the film, which were thematized as issues of cross-cultural dynamics. Bowman links this approach with the genre of self-portraiture in relation to her training in still photography:

> I remember being introduced to it a little bit by a teacher in high school, about still photography's history. . . . I know still photographers take self-portraits. . . . That's probably why it influenced me. (2015b)

While Bowman describes a personal dimension to her entry into the film as a form of "self-portraiture," this approach intersects with a long colonial history of the Diné people in photography and film that contributed to tensions during production. Throughout the film, Bowman is aligned with Western colonial practices, particularly the history of exploitation in Western visual culture. In her 1983 report, Bowman states that family and community members told her grandmother that she should not be filmed and that Bowman was "exploiting her," suggesting that Bowman was aware that Diné community members interpreted her project along a continuum of colonial practices. Lewis includes a comprehensive summary of the history of colonial fascination with images of "the Navajo" in portraiture, Hollywood cinema, and anthropology, which has generated a substantial body of scholarship examining Diné relationships to visual culture, as both "objects" of its gaze and as agents in its production and reception.[4] James C. Faris (1996) examines the extent to which the Diné have been the object of photography, first as a part of nineteenth- and twentieth-century ethnographic investigations of the colonial "Other," and increasingly in the twentieth century as tourist curiosities when photographic technologies became available to a mobile American population—so much so that "the impression is that few people crossed northwestern New Mexico and northern Arizona without pointing a camera at Navajo" (150). While recognizing Faris's important analysis of the visual regimes through which Indigenous people have been subject to the colonial gaze, subsequent scholarship has been more closely attentive to Diné agency throughout this history and in their relationships to film and photography.[5] Lewis (2012) and Limbrick (2010) examine Hollywood productions that were filmed in Diné territory that employed Diné actors and extras, and the negotiations between the Navajo Nation and these productions in which they defined the terms of their participation. This literature clearly identifies that the Diné people have long possessed a sophisticated understanding of the ideological and economic interests of photography and filmmaking, and that this knowledge motivates their wariness of Bowman's project. Thus, while *Navajo Talking Picture* uses "self-portraiture" to intervene in colonial representational practices, this approach did not resolve them, instead bringing to light complexities and striations internal to the Diné people resulting from colonial history.

MINORITY MEDIA HISTORIES AND INDIGENOUS STUDIES

As a photographer by training, Bowman brought a background in visual arts to bear on a film that was aligned with traditions of ethnographic filmmaking and direct cinema, which speaks to the history of minority-directed film production at UCLA that largely took shape through the Ethno-communications Program founded in the late 1960s. As David E. James details in *The Most Typical Avant-Garde: History and Geography of Minor Cinemas in Los Angeles* (2005), the Ethno-communications Program emerged in the context of the civil rights movement in the 1960s, and particularly the Watts Rebellion in Los Angeles in 1965. In response to these social pressures, UCLA founded ethnic studies centers and programs, and began recruiting students from minority groups, specifically African American, Asian American, Chicano, and Native American students. The ethnic studies centers were designed to support minority groups' greater control of and representation in research.

For the AISC, this has meant working toward self-determination for Indigenous people by "soliciting Indian priorities for research, training Indian researchers . . . and disseminating accurate information about American Indian peoples" (UCLA American Indian Studies Center 1980, 3). This statement voices founding principles of Indigenous studies as it took shape in North America. Elizabeth Cook-Lynn (Crow Creek Sioux Tribe) dates the discipline to the late 1960s and early 1970s and the interdisciplinary efforts of Indigenous academics, professional personnel, artists, and traditional historians of the era to create an academic discipline in which "a body of intellectual information such as the Natives of this land possess about the world be internally organized, normatively regulated, and consensually communicated" (1997, 10). This body of knowledge is held in oral traditional narratives that are bound to the geographies of Indigenous nations from which they emerge. Therefore, Cook-Lynn argues, Indigenous studies is inherently invested in communal efforts to defend Indigenous nationhood (11). Cautioning that Indigenous studies cannot be conflated with other areas of ethnic studies, she identifies that Indigenous studies

> would differentiate itself from other disciplines in two important ways: it would emerge from within Native people's enclaves and geographies, languages and experiences, and it would refute the exogenous seeking of truth through isolation (i.e., the "ivory tower") that has been the general principle of the disciplines most recently in charge of indigenous study, that is, history, anthropology, and related disciplines all captivated by the scientific method of objectivity. (11)

Thus, in its origins, the discipline gave rise to at least two premises: it positions Indigenous peoples as the source of expert knowledge, and therefore best equipped to produce research concerning Indigenous peoples, and undertakes research that works with and benefits Indigenous communities.[6] Bowman's project, funded by AISC, fits this mission. The film is framed as a research project in the AISC reports, with Bowman as principal investigator, and addresses the AISC's goals of preparing Indigenous researchers to produce knowledge about Indigenous peoples. However, *Navajo Talking Picture* complicates these premises as they are applied in the historical world via documentary film.

Along with the founding of the ethnic studies centers, thirteen students and faculty at UCLA formed the Media Urban Crisis Committee in 1968 (also known as the "Mother Muccers") to advocate for access to film training and resources, resulting in a pilot film program that enrolled the Mother Muccers as its first students. The program was modeled on UCLA's already-established film production program, though it operated independently and had its own instructors and curriculum. The Ethno-communications Program provided training and resources for minority students to represent their own interests and concerns and develop their own cinemas, a response to the exclusion of minorities from mainstream film industries, and to Hollywood cinema's frequently racist representations of minorities on screen (Hawkins 1970). The Ethno-communications Program paved the way for filmmakers like Bowman, whose own film can be seen as emerging from this history and ethic.

Navajo Talking Picture's original ethnographic design likely emerged from the influence of ethnography and anthropology in film production at UCLA during this period, which overlapped in certain regards with the political and ideological commitments of Ethnocommunications. Colin Young, a visual anthropologist and ethnographic filmmaker at UCLA, was the first chair of the Media Urban Crisis Committee, and his colleague and fellow anthropologist Richard Hawkins was the chair of the Theater Arts Department (now the School for Theater, Film, and Television), as well as Bowman's supervisor for her film (Hawkins 1970). Young and Hawkins participated in the "reinvention" of anthropology in the 1960s and 1970s motivated by the political and intellectual movements of the era that raised questions of the goals and methods of the discipline. Subsequent ethnographic work attempted more self-conscious processes that involved subjects in the production and interpretation of research.[7] Young and others recognized the influence of the ethnographer/filmmaker and camera on the behavior of their subjects, and argued that the film's subjects decided how to interact with the filmmaker in any scenario. The subjects therefore determined the film's project, and rather than projecting understandings of their subjects, the task of the ethnographer/filmmaker was to facilitate and make visible the negotiations between subject and filmmaker as a part of the filmmaking process. Bowman's original project design speaks to this ethnographic tradition, an attempt at more equitable, subject-directed interaction.

FORCING INTERACTION: THE CRISIS STRUCTURE

As Bowman relates in her report from 1982/1983, however, her grandmother stopped interacting with her and the crew after several days of filming and ordered them to leave. Bowman's solution was to add "interaction" and "interest" by inserting herself into the film. She states that this would create the "drama and conflict needed for the film," and that through this forced interaction, "a sense of my grandmother's personality could be depicted" (1983, 68). She suggests that the conflict could produce a more dimensional representation of her grandmother, a technique owing to methods of direct cinema. Stephen Mamber describes the function of the crisis structure in direct cinema of the 1960s as a way of revealing subjects' personalities, since a person's reaction to a crisis would reveal something of their character that would not be seen otherwise, resulting in a more multifaceted representation (1972). Bowman echoes this logic when she states that "either she could have spoken to me or not spoken to me. She *reacts* in either case" (1983, 68; emphasis mine). Creating a crisis structure was, in a sense, a functional solution to the scenario Bowman was facing to move forward the production.

A crisis structure also made it possible to thematize "cultural conflict" within the film, which Bowman identifies as the basis for her fraught interactions with her grandmother. Bowman explains that "the appearance of myself in the film, literally opened interaction and made the connection between both of our worlds. . . . She is coerced to speak to me. This is a central conflict and meeting of two cultures" (1983, 68). In interviews, Bowman describes experiencing a history of culture clashes, explaining it in terms of having been brought up in Phoenix, Arizona, and then undertaking her training in photography in San Francisco, and contrasts these experiences with working on the Navajo reservation several years before undertaking her work at UCLA, which she describes as "isolating" owing to her struggles to live and work in a "small town" after living in urban spaces (2015c). She elaborates that this sense of a "culture clash" carried into the film, stating, "maybe I didn't know enough about . . . Diné people who live on the reservation. . . . I'm so frank, and so blatant, and I don't think many Diné people are blatant and frank" (2015c). Bowman elaborated that her "frankness" took shape as a defense mechanism against the racism she experienced throughout her life, and the sexism she encountered while working in the film industry in Southern California, where such forthrightness and assertiveness served her well; as she states, "I usually fight back with my words" (2015a). Her demeanor was therefore a very rational response to the realities of living in settler colonial society. In the context of her interactions with her grandmother and community, however, Bowman felt this same demeanor alienated her and exacerbated cultural tensions. By inserting herself in the film not only does she "fix" the problem of noninteraction, but also reflexivity represents the cultural conflict that she understood was the core of the film.

Bowman's reports also identify that her grandmother's resistance to being photographed was a part of cultural taboos against photography, adding another axis of "cultural conflict" structuring the film. She states that her grandmother "believed in traditional ways regarding camera and sound equipment," and that "a granddaughter is not supposed to film her grandmother" (1983, 68). She discovers this during her third visit to the reservation, which forms the penultimate scene of the film. Biah keeps her back to the camera and repeatedly tries to leave the room, while pursued by Bowman and the camera, with the translator awkwardly trailing along. Biah finally sits on her bed, turns away from the camera and has the translator tell Bowman that the Diné never used to take photographs of their grandmothers, and when she was a child her grandfather told her stories that she remembered in her prayers; she never thought of taking pictures. Biah's response invokes cultural taboos against photography as explanation and context for her evasion of the camera, but also strategically addresses the immediate situation. When she explains that she remembers her grandfather's stories in her prayers, she identifies that she listened to him out of respect. She contrasts her actions to Bowman's: since Bowman is not listening to her grandmother, she is being disrespectful. While the film positions taboos against photography to emphasize the theme of "cultural conflict," the photographic apparatus is not the only issue here—more pressingly, it is Bowman's behavior, which invokes multiple historical dimensions of colonial incursions. In her discussion of the film, Beverly Singer is attentive to Ann Biah's perspective in order to identify the cultural and historical underpinnings to her responses, arguing that Biah's inability to fend off the camera "is reminiscent also of history when Native people were unable to defend themselves against white encroachment. Bowman's grandmother appears to be in her seventies; in her youth she would have heard stories about the campaign against the Navajo and of the 'Navajo Long Walk'" (2001, 77). By linking Biah's responses to the Diné history of forced relocation, Singer exposes layers of unvoiced traumas that Bowman's interactions with her grandmother invoke.

Following the scene of the "crisis" encounter, Bowman is shown in a close-up outside the hogan, anxious and exhausted, debating with herself and someone behind the camera whether she "forced" her grandmother, followed by a scene of her in a pen of lambs, chasing one until she catches it and, laughing and breathless, shows it to the camera. This scene comments reflexively on her dogged pursuit of Biah, the reasons for which are alluded to in her reports. These reports track the film's development over at least four years, and show that the film represented a significant investment of time and financial and personal resources. The film itself identifies Bowman's financial hardship in a scene where she looks for work opportunities at the student financial aid office. Bowman's master's degree depended on completing the film as her thesis. The possibility of not finishing the film would mean a major personal and professional loss. These dimensions of her production provide a way of framing her persistence in the face of her grandmother's resistance and despite her own apprehensions.

The film concludes with an interior shot in Bowman's car as she and the crew drive away from the reservation, and in voice-over, she reflects on the issues she felt were the basis for the conflict with her grandmother: the language barrier, her perception that her grandmother did not understand the project, and her own lack of understanding of Diné cultural and social prohibitions around photography. She states that she had set out to develop "understanding" between herself and her grandmother, and between herself and "the Navajo," a goal that she felt had actually been realized to a degree in the filmmaking process. She states that she also came to understand the limitations of her own position: despite being a Diné woman, her lack of familiarity with Diné cultural values and history created problematic cultural dynamics that she attempted to address through reflexive techniques of inserting herself in the film and commenting on her upbringing in the "white world." This is one of the key insights of the film, pointing out that shared ethnicity and heritage does not translate into shared cultural values and understandings: there is not a unified Diné perspective. Such assumptions do not take into account Indigenous peoples' historical realities of displacement and movement to urban areas to access resources not available on reservations, conditions underpinning the differences in Bowman's and Biah's cultural positions. Just as Lewis identifies that an Indigenous documentarian can make the same mistakes as any other documentarian, from an institutional standpoint it can be argued that the film makes the point that the power dynamics and representational issues of ethnographic practice are not necessarily resolved by involving a person of the same social or cultural position as their subjects; it is possible for researchers of Indigenous heritage to perform just as problematically as non-Indigenous researchers, and therefore makes visible the need for attention to methodologies for producing knowledge about and representing Indigenous groups and issues. This insight makes it possible to productively foreground the film's ethical issues as a part of the film's insights.

Though these ethical lapses can be considered "productive," they are no less distressing to witness and worth reflecting on to examine the issues relevant to academic research that they elicit. Lewis skillfully demonstrates how Bowman's techniques are not so different from those used in family portrait documentaries, and suggests that condemnation of the film is perhaps disproportionate when viewed within its historical context (2012). As Lewis points out in his discussion of the reception of *Navajo Talking Picture*, viewers frequently condemn Bowman, responses that Bowman alludes to from the first in her final report that states that she found that audiences "did not fully understand what [she] was trying to present about the conflict and reasons between Arlene [Bowman] and the grandmother over the filming at the beginning of the film, when they should have" (1985, 46). The language here is somewhat ambiguous, but it suggests that the issues of cultural conflict that emerged while Bowman attempted to create a portrait of her grandmother, and that Bowman sought to foreground, were overshadowed by the subsequent direction of the film. These responses are shaped by expectations that the documentary genre bears a close relationship to historical and social reality, and therefore involves ethical considerations regarding their "subjects." Such ethical considerations are compounded when engaging with socially and historically marginalized people. It is reasonable to assume that most audiences understand that Indigenous peoples have been historically oppressed, particularly if they view the film in a classroom setting, where the instructor is likely to provide this context. Even a general appreciation of this history compounds the impact of film's "crisis," as it depicts the revictimization of an Indigenous person by her own granddaughter, no less. It is therefore instructive to consider how techniques used in prevailing documentary practices create different sets of issues when applied to the representation of Indigenous groups, not necessarily because of different expectations of the documentarian, but out of recognition of the social and historical specificities of Indigenous peoples' experiences and the legacies of colonization that these approaches can and do replicate. Therefore, methodologies for knowledge production, which documentaries and research share, require attention and debate prior to undertaking such projects, a process that *Cry Rock* (2010) examines as its structuring narrative.

CRY ROCK (2010)

Navajo Talking Picture largely emerged in relation to one academic research institution, which has retained a set of production records that contribute to understandings of institutional discourses and representational practices contributing to the film's development. *Cry Rock* engages dynamically with multiple institutional discourses and practices owing to its production history and context, which traces the filmmaker's professional experience in film and media production and in Indigenous studies at a postsecondary research institution. Thus, *Cry Rock* requires a broader framework for institutional analysis than *Navajo Talking Picture* in order to elicit how the film brings together representational practices and discourses of Indigeneity from multiple sites. Further, while records exist for *Navajo Talking Picture* that enrich institutional analysis, such records are not the sole sources through which institutional discourses can be read; in the case of *Cry Rock,* I draw on websites, reports, and publicity materials in compliment with an interview with the filmmaker.

Cry Rock is a twenty-eight-minute documentary by Nuxalk filmmaker Banchi Hanuse, independently produced in 2010 by Smayaykila Films Inc. Combining documentary footage with animation, the film begins at a point of urgency: there are only fifteen fluent Nuxalk language speakers and storytellers left, including Hanuse's grandmother. As Hanuse relates in voice-over, she cannot speak the language and wants to ask her grandmother if she can record her stories on camera; however, she cannot bring herself to ask her. Instead, the film is an investigation of her apprehension, opening up an exploration of Nuxalk understandings of storytelling, and the potential repercussions of recording these stories using media and writing technologies. Her grandmother does appear in the film, though does not directly interact with the camera; instead, she is shown in a second narrative strand interwoven with the first in which she fillets and smokes a salmon.

Hanuse explains that she had been considering recording her grandmother for several years before undertaking the project, in the meantime undergoing film training largely at Capilano University (Vancouver, BC) while gaining experience on film sets and at the NFB, and complimenting her professional training at the FNSP and International Relations at the University of British Columbia (UBC) (Hanuse 2015). While Hanuse's experience is diverse and multisited, for the purposes of this discussion I concentrate on the institutional locations closest temporally and contextually to the production of *Cry Rock*. Hanuse identifies that her postsecondary education at UBC was "the base and the kick start . . . to continue to pursue film" and worked at the NFB during her postsecondary education leading up to the production of *Cry Rock* (2015).

Hanuse recounted that "When contemplating recording elders, such as my grandmother, questions came to mind that concerned me. Thinking of my grandmother turning 80, I realized there is so much knowledge my Grandmother has that I want to pass on" (2015). Historically, the Nuxalk language and stories were transmitted through oral traditional methods, and *Cry Rock* asks if recordings can capture the meaning of the language and the stories—and if, having been recorded, they can still be considered Indigenous cultural knowledge. The film ultimately presents cultural knowledge as a *modality*, and asks questions about what happens when certain forms of cultural knowledge are taken into a different cultural representational system. Indigenous languages emerge from cultural knowledge systems, and are understood as being key to transmitting traditional cultural knowledge. The Nuxalk language is endangered as a consequence of colonialism and the Canadian state's efforts to eradicate Indigenous cultures, which targeted Indigenous languages in particular. In *Cry Rock*, elders of Hanuse's grandmother's generation are shown to be fluent in Nuxalk, but we do not see people from Hanuse's *parents'* generation, a structuring absence that marks the break in language ability within that era. Questions about the effects of technology in cultural transmission thematize the generational cultural ruptures since, without the same language facility, these generations do not share the same framework for engaging traditional cultural knowledge. As a result, "mediation" is both a dominant visual motif and the focus for the film.

INTERINSTITUTIONALITY: INDIGENOUS STUDIES AND THE NATIONAL FILM BOARD

Cry Rock's examination of the value and meaning of oral traditions, and the mediations that take place when oral narratives are recorded, reflect debates that take place in Indigenous studies in the FNSP at UBC, from which Hanuse graduated in 2004. FNSP is a research-oriented undergraduate program designed to equip students with theoretical and methodological skills in order to undertake Indigenous community-based research (FNSP, n.d.). Its core courses focus on research methodologies that debate methodological approaches for undertaking Indigenous research, which includes questions about the effects of recording technologies on Indigenous cultures. While Hanuse was a student in the program in 2003, a unit of the required course FNSP 310–Theory Seminar focused on technologies and their effects on Indigenous peoples, including readings from Jerry Mander's *In the Absence of the Sacred: The Failure of Technology and the Survival of the Indian Nations* (1992) and Elsie Mather's "With a Vision Beyond Our Immediate Needs: Oral Traditions in an Age of Literacy" (1995); further, the course asked students to examine "the relation between technology and First Nations cultures" in a written or media-based assignment (Kesler 2003a). FNSP 320–Research Methods, a second required course, engaged even more deeply with debates surrounding research methods, and included workshops and readings on research ethics—including Maori scholar Linda Tuhiwai Smith's foundational text *Decolonizing Methodologies: Research and Indigenous Peoples* (1999)—in preparation for students' major assignment, an interview-based research project (Kesler 2003b). *Cry Rock* echoes these debates in its questioning of the applications and limitations of recording technologies for preserving and transmitting Indigenous cultural knowledge, a critical framework dovetailing with Hanuse's long-held deliberations about whether to record her grandmother's stories.

These debates intervene in and complicate institutional discourses around Indigenous cultural retention that circulate at the NFB, where Hanuse worked throughout the 2000s, and which was an associate producer of *Cry Rock*. Hanuse was the coproducer and project coordinator of *Our World,* an Indigenous language-based program that took shape in the early 2000s out of the NFB's west-coast-based Pacific and Yukon Centre (Hanuse 2015). *Our World* partnered the NFB with remote Indigenous communities in British Columbia and the Yukon to teach youth how to use digital technologies in order to make short films in their traditional languages (NFB, n.d.).[8] Filmmakers and digital animators visited communities whose traditional languages are endangered, and worked with youth ages eighteen to twenty-nine to develop projects that would engage with their traditional languages in ways relevant to their experiences, as described by the project's archived website:

> *Our World* is based on the concept of giving voice and inviting others to hear. The project aims to leave something behind that benefits both the individual and the community. By facilitating active communication and reception, we encourage positive social engagement. It is also about exposing young people to potential future career options by learning how to express themselves creatively with modern, digital media. (NFB, n.d.)

Social engagement and empowerment predominate as discursive frameworks for the project, wherein media technology acts as a facilitator that supports Indigenous people's connections with their cultures and communities. The "social engagement" framework is enhanced by the language of professionalization, in which participants would be equipped with skills transferrable to the employment realm.

This social engagement framework echoes long-established NFB discourses for minority and Indigenous production. As Zoë Druick argued, the NFB, as a national film agency, is responsive to Canadian law and social policy and seeks to reflect policy in its programs and productions (2007). Beginning in the 1960s in the context of Prime Minister Pierre Trudeau's liberal platform of a Canadian "participatory democracy," the NFB sought to equip disenfranchised social groups, including Indigenous people, with the film apparatus to produce their own representations with the mind that "media representation might effectively bring about improved political representation" (127).[9] This mission was reinvigorated in subsequent decades with increasing population and political shifts in Canada. From the 1980s onward, Canadian social policy was framed in terms of "diversity" to manage and govern population changes including increased immigration, the Québec sovereignty referendum of 1980, and Indigenous demands for autonomy (168). In response, the NFB prioritized youth, women, and minorities, and opened Studio I—the Indigenous studio—in 1991 (168). Through Studio I, the NFB sought to provide institutional resources—including training, equipment and technology, and facilities—to equip Indigenous filmmakers to undertake their own projects. Owing to its programs and resources for representing Indigenous social realities, the NFB has been discussed as facilitating Indigenous cultural continuity. In "Studio One: Of Storytellers and Stories," Maria de Rosa links NFB media practice with Indigenous cultural traditions, citing statements by Indigenous filmmakers, including Loretta Todd and Carol Geddes, who relate that filmmaking is a part of a continuum of "storytelling" (2002, 329–30). De Rosa evokes a discourse of Indigenous media as an extension of Indigenous cultural tradition, which overlaps with the NFB's social empowerment mission. *Our World*'s design explicitly brings together cultural revitalization with social empowerment:

> Before the projects are produced, we ask each community to identify young people interested in visual art and/or storytelling. . . . We then send instructors to the First Nations communities where they spend a week working with a group of young people who then create their own short films in the First Nations' language. At the end of the week, a public screening of their work is held to celebrate their accomplishments and to invite the community to come see and hear the stories. (NFB, n.d.)

The project thus engages with an urgent social issue, the decline in Indigenous language speakers, by seeking to equip Indigenous youth specifically with the media skills to develop projects to support language retention. In this configuration, film and media play a role in cultural continuity. However, *Cry Rock* reflects on the role of digital technology in transmitting Indigenous cultural knowledge, and what is changed, or even lost, when cultural knowledge is recorded. *Cry Rock* intervenes in prevailing discourses of media's relationship to Indigenous cultures, arguing that this dynamic risks conflating oral traditions with recording technologies. *Cry Rock* thereby enters into a critical dialogue with national cultural policy and institutional discourses that challenge their underpinning logics in order to create space to reflect on the specificities of oral traditions.

VISUALIZING CULTURAL MEDIATIONS

The pervasiveness of Western cultural influences on Indigenous communities is visually conveyed through the representation of a broad range of media technologies: notebooks, a reel-to-reel recorder, photographs, DVDs, and video cameras. The film is ambivalent about the use of these technologies, at once acknowledging that they play a role in cultural preservation, while at the same time arguing for the distinctiveness and value of oral traditions. Hanuse's voice-over rhetorically enacts this ambivalence: it is structured as a series of questions about her reluctance to record her grandmother's stories and reflections on her childhood, bracketing her perspective to create a point of departure for representing others. Hanuse's cousin, Deborah Nelson (Nuxalk), is shown in the process of video-recording her father's stories so that she can both preserve and learn from them. She is particularly interested in the more recent history of when the entire village was moved from the north side of the river to the south side due to a historical smallpox epidemic. She both records him at home speaking Nuxalk and travels with him to the old site of the river where the village once stood, recording her father's memories on a small digital camera. Nelson could be said to be using a "mixed mode" approach to oral history, in which electronic recording and oral narratives are both involved to record cultural knowledge. Hanuse, however, is interested in the specificity and value of oral traditions. Though Nelson asserts that recording is imperative because every time an elder dies, those stories are lost, Hanuse states in voice-over, "And still, when I turn my camera on my grandmother, I can't bring myself to ask her for her stories." Though Hanuse gives space to represent a perspective supporting the use of recording technologies, the film distinguishes the two in order to give oral traditions their due. In addition to interviews with community members, the film features evocative watercolor animation of Hanuse's memories of her youth learning from elders in the community. These sequences are warm and intimate, and as Nuxalk is spoken, the words appear in watercolor on-screen, conveying that the Nuxalk language is "animated" and alive in these environments. *Cry Rock* describes language and stories as living entities that are a part of the cultural history, and this cultural history lives within a physical and social world. In "Oral Tradition and Oral History: Reviewing Some Issues" (1994), Julie Cruikshank describes the unique social and historical character of oral narratives. Cruikshank, an anthropologist who has done extensive ethnographic work with Indigenous peoples to theorize oral traditions, evaluates prevailing analytic approaches to oral traditions: they have been considered material culture that give evidence of the past, and have been theorized as a method for interpreting and understanding social conditions in the present. To these dominant interpretive methods she adds more contemporary approaches that recognize that the meanings of oral narratives are not self-evident but must be understood in social practice where meaning is enacted. Context is particularly meaningful for oral histories because they bear an intrinsic relationship to place. Cruikshank cites a case study of an anthropologist conducting field research with Indigenous groups in the Philippines, in which he came to understand that in oral traditional modes, "events are anchored to place and people use locations in space to speak about events over time" (1994, 409). Thus, by relating events to place, oral narratives shape perception of the landscape as a part of history. Oral narratives resist codification—which would render them into a static form—because their meaning comes from the context of their telling, enacted by the person relating the narrative in a particular place where that narrative is "located."

Cry Rock explores dimensions of oral narratives that convey place relationships. The film crew travels with Clyde Tallio, a young Nuxalk speaker, and Alvin Mack, a local Nuxalk artist, to a site that they believe might be the Cry Rock, a spot in a local river where, as Clyde describes, a supernatural being called the Sniniq once sat crying for her dead child. Two local boys heard her crying and approached her in their boat, and when one boy stepped out on the rock next to her, he began crying too. After a while the Sniniq turned to him and thanked him for crying with her. Alvin's voice is heard over a long shot of the bend in the river that he believes could be the site of the story, and the camera slowly zooms in to consider the spot. The story is shown to have a physical and historical location, which transforms perceptions

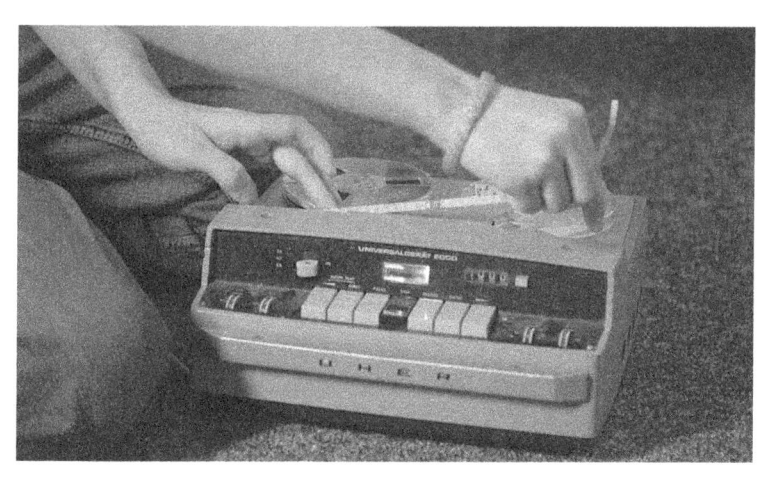

FIGURE 20. Snxakila (Clyde Tallio) loads reel-to-reel tape of Nuxalk language recording in *Cry Rock* (2010). Image courtesy of Banchi Hanuse.

of the site; the story "becomes real" in the world, living in a particular territory. This scene links storytelling to place, something the film can point to but cannot reproduce or embody. The Sniniq story also tells another story, one about the limitations of electronic recordings to communicate the full meaning of oral narratives. The young boy who joins the Sniniq on the Cry Rock experiences her grief empathetically, but does not share the source of her grief. The Cry Rock becomes a site of mediation, where a certain social and cultural interaction can take place, but a fullness of understanding through shared experience is not realizable. It is telling that the Sniniq is a mother, and the boy a child—in the story's telling in the film, they are from different generations. Generational difference is therefore the framework for the disjuncture between them, echoing the generational ruptures experienced within Indigenous communities. Elsewhere in the film, the presence and influence of the elementary school in the community is foregrounded, evoking the colonial education system and its impact on Indigenous communities and cultures. As Clyde Tallio relates, the provincial educational curriculum limits the amount of time that the Nuxalk language can be taught in class to thirty minutes a week—in effect, perpetuating the colonial project of cultural erosion through its inadequate language programming.

The relationship between the boy and the Sniniq allegorizes Hanuse's own relationship with her grandmother. Like the boy, she is at a remove from her grandmother's conceptual and cultural frameworks by virtue of descending from a generation in which a profound cultural disruption took place. Her relationship with her grandmother is therefore mediated by a generational cultural shift. This should not, however, be understood as an inflexible barrier to understanding. Though Indigenous communities have experienced an irrevocable cultural change over the past several centuries, Julie Cruikshank helps us to understand that oral traditions are used to make sense of contemporary circumstances and gain meaning in practice as they relate to those circumstances (1994). Oral narratives are thus flexible and adaptive, constantly making sense of the present in particular places. As illustrated by the film, the Cry Rock story allegorizes the generational rupture and reflects on the cultural and social changes that have taken place in the community as a result. It simultaneously identifies the limitations of the documentary mode, since we cannot be in the

FIGURE 21. Alvin Mack and (Snxakila) Clyde Tallio at the site of the Cry Rock (Kwanatulhayc) (*Cry Rock*, 2010). Image courtesy of Banchi Hanuse.

physical place to which the story refers and in which it is meaningful. The film thus argues that oral narratives are able to both account for cultural and historical change—and in fact, are meaningful in that they do address the present—while at the same time require certain conditions in order to be more fully meaningful: the language in which they are relayed and the environment in which they live. Oral traditions are both flexible and finite, and the film registers this tension, particularly since the conditions through which these stories are meaningful are increasingly under threat. Though different conceptual frameworks will be at play due to generational differences, the film makes the case that given the right conditions, the knowledge that the stories possess can be transmitted across that divide.

As in *Navajo Talking Picture,* the representation of Hanuse's relationship with her grandmother is a central trope of the film. Where the conflict-based interactions between Bowman and Ann Biah thematized cultural conflict as the structuring device of the film, Hanuse and her grandmother do not interact on camera for the majority of the film; rather, her grandmother appears in a sequence in which she prepares and smokes a salmon, which is intercut throughout the film and which the camera observes discreetly. I would argue that it functions pedagogically, modeling a kind of careful attentiveness required of in oral traditions. The camera is aligned with Hanuse's perspective, enhanced by the film's first-person narration and Hanuse's memories. As grandmother prepares the salmon, the camera-as-Hanuse patiently observes. While the film ultimately argues that oral traditions cannot be fully realized through the film apparatus, it guides the viewer toward recognition of the interpersonal dynamics necessary to participate in them. At the end of the film, Hanuse states that she decided to learn the Nuxalk stories following the oral tradition, and in a long shot, runs from behind the camera up to her grandmother's porch steps to embrace her. This shot compliments the salmon preparation sequence in that it suggests that attentiveness, modeled throughout the film, has prepared her for the interpersonal relationships required of oral traditions. *Cry Rock* intervention is particularly timely given the proliferation of Indigenous film and media production worldwide. The film's attention to the value and relevance of oral traditions and critique of the applications and limitations of recording technologies is crucial ballast for social and institutional discourses that align media with oral traditions. It thus brings together critical frameworks from Indigenous studies with discourses around Indigenous production from state-sponsored film institutions. Attention to the institutional dimensions of the film illuminates an area of discursive convergence that enables a productive critique of discourses conflating filmmaking with oral traditions, enabling closer examination of these two modes and their specificities.

FIGURE 22. Anuximana (Violet Tallio) bagging salmon (*slaq'k*) (*Cry Rock*, 2010). Image courtesy of Banchi Hanuse.

CONCLUSION: REPRESENTING THE UNREPRESENTABLE

In a sense, the insights of both *Navajo Talking Picture* and *Cry Rock* pivot around the limits of representation. *Navajo Talking Picture* shows the audience Bowman's "failure," which demarcates the boundary of what she sought to represent—her grandmother's traditional lifestyle—and what she is unable to, which is ultimately attributed to the irreconcilability of their cultural positions. *Cry Rock,* meanwhile, shows the audience what it cannot show, since the film apparatus, and indeed any other recording technology, cannot represent the fuller meaning of oral traditional narratives.

Though produced in different national contexts, both *Navajo Talking Picture* and *Cry Rock* give evidence of their negotiations with institutional discourses and practices in their production and ultimately in their screen content. At UCLA, the "reinvention" of anthropology sought to involve Indigenous people in the production and interpretation of research, but did not anticipate or understand how colonial processes might be replicated in what was intended to be a culturally empowering project. In trying to better represent Indigenous needs, the NFB designed programming to support Indigenous social empowerment that aligned Indigenous media with traditional cultural practices, perhaps not fully cognizant that even with the best of intentions, contemporary applications of media for engaging with Indigenous cultural knowledge risks displacing traditional modalities. These films do, however, make visible the complexities arising out of such efforts and contribute to understandings of the possibilities and limitations of particular institutional approaches, valuable insights that can advance institutional and disciplinary practices in Indigenous studies and other studies of marginalized groups.

5

Resisting Colonial Relations in Virtual Reality

HIGHWAY OF TEARS

By bringing greater visibility to the institutions of media culture that form the backdrop for the Indigenous media wave in Canada, this book has maintained that attention to institutional contexts of Indigenous media that enriches analysis of screen content, deepening understandings of their aesthetic and critical transformations and insights. The spectrum of media-producing institutions should be recognized for their significance to Indigenous media development in Canada, and as foci for social and political dynamics that Indigenous producers reflect on, debate, and critique through their work. The case studies at the center of each chapter have been chosen for being meaningful to particular eras of Indigenous production emerging from different institutional contexts, but they do not represent the full scope of media formats available at the time—in particular, digital media platforms. As has been shown throughout this book, media genres and their platforms are accompanied by discourses specific to them (documentary film, educational television, public service announcements, reality television, etc.), which Indigenous media-makers take up, challenge, and transform. Digital media is no different, and in fact has been an area of development for Indigenous artists and developers that accelerated in the early 1990s alongside other media formats. A discussion of Indigenous digital media, therefore, must avoid reproducing a developmental narrative that positions digital media as an end point to the evolution of media technologies, and instead must recognize that digital media has been a part of the media ecosystem composed of other media formats and developments discussed throughout.

As with the preceding chapters, the focus for this chapter brings together the institutional context for developments in media technologies—specifically virtual reality (VR)—with Indigenous concerns contemporaneous with these technologies. This chapter examines

Highway of Tears (2016), a four-minute, 360-degree immersive documentary that was conceptualized and produced at *The Current*, CBC (Canada Broadcasting Corporation) Radio's daily news affairs program, for which renowned Anishinaabe filmmaker Lisa Jackson was hired to direct it. *Highway of Tears* emerged at the intersection of reconciliation-era politics, industry trends toward VR technologies, and the phenomenon of "immersive journalism." The film uses VR technology to speak to a high-profile case that contributed to the National Inquiry into Missing and Murdered Indigenous Women and Girls (MMIWG) in Canada, which formally operated from 2016 to 2019 and investigated the history and conditions contributing to the disproportionate violence inflicted upon Indigenous women in Canada. The film provides a 360-degree view from the air and at ground level of the landscape of Highway 16, a notorious 724-kilometer section of the Trans-Canada Highway that runs through central British Columbia linking Prince Rupert and Prince George, where at least eighteen and up to fifty Indigenous women and girls have gone missing or have been murdered (Levin 2016).[1] Shots of the highway and neighboring land are intercut with Matilda Wilson's (Gitxsan) living room, where Wilson discusses the murder of her sixteen-year-old daughter, Ramona Wilson, who disappeared along the highway in 1994 and whose body was found near Smithers in 1995. The experience of viewing the film is striking, as the scenes in Wilson's living room place the viewer directly in front of her as she sits in her armchair and tells her story. There is a marked contrast between the open space of the highway and vistas of the surrounding landscape, and the almost disconcerting closeness of the viewer to Wilson in the living room. My own response has been echoed by Chelsea Barnett:

> I had to break [Matilda Wilson's] gaze to relieve my discomfort, turning instead to the domestic intimacies of their living quarters. Each time I looked away, I faced failure as the focus in the room wouldn't shift from the foreground to the background, or the wall began to warp as I swiveled in my lounge chair. I was instantly reminded that I was in a gallery, watching cinema, despite the absence of the screen. (2016)

The discomfort generated by proximity and the "interference" of the formal properties of the virtual space are productive: they disrupt pre-

FIGURE 23. Matilda Wilson shows a photograph of her daughter, Ramona, in *Highway of Tears* (2016). Image courtesy of *The Current,* CBC Radio.

vailing claims that VR amplifies empathy and transparency—claims that circulate around VR and immersive journalism—and, I argue, in so doing refuse the colonial gaze that craves the spectacle of Indigenous trauma that accompanied the national media coverage of Indigenous issues, including the MMIWG inquiry.

THE MMIWG CRISIS: GENDERED COLONIAL VIOLENCE

The Highway of Tears is a major symbol of the MMIWG crisis, which refers to the systemic, ongoing, disproportionate violence inflicted on Indigenous women in Canada, the United States, and Latin America. In Canada, the crisis erupted into public consciousness and international attention at the turn of the twenty-first century in no small part due to the largest serial murder investigation in Canadian history that began in February 2002 on a farm in Coquitlam, BC, owned by Robert Pickton. After his arrest in 2002, Pickton ultimately confessed to killing forty-nine women over at least a decade, and sought his victims from Vancouver's Downtown Eastside, one of Canada's most impoverished communities. As Shari M. Huhndorf (Yup'ik) explains, the Downtown Eastside is associated with poverty, rampant drug use, and sex work, "a space of violence and death" linked to perceptions of the "degeneracy" of those living there that, she argues, naturalizes the violence inflicted on community members, and explains why for so long the disappearances of Indigenous women from the neighborhood attracted little public attention and were not adequately or meaningfully investigated by police (2021, 561). Huhndorf pointedly notes that at least half of Pickton's victims were Indigenous even though Indigenous people make up only 3 percent of people in Vancouver, a pattern that was not widely noticed outside of Indigenous communities (2021, 561).

To take Huhndorf's point, it took these extraordinarily high-profile cases, and the widespread and sensational international media coverage that accompanied them, to jolt the national public, Canadian government, and police forces out of their complacency and begin to take seriously the disappearances and murders of Indigenous women and girls across the country, even though their families, communities, and advocates have been calling for an investigation for decades. As Huhndorf argues, this complacency is bred from gendered colonial stereotypes of Indigenous degeneracy, which conflate Indigenous women with sex work and frame missing women—whether they are sex workers or not—as "drug addicted sex workers, as 'blameworthy,' thereby defecting attention from the structural dimensions of the violence" (2021, 565). The media is particularly culpable for such framing: as Yasmin Jiwani and Mary Lynn Young argue, posters circulated by the police to the media used mug shots for many of the women, which "not only reinforced the women's association with criminality . . . but also highlighted the Aboriginal heritage of many of the missing women" (2006, 898).

The discourses of sexualized degeneracy enfolding Indigenous women emerge from colonial ideology. As Huhndorf explains, colonial ideology is organized around the removal of Indigenous peoples from their lands to make way for European settlement. Removal is advanced by the colonial perception that Indigenous people are antithetical to modernity, linking Indigenous with the temporal notion of "pastness" or the distant geographical space of the "reserve/reservation" that rationalizes Indigenous territorial dispossession (2021, 564). Huhndorf further explains that Indigenous women's vulnerability is innately tied to the gendered dimensions of colonial dispossession and removal. Colonial law, particularly the Indian Act, 1876, forcibly disenfranchised Indigenous women if they married a non-Indigenous man, forcing them to leave their communities, while the residential school system enforced strict European gender roles on Indigenous children that subordinated Indigenous girls (563). Consequently, "contemporary violence, including gendered violence, enacted on Indigenous bodies extends from and repeats the colonial subjugation of Indigenous communities and their eviction from traditional homelands" (564). Both Indigenous women's bodies and the land, therefore, are the "terrain" of the exercise of inherently gendered colonial power and dispossession.

MMIWG AND DOCUMENTARY INTERVENTIONS

Highway of Tears is directly contextualized by colonial discourses that enfold Indigenous women *and* the land, and confronts and disrupts these discourses via its textual strategies within an immersive VR environment. In this respect, I connect *Highway of Tears* to a cluster of documentary films by Indigenous filmmakers in the 2000s linked to the MMIWG crisis that seek to transform these gendered colonial discourses, which I use as touchstones for framing my analysis of *Highway of Tears*. The first is *Donna's Story* (2001) by Doug Cuthand, the subject of chapter 1 of this book. The film is a portrait documentary of Donna Gamble (Cree), a former sex worker and recovering addict who now works as an educator and counselor with her community. I argued that Cuthand employs the portrait documentary genre because it focuses on the personal as a window on broader social issues that shape a person's lived experience. In the case of Donna Gamble, the film addresses the intergenerational trauma and sexual abuse that has been imposed on her and her family by settler colonial society, which has dehumanized her instead of recognizing the complex and painful conditions shaping her background. The documentary is profoundly empathetic in its depiction of the highs and lows of Donna's everyday life, her family life, her efforts to connect with traditional cultural practices, and particularly around her struggles with sobriety. Toward the end of the film Donna discusses her recent experience of "falling off the wagon," explaining pragmatically that it is a part of the recovery process. The film refuses to end on a neat resolution or statement about Donna's life; it is instead structured as a circle, echoing the lived, cyclical process of recovery. Though the ending might be considered "ambivalent," Donna's determination and tenacity suggest that she will survive and thrive. *Donna's Story* is a humanizing, dimensional portrait of a person that settler colonial society typically overlooks or vilifies; in the process, it maps the systemic nature of gendered colonial violence that has shaped her and her family's lives. Thus, while Donna's story is uniquely her own, it is not a standalone or exceptional case for Indigenous women in Canada.

Donna's Story was produced before the horrific discoveries of the Pickton farm. Five years later, Métis filmmaker Christine Welsh produced *Finding Dawn* (2006), a documentary that followed the Pickton farm investigation and his arrest, as momentum was gathering for a national inquiry into the MMIWG crisis. Pamela Palmater (Mi'kmaw) has provided an invaluable account of the milestone actions, investigations, and missing and murdered cases that led to the national MMIWG inquiry (2019). This timeline includes the 2004 Amnesty International report, *Stolen Sisters: A Human Rights Response to Discrimination and Violence against Indigenous Women in Canada* (2004), which gave scope to the extent of gender-based violence against Indigenous women and used an international human rights framework in order to hold the Canadian state accountable for the human rights abuses this violence represents. Further, in 2005, the Native Women's Association of Canada created a database tracking Indigenous women and girls who have been murdered or gone missing, and in 2010 reported 582 cases (2010, i). By 2014, that number had been revised by the Royal Canadian Mounted Police's national operational overview to 1,181 cases between 1980 and 2012 (2014, 3).

These major initiatives and reports made clear that the serial murders on the Pickton farm and the disappearances and murders along the Highway of Tears are far from exceptional or isolated events and tragedies: not only is this violence much more widespread than anyone ever imagined,[2] but they are all linked by their common root of gendered colonial violence that is the foundation of the settler colonial project of the Canadian nation-state. It is precisely this relationship that structures *Finding Dawn*, which links the disappearances and murders of Indigenous women in Vancouver's Downtown Eastside with those on the Highway of Tears, including Ramona Wilson, and finally with the murders of three Indigenous women in Saskatoon, Saskatchewan, by serial killer John Martin Crawford in the 1990s, three highly visible instances of violence against Indigenous women spread over a wide geography. While the Pickton case is a starting point for the film, Welsh challenges mechanisms by which systemic violence is "exceptionalized," such as by attributing murders to an individual, which is typically the route through which a murder gains notoriety and even celebrity. Welsh refuses to name Pickton in the film, and only briefly shows footage of the outside of the farm, which by that time had been reduced to mounds of dirt and debris from the police investigation surrounded by nondescript industrial fencing. The film spends less than two minutes on the crime itself before Welsh's voice-over names the twenty-third woman whose DNA was identified on the farm as Dawn Crey (Stó:lō), and states that finding her DNA "raised more questions than it gave answers. Who was she and how did we lose her?" Stating that "I need to put a human face to what's happened," the film develops a fuller portrait of Dawn and the circumstances that led to her life on the Downtown Eastside, where she ultimately disappeared. The film briefly shows a wall of mugshots used to identify the women missing from the Downtown Eastside before transitioning to show only family photographs of the women, pointedly intervening in the police and media's practice of using the women's mug shots to identify them. Interviews with Dawn's brother and sister, Ernie Crey and Lorraine Crey, reveal that all of their siblings were apprehended by the child welfare system in British Columbia as a part of the Sixties Scoop, a period of time from the 1950s and 1960s onward when Indigenous children were taken by the state from their families and fostered or adopted out to non-Indigenous families (Fournier and Crey 1997). The Sixties Scoop is widely understood to have picked up where residential schools left off, separating Indigenous children from their families and communities in order to eradicate their relationships to their lands, languages, cultures, and families. The Sixties Scoop tore apart the Crey siblings, placed them in abusive homes far from their family members, and led Dawn in her teenage and adult years to the Downtown Eastside. The film demonstrates that circumstances of Dawn's life, and the tragedy of her death, are directly linked to the colonial practice of child apprehension, which makes Indigenous children—and particularly women and girls—vulnerable to violence throughout their lives.

Finding Dawn then moves north to the Highway of Tears to focus on the disappearance of Ramona Wilson, who ten years later is the focus for the immersive documentary *Highway of Tears* (2016). While the discourse of Indigenous "degeneracy" produces a narrative that blames victims for the violence they experience, usually due to their association with "high risk" activities, this sequence illustrates that Indigenous women are at risk of violence no matter who they are, where they live, or what they are doing, even if simply travelling along the sole thoroughfare between communities in central British Columbia. Ramona's youth and wholesomeness, and her strong family bonds, disrupt associations of Indigenous women with "high risk" activities, which is emphasized by other Indigenous women interviewed for this segment, who include Wilson's family members, a local radio host, and community members who take part in an annual memorial walk for Wilson. As the film then moves to Saskatoon to interview Janice Acoose (Salteaux/Métis), a former journalist and university professor, it is clear that viewers are being presented with a remarkably diverse range of Indigenous women's backgrounds over a vast geography, who nonetheless share the common experience of gendered colonial violence, a system that binds them together as concretely as the highways that Welsh traverses to visit them to hear their stories. In this way, the film dismantles notions that incidents of violence against Indigenous women can be thought of in isolation, and instead places them in direct relation linked by the very conditions that have produced the Canadian state.

THE MMIWG INQUIRY IN/AS RECONCILIATION POLITICS

By the time that *Highway of Tears* was produced in 2016, the MMIWG crisis had been recognized as a national issue and the Canadian government had initiated an official inquiry. The inquiry took shape directly out of reconciliation politics, which, as Glen Coulthard (Yellowknives Dene) has argued, has shaped Indigenous–state relations since the 1990s (2014, 106). Perhaps the defining moment of this era was Prime Minister Stephen Harper's June 11, 2008, official apology on behalf of Canada to the survivors of the residential school system. Canada's apology followed the 2007 Indian Residential School Settlement Agreement that was negotiated between Canada and approximately 86,000 residential school survivors, resulting in—among other measures—a C$1.9 billion compensation package set aside for former residential school students, and the creation of a Truth and Reconciliation Commission (TRC) tasked with documenting the history of residential schools and testimony of survivors. The TRC operated from 2008 to 2015, producing a multivolume report and an executive summary with ninety-four calls to action to redress the legacies of residential schools. Call to action 41 specifically calls for the federal government to appoint a public inquiry to investigate "the disproportionate victimization of Aboriginal women and girls" and examine the links between this phenomenon and intergenerational legacy of residential schools (TRC of Canada 2015b, 4).

Following the conclusion of the TRC in 2015, the MMIWG inquiry began almost immediately—some might say expeditiously—in early 2016. Whatever the motivations on the part of the state to move forward so quickly, both the TRC and MMIWG inquiry served as mechanisms by which to affirm Canada's accountability for the residential school system and systemic gendered violence against Indigenous women and girls by constructing a shared discursive framework for both. Both the TRC and MMIWG reports framed the legacy of the residential school system and MMIWG as "cultural genocide," a concept both final reports define and employ to produce a mutually reinforcing interpretive schema for understanding the Indigenous experience of the formation of the Canadian nation-state. The TRC defines cultural genocide as the opening paragraph of the final report:

> For over a century, the central goals of Canada's Aboriginal policy were to eliminate Aboriginal governments; ignore Aboriginal rights; terminate the Treaties; and, through a process of assimilation, cause Aboriginal peoples to cease to exist as distinct legal, social, cultural, religious, and racial entities in Canada. The establishment and operation of residential schools were a central element of this policy, which can best be described as "cultural genocide." (2015a, 3)

The 2019 final report of the MMIWG builds on this definition in relation to the ongoing and disproportionate violence experienced by Indigenous women and girls by identifying that the abuses and community and family ruptures inflicted by the residential school system have resulted in intergenerational trauma that has produced "a cycle of violence that is extremely difficult to break collectively, as it affects all those who are caught up in the cycle" (National Inquiry into MMIWG 2019, 96). Without diminishing the violence overwhelmingly originating from settler colonial racism and misogyny, the report traces the interlocking systemic, socioeconomic, and familial issues that create conditions in which "Indigenous women and girls are almost guaranteed to be exposed to one form of violence or another in their lifetime"

(National Inquiry into MMIWG 2019, 96). These reports provide historical context for the MMIWG crisis that roots it within the settler colonial state's agenda to terminate Indigenous peoples, thus affirming that it is a national issue, one for which Canada is ultimately responsible.

HIGHWAY OF TEARS: THEORIZING INDIGENOUS DIGITAL ENVIRONMENTS

That *Highway of Tears* employs immersive technology places it on a continuum of Indigenous digital engagement and innovation, as much as it is an outcome of the availability of this technology in Canadian news media industries. Indigenous engagement with "new" or digital media is far from a recent phenomenon; Joanna Hearne, for instance, discusses an early instance of Indigenous digital experimentation by examining Cree artist and musician Buffy Sainte-Marie's pixel art that she created using MacPaint on Macintosh computers in the mid- to late 1980s (forthcoming). However, the early 1990s does mark a period in which digital work by Indigenous artists flourished, accompanying the rise of Indigenous media across available formats and platforms. VR produced by Indigenous artists in Canada dates to Cowichan/ Syilx visual artist Lawrence Paul Yuxweluptun's *Inherent Rights, Vision Rights* (1992), which has been described as a "virtual [Coast Salish] longhouse" that employs first-person perspective that allows users to move through the "space" of the longhouse, where singing and drumming can be heard (King 2017, 190). Users can approach fires and stylized "ovoid" beings in the longhouse, who react and move as users approach. *Inherent Rights, Vision Rights* was created while Yuxweluptun was a visiting artist at the Banff Centre for the Arts[3] as part of a residency for the Virtual Seminar on the Bioapparatus, which brought together experts in VR technology with artists and researchers in the humanities and social sciences (MacLeod 1996). The project was one of the first VR projects in Canada, as well as the first VR piece exhibited at the National Gallery of Canada (Hampton 2017).

Inherent Rights, Vision Rights not only marks an early and groundbreaking moment in Indigenous implementations of VR—and VR in Canada in general—but it also points to the Banff Centre for Arts and Creativity as an institutional site that has historically supported the development of Indigenous digital media. Chapter 2 of this book examines the Banff Centre's partnership with the Aboriginal Film and Video Art Alliance (AFVAA), but Indigenous artists participated across Banff Centre's programs, including in residencies and as visiting artists, as was the case with Yuxweluptun. The early 1990s, however, coalesced energy and momentum to expand Banff Centre's capacities for Indigenous engagement, research, and media-based production in its partnership with the AFVAA, which intersected with tectonic shifts in the digital media landscape. Sara Diamond, the founding director of the Banff New Media Institute, states that the early 1990s through the 2000s was an era of massive technological shift characterized by the adoption of "new media," later termed "digital media," and the rise of "an information-, technology-, and communication-boom economy" (Cook and Diamond 2012, 21). The Banff Centre—as a preeminent art institution in Canada—quickly adapted in its strategic programming development, including research, symposia, and workshops on virtual environments and immersive experiences as early as the late 1980s into the early 1990s that contributed to the eventual formation of the Banff New Media Institute in 1995 (Cook and Diamond 2012, 25).

The Banff Centre's partnership with the AFVAA became a major pillar in the development of Indigenous digital media. The partnership was established at a major gathering in February 1993, and six months later in August 1993, the Storytellers and Media Gathering took place where there was consensus for developing an online communications network for Indigenous artists, a "multi-media distribution system" to share and view Indigenous artwork, and training and workshops for "new media design and authoring" with the goal of advancing Indigenous "economic self-sufficiency and self-determination" (Banff Centre for the Arts 1994, 2–3). Banff subsequently hosted a number of initiatives and events through the 1990s and into the 2000s, including two iterations of Drum Beats to Drum Bytes in 1994 and 2002, gatherings that examined Indigenous presence on the internet; and the Aboriginal Interactive Media: Electronic Publishing and Multimedia workshop in 1997 in partnership with the AFVAA (Cook and Diamond 2012, 512). While the telecommunications network and distribution system the AFVAA envisaged has been more aspirational than fully realized, these activities illustrate the comprehensive approach that Indigenous innovators took to internet-based and digital media technologies and infrastructures as a part of advancing Indigenous sovereignty.

The Banff Centre's collaborations with Indigenous artists and organizations have played an undeniably significant role in the history of Indigenous digital media in Canada, but this very brief overview is not meant to cover over major contributions during this era beyond the Banff Centre that illustrate how Indigenous artists engage digital technologies to advance Indigenous priorities and interests. For instance, CyberPowWow, created and curated by the collective Nation to Nation (consisting of Skawennati [Mohawk], Ryan Rice [Mohawk], and Eric Robertson [Métis/Gitxsan]) was conceptualized in 1996 and operated from 1997 to 2004 in four iterations: CyberPowWow, CyberPowWow 2, CPW 2K: CyberPowWow Goes Global, and CPW04: Unnatural Resources (Nation to Nation, n.d.). As its name suggests, CyberPowWow was a virtual space for Indigenous gatherings built using "The Palace," a program by Time Warner that allowed users to design and customize graphical avatars and access "palaces," or graphical chatrooms, to interact with each other. Part of the intent of the project was to challenge notions that somehow Indigenous artists and technology are antithetical, as Skawennati explained:

> CyberPowWow started off as a virtual exhibition and chat
> space that would dispel the myth that Native artists didn't (or
> couldn't!?) use technology in their work. In addition to that, we
> wanted to claim for ourselves a little corner of cyberspace that
> we could nurture and grow in the way we wanted. (n.d.)

Nation to Nation invited Indigenous participants to CyberPowWow to create and interact with one another and their digital artwork, certainly confronting the specter of the "primitive Indian" that has haunted Indigenous engagement with modern technology, while creating the kind of personal and professional network that was envisioned through the AFVAA at Banff. Moreover, CyberPowWow engaged with concepts of space and territory accompanying the internet that Skawennati's use of the term "cyberspace" indicates, which David Gaertner defines as a "notional environment generated through computer networks" (2015, 56). As Gaertner argues, CyberPowWow is a "remediation" of cultural practices, an act of "translating events such as the powwow into alternative forms and spaces" (58), producing "a singular indigenous space for installation art, performance, and community building" (57). CyberPowWow's translations of cultural practices into digital realms do not represent a break with tradition, but rather, as Gaertner points out, are an innovative extension of tradition using digital and networked technologies (59).

Through their efforts to produce "Indigenous space" online, the organizers of and participants in CyberPowWow are engaged with a fundamental debate in Indigenous media studies that is concerned with the ideological basis of digital technologies and the extent to which these ideologies (Western and colonial) are inherently reproduced by using them. Filmmaker Loretta Todd (Cree/Métis) captures this debate in her foundational essay, "Aboriginal Narratives in Cyberspace."[4] Todd confronts the techno-utopianism that tends to accompany the introduction of new technologies by asking, "What ideology will have agency in cyberspace?" (Todd 1996, 180). Challenging the idealism of ideas that "in cyberspace, everyone will have free and equal access regardless of origins," (180), Todd argues that cyberspace is deeply rooted in Western ontologies, a critique that Joanna Hearne summarizes: "a place of symbolic violence, not visual sovereignty; a space where artifacts of settler imagination are simply rehearsed and (re) distributed in newly monetized ways using powerfully intensified infrastructures" (2017, 17). Todd questions if cyberspace reproduces the mind/body dualism of Western thought that seeks to transcend the limitations of the body and physical world and achieve the rarified and dominant state of all-knowing, "to emulate *visio Dei*" (181; the vision of a god). Such dualisms sever the relations between body, place, territory, and nonhuman beings on which Indigenous knowledge systems are based, and which seek "harmony and balance with the self and the universe" (183). Todd's essay is not a wholesale condemnation of virtual space, but is structured as a series of crucial questions to incite careful reflection on the impact of digital technologies on Indigenous epistemologies, and emphasize the need for such critical rigor in the process of adopting new technologies for Indigenous purposes.

A project like *CyberPowWow* is clearly built on careful thought about how digital technology and networked computers can be adapted to enhance Indigenous communities and equip Indigenous artists with a platform and digital tools for creative self-expression; it also anticipates the kind of critical reflection that Indigenous digital artists invariably undertake as they develop innovative and creative strategies for resisting "artifacts of settler imagination" that accompany the technologies they use. Throughout this book I have argued that Indigenous artists have developed sophisticated techniques for navigating and transforming colonial discourses that undergird media technologies and inform screen aesthetics; these sentiments resonate with Heather Igloliorte (Inuk), Julie Nagam, and Carla Taunton's assertion, in the special issue of *Public* on Indigenous digital media art, that "Indigenous artists have always been innovators, and have therefore been at the forefront of practice and technologically orientated methods and methodologies" (2016, 7).

As the AFVAA and *CyberPowWow* illustrate, Indigenous creatives and artists have long formed alliances, collectives, and organizations—often in association with research and art-based institutions—to work collaboratively to produce research, public events, creative works, and exhibitions advancing the field of Indigenous digital media. In Canada, Skawennati and Dr. Jason Edward Lewis (Cherokee, Hawaiian, and Samoan) are cofounders and codirectors of Aboriginal Territories in Cyberspace, a research network that originated with *CyberPowWow* and launched in 2005 at Concordia University in Montreal with the aim to "ensure Indigenous presence in the webpages, online environments, video games, and virtual worlds that comprise cyberspace" (Aboriginal Territories in Cyberspace n.d.). Igloliorte, Nagam, and Taunton comprise the GLAM Collective (Galleries, Libraries, Archives, and Museums), a group founded in 2018 to examine the intersections of performance and public art, digital technologies, and curatorial practice through Indigenous theory and methodologies (GLAM Collective, n.d.). These groups are playing a crucial role in developing Indigenous knowledge, research, and creativity within digital contexts, contributing to defining the field of Indigenous digital media as one based in and driven by Indigenous interests and concerns.

In this fundamental respect—their commitment to advancing Indigenous priorities in digital contexts—these groups overlap with other forms engagement with digital platforms and technologies to support Indigenous self-determination, sovereignty, creativity, and knowledge production. Social media played a major role in mobilizing support for Indigenous grassroots social movements in North America in the 2010s that gained enormous international attention, most visibly Idle No More and the #NoDAPL (No to the Dakota Access Pipeline) movements. Idle No More began in 2012 in protest of an omnibus bill, Bill C-45, that was introduced by Prime Minister Stephen Harper. The 450-page document proposed changes to dozens of acts that undermined First Nations rights, including unilateral amendments to the Indian Act, and changes to environmental legislation that eroded environmental protections that would make it possible to expedite resource extraction projects, such as oil and gas pipelines (Coates 2015, 1–2). Idle No More was founded in 2012 by a group of four Indigenous and non-Indigenous women in Saskatchewan, who used Facebook to bring visibility to their concerns about Bill C-45. Shortly thereafter, supporters began amplifying these messages on Facebook and Twitter, where the hashtag #IdleNoMore began trending. Supporters used social media to mobilize teach-ins, rallies, and round dances in, to that point, an unparalleled public demonstration of Indigenous discontent, and efforts to unite Indigenous peoples across Canada and internationally around common issues affecting Indigenous rights, sovereignty, and their cultural and economic futures (Raynauld, Richez, and Boudreau Morris 2018, 627). Only a few years later in 2016, another Indigenous-led grassroots movement known as #noDAPL—the Dakota Access Pipeline protests—arose in North Dakota and gained global attention. #noDAPL was a social media and hashtag campaign in protest of the construction of the Dakota Access Pipeline that would run through Standing Rock Sioux treaty lands, sacred sites, and burial grounds in violation of the tribe's treaty rights, and pass under the Missouri River, threatening the primary water source for communities along the river (Ostler and Estes 2019, 98–99). Social media campaigns initiated by Indigenous youth, including Rezpect Our Water and Water Is Life/Mní Wičóni, captured social media attention and brought extraordinary support for the Water Protectors, as they came to be known. It is estimated that well over ten thousand Indigenous and allied supporters flocked to Standing Rock from around North America and the world, resulting in one of the largest pan-Indigenous mobilizations in history (Ellis 2019, 172–73).

In addition to making visible the ongoing colonial projects of the contemporary Canadian and U.S. nation-states and the scope of Indigenous resistance to them, #IdleNoMore and #noDAPL demonstrated how social media can be used strategically to galvanize support for Indigenous sovereignty and protection of Indigenous rights. The incredible visibility of these social media campaigns is also a product of the historical confluence of Indigenous social movements and the evolution of social media platforms: the issues driving these movements have very deep historical roots that are activated by ongoing violations of Indigenous treaties and rights, which occurred during a period in which Twitter and Facebook were experiencing massive user growth. This is not to say there is a causal relationship between social media and the formation of social movements, but rather to identify that social and technological phenomena are inextricably linked, a dynamic that this book has traced and which forms the context for the immersive documentary, *Highway of Tears*.

VR RESURGENCE AND NATIONAL CRISIS

Investigations into virtual environments at the Banff Centre for the Arts in the late 1980s and early 1990s represent an early and key moment for creative and critical attention to VR technologies, in no small part due to the resources and interests of administrators, programmers, and creators at the Banff Centre. *Highway of Tears* emerged when VR and augmented reality (AR) received renewed and substantial attention and investment in Canada in the mid-2010s, which was reflected in Indigenous media production opportunities, as reflected at the imagineNATIVE Film + Media Arts Festival in 2017. The imagineNATIVE festival seeks to reflect industry opportunities in its annual programs and during its annual festival in Toronto, particularly through its Industry Days, which bring together media industry professionals with Indigenous creators to "provide Indigenous-led professional development opportunities to address gaps within the industry" (imagineNATIVE 2021). Indigenous AR and VR were the thematic focus for the festival in 2017 largely through *2167*, a set of four VR projects by Indigenous artists commissioned by imagineNATIVE as a major capstone for the festival that year. *2167* consists of two- to six-minute VR projects by Kent Monkman (Cree), Scott Benesiinaabandan (Anishinaabe), the arts collective Postcommodity (composed of Raven Chacon [Diné], Cristóbal Martínez [as Genizaro, Pueblo, Manito, and Chicano people of Northern New Mexico], and Kade L. Twist [Cherokee]), and Danis Goulet (Cree-Métis). At the introduction of an artist panel titled "*2167*: Indigenous Storytelling in VR," Sandra Collins, chief financial officer and vice-president of operations of the Canadian Media Fund (CMF), announced that the CMF had contributed C\$24 million to VR and AR projects from 2013 to 2017 (imagineNATIVE Film + Media Arts Festival 2017), representing a significant industry investment in creative implementations of the technology and signaling potential opportunities available to Indigenous creators. Given that *Highway of Tears* was produced in 2016, the same timeframe as *2167*, there are meaningful indications that Canadian media industries were taking VR and AR implementation seriously during this period.

The combination of the availability of and industry interest in immersive technology with the immediacy of the national MMIWG crisis contextualizes *Highway of Tears*. CBC Radio's *The Current* airs daily and was hosted by radio and television journalist Anna Maria Tremonti from 2002 until 2019 (Canadian Communications Foundation 2022).[5] The program focuses on national current affairs, and as a part of Canada's national broadcaster addresses the MMIWG crisis as a national issue. *Highway of Tears* engages the crisis using conventions of documentary journalism within 360-degree immersive technology. The film was conceptualized at *The Current*, and was produced to accompany a series of five CBC public forums on the MMIWG crisis that were held across Canada (Goldhar and Bloch 2016). Lisa Jackson was hired to direct the film in collaboration with Secret Location, a production company specializing in immersive technologies (Doty 2017). Jackson notes that *Highway of Tears* was a departure from her usual work in the sense that she did not originate the idea and development, but rather "lent her skills to" the project (Crey, forthcoming). Jackson is a well-established and respected artist with a body of work, at that point, that cut across film, television, animation, and performance art film, including at least two documentaries that aired on CBC television, *Reservation Soldiers* (2007) and *How A People Live* (2013) (Jackson, n.d.). Moreover, in 2012, Jackson participated in the Stolen Sisters Digital Initiative, an initiative produced by imagineNATIVE Film + Media Arts Festival in partnership with Amnesty International Canada. Four Indigenous artists were commissioned to each produce a short digital media project that would be exhibited nationally in public transportation spaces, including on digital subway platform screens, in shopping centers, and at airports (NationTalk 2012). Jackson's 3.5-minute contribution, *Snare* (2013), is an acrobatic, performance-art-based film examining the violence against Indigenous women and the possibility of healing.

Unlike *Snare, Highway of Tears* is rooted in documentary realism, a stark difference from *Snare's* more poetic and evocative imagery.

Highway of Tears engages and challenges prevailing discourses surrounding VR, specifically that which links the technology to empathy. This association has been circulating since the 2000s, and has been enthusiastically taken up as a part of "immersive journalism." Robert Hassan argues that news journalism was an early adopter of VR technologies owing to the erosion of print media's relevance and influence in the public sphere, stating that the technology is not only attention grabbing, but also "provide[s] the means for strengthening the fourth estate's civic role in informing and enlightening the public through absorbing informational stimuli on political events, conflict, natural disasters, and the like" (2020, 196).[6] "Immersive journalism" has arisen as a result, a news format in which viewers are given a first-person experience of an event from news stories in an environment created using immersive technologies (de la Peña et al. 2010, 291). The shift from third-person to first-person perspective, from the "abstract" to the immediate and tangible, has led many to argue that VR can produce empathy in the viewer by immersing them in the event or situation, through which they gain a deeper understanding of the issues (Hassan 2020, 196). This effect is captured by the term "empathy machine" that is invoked in discussion of immersive journalism, and which CBC producer Josh Bloch explicitly cites while discussing the choice to employ VR technology for *Highway of Tears,* situating the film within this particular discursive milieu (CBC Radio 2016). By extension, Bloch suggests that VR enables viewers to have a more affective and therefore more meaningful engagement with Matilda Wilson's story and the MMIWG crisis than they might through traditional news coverage.

There are obvious problems with this formula, of course. The idea that a viewer inside a simulated immersive environment would experience an ideal response takes much for granted, implying that viewers have a fairly consistent capacity for empathy despite wide variation in individual psychology, and that, as Robert Hassan argues, simulated proximity to events or situations can transform a viewer by generating "psychological affinity" (2020, 205). Moreover, proximity and empathy hardly correlate; human proximity can equally result in more hostile responses, such as alienation and resentment. Further, psychology is shaped by cultural and social experiences, which obviously vary widely and can result in very different affective responses to the same stimuli or context. Perspective is not just psychological, but ideological: not only does ideology shape perspective, but the very notion of being able to align one's perspective with that of another, whatever their cultural background, is ideological; and further, it carries very troubling associations within Indigenous contexts. The suggestion that viewers might have more "transparent" access to others via proximity and immediacy, and that they might thereby become "knowable," carries resonances with the colonial gaze, which filmmaker Danis Goulet (Cree/Métis), one of the artists commissioned for *2167*, named and reflected on during the artists' panel:

> I'd seen a lot of VR pieces that are, wow, go into this Amazon tribe and sit by the fire with an elder and experience.... You know, that old exotic colonial gaze, it's now playing out in a hyperimmersive environment. We've been having these talks at imagineNATIVE and also within documentary talks, a lot about ethics and "Whose gaze?", and I think VR also has to be very engaged.... To talk about this medium we have to keep talking about these issues. (imagineNATIVE Film + Media Arts Festival 2017)

Goulet's comments make crucial observations about the colonial ideology undergirding discourses of VR technologies and their implementations, namely, notions of "access" combined with the spectacle of Otherness. Such observations have long been a concern of Indigenous artists and thinkers such as Loretta Todd, who pointed to the close relationship between VR's promise of transparent immediacy and the Western tradition's "need to know all" (2005a, 155). The desire to see, to surveil, and thereby to "know" is well known to Indigenous peoples, who have long been objects of colonial, disciplinary, and extractive scrutiny. The discourse or exercise of the "empathy machine" is by no means a remediation of such spectatorial regimes or the ideology producing them. As Lisa Nakamura argues, VR has been marketed as an empathetic technology to counter "the popular perception that Big Tech is rapacious, self-interested, and invasive" (2020, 50), which has resulted in "virtuous VR" as a means of contributing to social good by inducing in viewers empathy for victimized people. Framed as technology that creates empathy across social difference, virtuous VR actually creates "non-white, non-male experiences for a white male industry that needs to feel differently" (51). Consequently, virtuous VR reproduces the colonial, white spectatorial position and is, as Nakamura elaborates, part of the tradition of "empathy media" in

Western visual culture that can and historically has "completely misfired by exploiting their subjects and reducing their humanity through simplistic and moralistic framing" (54). Indigenous peoples have long experienced such positioning, and have developed strategies to resist such exploitation in digital terrains. This is not to say that non-Indigenous VR creators are not conscious of the problems of virtuous VR; *Highway of Tears* is, after all, a collaboration between Indigenous and non-Indigenous creatives that has resulted in representational strategies that push back against the issues that attend the empathy machine.

Highway of Tears confronts VR's colonial implications of access, proximity, and spectacle, which were particularly keen concerns during the public activities of the TRC and MMIWG inquiries. Dylan Robinson (Stó:lō) identifies that the stage of the TRC inquiry involving Commissioners Sharing Panels, which heard public testimonies from residential school survivors and families, "has been repeatedly criticized by Indigenous and settler critics alike as a compromised space that privileges performances of testimonial suffering. In its adoption of a confessional model, survivors are expected to purge negative emotion in the service of moving toward a certain strand of 'reconciliation'" (Robinson 2015, 60). As one of its recommendations, the MMIWG inquiry was launched at the tail end of the TRC, and like the TRC, held public community hearings. These allowed families and survivors to submit testimony privately if they preferred, but these hearings nonetheless illustrate that the 2010s was a period in which Indigenous trauma experienced intense scrutiny and visibility, accompanied by the colonial gaze and its appetite for Indigenous suffering. This does not mean, however, that Indigenous people were necessarily subjects of these testimonial spaces, or the colonial gaze. As Robinson points out, Indigenous participants in the TRC used the public panels in ways that refused the spectacle of suffering: speaking to one another, or taking an educational rather than emotional approach to testimony that created distance between their experiences and those of others (61).

In the same vein, *Highway of Tears* employs strategies that refuse viewer consumption of Matilda Wilson's pain. Lisa Jackson was very mindful of the colonial dynamics of the reconciliation era; in an episode of *The Current* in 2017, she reflected on *Highway of Tears*:

> For me personally as a filmmaker, working with a lot of traumatic issues, I think that one of the antidotes to media coverage—which can be salacious, detail-oriented, re-traumatizing, not complete—is to actually put, the way I look at it, is putting viewers in a space where they have to reflect and it's uncomfortable and they have to be in a space with a truth that isn't put forward in a conclusive way. (CBC Radio 2017)

Thus, while viewers may be "immersed" in Wilson's living room, it is discomfiting to appear suddenly in someone else's space as an "uninvited guest" and be directly addressed by them. The abrupt immersion in Matilda's living room is uncomfortable, even alienating. Wilson's direct address to the viewer, which is intercut with scenes of the highway and surrounding territory, resists viewer immersion in the 360-degree world of the film. Wilson's direct, eye-to-eye address to viewers involves them in the story she tells. The viewer is effectively "put on the spot" and becomes involved in her story as its recipient. Viewers are not so much an audience as much as they are witnesses, an important shift from spectator to a position that implicates the viewer in the social issue of missing and murdered Indigenous women and girls, while simultaneously pushing back against the colonial gaze and its appetite for Indigenous lives and especially Indigenous suffering. This textual strategy invokes questions of how we "see" or consume images, and thereby in issues of ethics and accountability as viewers. The ethical implication of viewers in Wilson's story and the broader MMIWG crisis advances the crucial understanding that this is not an issue of individual tragedies but one involving a broader public. Given the national mandates of both the MMIWG inquiry and the CBC, this public is, at the very least, a national one.

Scenes of Highway 16 and the surrounding land amplify the national scope of the issue, and Canada's accountability for it. The film opens with a shot on the side of the highway in daylight, with the film's title overlayed. The shot fades to images from the same perspective but at night, with only car headlights as the source of brief and sporadic light. A shot of Wilson speaking in her living room then fades to the highway at dusk from the same perspective as the first two shots, which then fades to an aerial shot of the highway and adjacent land in daylight. In each of these shots, the highway is largely benign, and in

FIGURE 24. An aerial shot of Highway 16 in *Highway of Tears* (2016). Image courtesy of *The Current*, CBC Radio.

the aerial shot in particular, actually quite beautiful. For a region that has become a symbol of gendered and racialized violence, depicting the land as beautiful is an important intervention. The film conveys that the geography is not in and of itself dangerous. Even the night shot, though somewhat isolating, is not as much frightening as it is revealing: the highway is very poorly lit. The viewer can see how the highway puts at risk women who hitchhike and travel along it. The lighting, or lack of it, is an apt metaphor for how colonial violence is reproduced through the provincial government neglect: the lack of basic safety measures along the highway makes Indigenous women even more vulnerable.

Jackson is clear, however, that the issue of MMIWG has to do with Highway 16, not the surrounding landscape. In an interview with *VICE*, Jackson points out that "the problem isn't that these Indigenous communities are in the middle of nowhere—they're actually in the middle of their territory" (Berman 2017). Jackson reminds us that this is not some desolate geography, but the traditional territory of local Indigenous communities. The highway is an imposition on these territories, a part of settler colonial infrastructure cutting through Indigenous lands. Because the highway is not properly lit, predators exploit its lack of basic safety measures, placing Indigenous women traveling the highway in grave danger. By delinking the territory from the highway, Jackson "rehabilitates" the territory's reputation. Violence has nothing to do with the land itself but is a result of the province's neglect of highway safety and of the well-being of the Indigenous communities whose lands it appropriated for the highway system. The responsibility is clear: this is not an "Indian problem," but a state problem for which it needs to be held accountable.

CONCLUSION: INDIGENOUS TRAUMA AND DOCUMENTARY REFUSAL

That Matilda Wilson and her daughter Ramona Wilson figure centrally in both *Finding Dawn* and *Highway of Tears,* filmed ten years apart, is a gutting testament to the lack of closure in her disappearance and murder, which remains unsolved. Wilson's case is a part of Project E-PANA, an RCMP task force created in 2005 charged with investigating the unsolved murders along the Highway of Tears, which at present includes thirteen homicide cases and five missing person's cases (Royal Canadian Mounted Police 2016). None of these cases have been solved.

The investigators for E-PANA do not believe that a single killer is responsible for all of E-PANA cases, which as Shari M. Huhndorf reminds us, indicates that these murders do not derive from the singular perspective of a dangerous and deranged individual, but instead betray a widespread attitude toward Indigenous women as prey and the land as a hunting ground and a place to dispose of their bodies (2021). This perspective appraises Indigenous women and girls and the land with the same gaze, and is grounded in settler colonial attitudes that gender domination, occupation, and extraction. As Jackson and others have pointed out, the colonial gaze has an appetite for the spectacle of Indigenous "degeneracy" as manifested in the mainstream media's coverage of the MMIWG crisis, seeking to consume the spectacle of Indigenous trauma. *Highway of Tears* confronts this gaze and its appetite in its critical conversation with discourses of immersive technology operative in the sphere of news journalism via the CBC. By doing so, the film resists many of the premises of VR—such as transparency, access, and spectacle—that are touted by industry players but of which Indigenous artists have long been wary, seeing the broader colonial ideology in which they are couched. Consequently, the film's techniques of alienation disrupt spectatorship in favor of a form of address that implicates the viewer in the topic at hand, carrying an ethical weight that spectatorship disavows.

This chapter began by placing *Highway of Tears* in relation to other documentaries from the 2000s that, when considered together, trace the evolution of public discourse about, the national response to, and media representation of the MMIWG crisis, and Indigenous critical perception and response to these dimensions of the crisis. In addition to their shared thematic concerns, these documentaries all have in common a refusal to provide narrative or textual closure, though they do offer hope. *Donna's Story* is bookended by scenes of a candlelight vigil for victims of the sex trade. At the end of the film, Donna relates in voice-over that the encounter that led her to recovery was when a women saw her on the street and gave her a hug, both seeing her and acknowledging her humanity. *Finding Dawn* also has a bookend structure, beginning and ending the film with footage from the annual women's memorial marches and vigils shown throughout the film, and a scene of volunteers in safety vests searching a field, clearly looking for traces of the missing. *Highway of Tears* ends with Matilda Wilson saying in voice-over, "I'm not going to give up," as an aerial shot of Highway 16 fades to black. These films refuse the emotional satisfaction of some kind of resolution, instead insisting the viewer sit with the discomfort of ambivalence, knowing that not only have these cases not been solved, but that these crimes continue to be committed. The films all end with the clear message that even as these cycles of violence continue across the country, the strength and commitment of survivors, the families and loved ones of the missing and murdered, and their communities is without doubt—though this is as much an indictment of insufficiency of national measures taken to address the crisis as it is a statement about hope.

Afterword

This book has argued that Indigenous media has flourished in no small part because of the resources that circulate around and through federal and provincial funding and public media institutions in Canada. Comparably, as I write these words, it was just announced that the groundbreaking sitcom, *Rutherford Falls* (2021–2022), was cancelled after two seasons on Peacock, a streaming service of NBCUniversal. Sierra Teller Ornelas (Navajo), one of the show's creators and showrunners (with Ed Helms and Michael Shur), oversaw a writer's room with four other Indigenous writers, a first in television history (Goldberg 2022). The show also showcased the extraordinary range of Indigenous on-screen talent, including Michael Greyeyes (Cree), Jana Schmieding (Lakota), Dallas Goldtooth (Mdewakanton Dakota and Diné), Kaniehtiio Horn (Mohawk), and Kawennáhere Devery Jacobs (Mohawk). Despite the show's excellent reviews and the extraordinary depth of its examination of Indigenous history and perspectives, lack of viewership led to its demise. While it is exceptional television, the series was also exceptional within the usual profit-driven mainstream film and television industry. It is a harsh reality that state film and television industries cannot compete with corporate media in terms of reach and capital, nor are they a panacea for Indigenous representation. However, their imbrication in national law and policy, funding structures, and the mandates of public broadcasting and film production have produced an infrastructure through which Indigenous media has thrived.

By bringing greater visibility to the institutions of media culture that form the backdrop for the Indigenous media wave that began in Canada after 1990, this book has maintained that attention to institutional contexts of Indigenous media enrich analysis of screen content, deepening understandings of their aesthetic strategies and discursive negotiations. The spectrum of media-producing institutions must be acknowledged for their significance to Indigenous media development in Canada, and as foci for social and political dynamics that Indigenous producers reflect on, debate, and critique through their work. The case studies at the center of each chapter are not intended to be representative of the scope of institutions that undergird Indigenous media history in Canada, nor are they meant to represent the scale and range of Indigenous media production, which far outstrips the capacity and intent of this book. Instead, the case studies provide an opportunity to look deeply at the representational and discursive complexities of these media objects, and model an approach to institutional analysis that illustrates their keen critical and theoretical insights. There are still many institutions to examine, including museums and galleries, media collectives, and independent production companies, let alone the presence of streaming giants like Netflix in the Canadian production landscape. Furthermore, as stated in the introduction, institutions undergo change over time in response to industrial shifts, changes in political economies, and transformations in the social and political fabric in which they are enmeshed. Much work is to be done tracking how these shifts alter institutions over time, and how Indigenous producers have responded to them in their work. To state an obvious implication to this last point, Indigenous media strategies are as historically contingent as they are culturally rooted, which is worth reemphasizing not only to avoid cultural essentialist readings of this work, but to look at how the disruptions and changes that Indigenous people make within dominant industrial and representational systems can change how these systems operate.

While avoiding reproducing developmental narratives surrounding Indigenous media, it is worth identifying that sovereignty has always been, and continues to be, an objective that guides the direction and development of Indigenous media in Canada. This commitment has led to the founding of the Indigenous Screen Office in 2017–2018. The ISO represents a pivotal moment in Indigenous media history, not only because it is an advocate for Indigenous media practitioners and a source of production funding, but also because it defines protocols and ethical practices for working with Indigenous communities and narratives to inform, guide, and compel Canadian media industries to both respect and incorporate principles of Indigenous sovereignty into development and production processes (Indigenous Screen Office 2022). The ISO thereby represents both the kind of transformative industry engagement that defines Indigenous media history in Canada, and the realization of Indigenous stewardship within Canadian media industries that has shaped and defined the field of Indigenous media for decades.

Acknowledgments

There are many people I would like to thank for their help, support, and encouragement while writing this book. I am deeply grateful to the filmmakers, producers, artists, organizers, and other media professionals who shared their time, experiences, expertise, and insights with me during the research and revision process. I am constantly inspired by your accomplishments and commitment to the Indigenous media community.

This book began as my dissertation in cinema and media studies in the School of Theater, Film, and Television at the University of California, Los Angeles. I would like to thank my dissertation committee: John T. Caldwell, Jasmine Nadua Trice, Michelle Raheja, and especially my supervisor, Chon Noriega. Thank you for your mentorship and guidance, your advice and motivation, and your generous feedback on my work. My thanks also to current and former faculty and staff of the Cinema and Media Studies Program elsewhere at UCLA, including Janet Bergstrom, Brian Clark, Barbara Dube, Rebecca Epstein, Allyson Field, Rebecca Frazier, Connie Heskett, L. S. Kim, Diana King, Steve Mamber, Kathleen McHugh, Christopher Mott, Mark Quigley, Darling Sianez, Vivian Sobchack, and Ken Wade. I am also exceptionally grateful to the American Indian Studies Center, the AISC Library, the UCLA Film and Television Archive, and VTape for so generously contributing time and resources in supporting my research and supporting me as a graduate student.

My thanks always to PhD cohort members and Los Angeles friends who made hard things easier and a lot more fun, especially Andrew deWaard, Bryan Wuest, Terra Stuart, Jen Porst, and Lindsay Giggey. Thank you for your feedback and conversations, dinners, road trips, concerts, screenings, and karaoke.

This research was generously supported by fellowships and awards from the UCLA Department of Film, Television, and Digital Media; a Dissertation Year Fellowship from the UCLA Division of Graduate Education; the UCLA Office of Instructional Development (now the

Center for the Advancement of Teaching); the Ford Foundation; and the New Relationship Trust. It was also made possible by the support of two awards from the Social Sciences and Humanities Research Council of Canada: a Joseph Armand Bombardier Canada Graduate Scholarship and a SSHRC Doctoral Fellowship. The publication of this book was also supported by SFU's University Publication Fund.

I am also deeply grateful to Cheam First Nation for their constant support of my postsecondary education—without it, my research and this book would not have been possible.

My dissertation started to become a book once I joined the School of Communication at Simon Fraser University, where I received generous support from the Faculty of Communication, Art and Technology to give me time and resources for my research, and for helping me in my transition from graduate student to faculty member. I have been extraordinarily fortunate to work with colleagues in the School and at SFU whose friendship and encouragement helped me over the past six years acclimate to my role as a faculty member and kept me motivated to finish the book: Kirsten McAllister, Adel Iskandar, Cait McKinney, Daniel Ahadi, Svitlana Matviyenko, Milena Droumeva, Sarah Ganter, Wendy Hui Kyong Chun, Peter Chow-White, Deanna Reder, Cliff Atleo Jr., and Dorothy Christian. My thanks especially to Cait, for your feedback and comments on drafts that helped me find my way forward again. My deepest thanks also to Julia Werkman, for your methodical and meticulous editorial assistance.

The feedback and encouragement of the reviewers of earlier versions of the manuscript have shaped almost every aspect of this book—thank you for your kind, supportive, and incredibly helpful feedback. To the staff at the University of Minnesota Press, particularly editorial director Jason Weidemann: thank you for guiding me through the publication process at every stage. My thanks also to Wendy Holdman, Ana Bichanich, Daniel Ochsner, and Siusan Moffat, and the production staff for their support.

Beyond UCLA and SFU, I have been very lucky to have the amazing friendship and support of Danika-Medak Saltzman, Joanna Hearne, Dara Kelly, and Aleena Chia, who have shared their time, support, and knowledge that enriched my thinking, and for seeing me through the ups and downs of life and work. Thank you too, Danika, for so generously reviewing drafts in record time to keep me on track.

I am also grateful to my family—Mom, Dad, Naomi, Aaron, Amber, Saul, Keith, and Jan—for wanting me to succeed in whatever I tried and no matter how far I travelled, and to my lifelong friends Ryan Petersen and Leona Hwang. Though Jan and Leona couldn't be here to see the finish, I am so grateful they stayed as long as they could.

Notes

INTRODUCTION

1. Formally the Constitution Act, 1982 Section 35. While Canada had been self-governing, prior to 1982, amendments to the Constitution could only be made by British Parliament. The patriation of the Canadian Constitution allowed the Constitution to be amended in Canada (Department of Justice 2021).

2. The history of northern television is explored in greater detail in chapters 1 and 3.

3. Databases and catalogues include VTape (Toronto), Video Out Distribution (Vancouver), Moving Images Distribution (Vancouver), the National Film Board of Canada (Montreal), as well as university library databases.

4. These numbers do not include narrative film, television, video, or digital media, which would significantly increase this count of media output during this period.

5. Whenever possible, tribal or national affiliations indicated in this book refer to how a person self-identifies, which may differ from official or scholarly terminology. As a result, affiliations referring to the same Peoples may at times vary.

6. Historically "outsiders" has referred to Indian agents, representatives of Indian and Northern Affairs who had the authority to scrutinize tribal affairs without their consent, and from whom Aboriginal people would have to seek permission to travel off-reserve and to sell livestock and other resources cultivated on reserve lands, among other restrictions. Over time, "outsiders" has come to encompass the state more broadly (Indian Chiefs of Alberta 1970; Milloy 2008).

7. These were not the only direct actions taken by Indigenous people in this period; Georges Erasmus lists seven additional notable actions, including Haida logging blockades in British Columbia, road blockades by the Lubicon in northern Alberta to protect their traditional territories, and the Gitxsan-Wet'suwet'en court battle over land jurisdiction that spanned the late 1980s (1989, 9–10).

1. PRAIRIE VOICES

1. An "envelope" is a term typically used by the Canadian federal government to refer to an allocation of funds, see CMF 2016c.

2. Now named Oskāyak High School.

3. Now the Assembly of First Nations, a national organization consisting of the elected chiefs of Indigenous groups across Canada.

4. These rumors would be confirmed with the 2002 arrest of Robert "Willie" Pickton, whose pig farm in Coquitlam, BC, was used as the site for the murders of dozens of women, of whom many were Indigenous. Pickton was convicted of six counts of second-degree murder.

2. THE ABORIGINAL FILM AND VIDEO ART ALLIANCE

1. Formerly named the Banff Centre, and the Banff Centre for Continuing Education.

2. As Monika Kin Gagnon explains, "Minquon Panchayat" translates to "Rainbow Council": "Minquon" means "rainbow" in Maliseet and other related Indigenous langauges, while "Panchayat" is a word in several South Asian languages to refer to a Hindu village "council of five" (1999, 63).

3. In 1995, ANNPAC was replaced by a new association called the Artist-Run Network (Robertson 2006, 40).

4. Such activities included funding for initiatives such as "Drumbeats to Drumbytes" in 1994, a gathering coordinated by Ahasiw Maskegon-Iskwew and Sara Diamond and held at the Banff Centre that focused on Indigenous engagement with and presence on the internet, an event that signaled the AFVAA's concern with telecommunications and new media contemporaneous with their attention to film, video, and television.

5. The Royal Commission on Aboriginal Peoples, which was established in 1991, identified that Indigenous people's access to film and media was a priority, stating that "access to mainstream media is critical to achieving wider understanding of Aboriginal identity and realities" because the mainstream media "often contain misinformation, sweeping generalizations, and galling stereotypes about Natives and Native affairs." The commission identified that Indigenously controlled media—which includes film, communications, and journalism—plays a critical role in "the pursuit of Aboriginal self-determination and self-government" (3.6.11–3.6.16); see Royal Commission on Aboriginal Peoples 1996.

6. Credited in publications and records as Cliff Redcrow.

3. PROGRAMMING INDIGENEITY

1. APTN was granted mandatory carriage by the Canadian Radio-Television and Telecommunications Commission (CRTC), the federal regulatory agency for broadcasting and telecommunications in Canada.

2. In-house production is largely restricted to its news and current affairs programs, including *APTN National News, APTN Investigates, Nation to Nation,* and *Face to Face.*

3. "An 'independent production company' is defined as a Canadian company that is carrying on business in Canada with a Canadian business address, that is owned and controlled by Canadians, whose business is in the production of film, videotape or live programs for distribution, and in which the licensee and any company related to the licensee owns or controls, directly or indirectly in the aggregate, less than 30% of the equity" (APTN 2018, 49).

4. Broadcasting Act, 1991, Statutes of Canada c. 11. https://laws.justice.gc.ca/eng/acts/B-9.01/.

5. Broadcasting Act, 1991, 5.

6. At the time *Indians + Aliens* was produced, APTN's subscriber fee was C$0.31. In 2018, its subscriber fee was raised to its current rate, C$0.36 (CRTC 2018).

7. As previously mentioned, *Rez Rides, Indians + Aliens,* and *Mohawk Girls* draw on U.S. television counterparts, while *Working It Out Together* features former Olympian Waneek Horn-Miller (Mohawk) and *Moose TV* star Adam Beach (Anishinaabe), who gained fame as one of the stars of *Smoke Signals* (dir. Chris Eyre, 1998).

8. Rezolution Pictures also has established Minority Media, a studio dedicated to virtual reality game development, which further enhances its "cutting edge" profile.

9. While explicitly citing reality television precedents for this series, the use of "documentary series" to describe *Rez Rides* is largely rhetorical in response to CRTC policy guidelines for Canadian programming, which historically has defined nonfiction television federally-recognized categories such as 2(b) "Long-form documentary" (CRTC 2010). The designation of "reality television" in this chapter is therefore analytical, and is intended to identify generic conventions employed by these shows.

10. In the realm of drama series, APTN has since 2014 aired *Mohawk Girls* (Rezolution Pictures), a comedy-drama series modeled after *Sex and the City.*

11. My argument follows Bill Nichols's definition of a documentary as an argument about the historical world (1992, 111), and so approaches analysis of *Indians + Aliens* in terms of the argument it makes about Cree and Western epistemological systems.

4. INDIGENOUS DOCUMENTARIES AND ACADEMIC RESEARCH INSTITUTIONS

1. Carolyn J. Marr provides an invaluable overview of the boarding school system in the United States (n.d.). Eric Hanson, Daniel Games, and Alexa Manuel provide a concise summary of the history and effects of the residential school system in Canada (2020).

2. The First Nations Studies Program has since become the Institute of Critical Indigenous Studies. I use "FNSP" throughout to be consistent with the time period in which Cry Rock was produced.

3. "Diné" is the traditional name of the Navajo people, which I use throughout this chapter except when directly quoting sources.

4. Perhaps most widely known is Sol Worth and James Adair's Navajo Film Project, an anthropological endeavor that sought to discover a Diné worldview by equipping Diné community members with film cameras to shoot their own short documentaries. The results were more telling of the anthropologists' assumptions about Indigenous culture, authenticity, and documentary verisimilitude, and the project has subsequently become a touchstone for debates about Indigenous self-representation and the mediating effects of the cinematic apparatus (Worth and Adair 1972.)

5. Terence Turner (1992) and Joanna Hearne (2012) have critiqued Faris for his claims that the film and photographic apparatuses are inherently colonial because they construct their subjects always as "the Other." They argue that this position denies the agency of Indigenous filmmakers and overlooks the specific social relations that Indigenous viewers may have with the images, relations that Taskigi/Diné artist Hulleah J. Tsinhnahjinnie (1998) theorizes in terms of "photographic sovereignty," which describes Indigenous reinterpretation of Indigenous images. Sam Pack's (2007) ethnographic work of Diné audiences' responses to film and television representations of Diné people can also be understood in terms of Indigenous reception studies.

6. While these emphases center Indigenous knowledge and experiences, Indigenous studies is, and has always been, an interdisciplinary field with a wide range of Indigenous and non-Indigenous specialists.

7. Faye Ginsburg (1995) provides a concise summary of this epistemological shift in light of political movements of colonized peoples beginning in the 1960s onward, and Indigenous people's increased participation in self-authored media.

8. Snapshots of the *Our World* website were located through the Wayback Machine, which do not retain its full content, an unfortunate reality of the ephemerality of internet-based records.

9. Called *Challenge for Change,* this activist documentary initiative has been widely discussed, and has received extensive examination in Waugh, Winton, and Baker 2010.

5. RESISTING COLONIAL RELATIONS IN VIRTUAL REALITY

1. As stated in the MMIWG's inquiry's 2017 interim report, "Our Women and Girls Are Sacred," the true number of missing and murdered Indigenous women and girls is not known (National Inquiry into MMIWG 2017).

2. So widespread that it directly informs my own life. Dawn Crey, to whom the title *Finding Dawn* refers, is my aunt, my father's (Ernie Crey) sister.

3. Now named the Banff Centre for Arts and Creativity.

4. Published the same year that CyberPowWow was conceptualized, in *Immersed in Technology: Art and Virtual Environments* (1996), a collection produced as a result of the Art and Virtual Environment Project that began at Banff Centre for the Arts in 1992, an initiative that continued support for Lawrence Paul Yuxweluptun's *Inherent Rights, Vision Rights* following the Virtual Seminar on the Bioapparatus that took place the previous year.

5. Tremonti left *The Current* in 2019 to produce and host podcasts at the CBC; Matt Galloway stepped in as host of *The Current* in early 2020 (Canadian Communications Foundation 2022).

6. The "fourth estate" refers to the press and news media.

Bibliography

AAMP Board of Directors. 2013. Letter to Ms. Valerie Creighton, president & CEO of the Canada Media Fund. Paul D. Fleck Library and Archives, Banff, Alberta.

Abbott, Lawrence. 1998. "Interviews with Loretta Todd, Shelley Niro and Patricia Deadman." *Canadian Journal of Native Studies* 18 (2): 335–73.

Aboriginal Film and Video Art Alliance Steering Committee. 1993. *National Aboriginal Training and Employment Project: Towards Self-Government in Art.* Banff, AB: Banff Centre for Continuing Education.

Aboriginal Territories in Cyberspace. n.d. "Home." http://abtec.org/#home.

Acland, Charles R. 2003. *Screen Traffic: Movies, Multiplexes, and Global Culture.* Durham, N.C.: Duke University Press.

Alia, Valerie. 1999. *Un/covering the North: News, Media and Aboriginal People.* Vancouver: UBC Press.

Amnesty International. 2004. *Stolen Sisters: A Human Rights Response to Discrimination and Violence against Indigenous Women in Canada.* https://www.amnesty.ca/sites/amnesty/files/amr200032004enstolensisters.pdf.

Appadurai, Arjun. 2002. "Deep Democracy: Urban Governmentality and the Horizon of Politics." *Public Culture* 14(1): 21-47.

APTN (Aboriginal Peoples Television Network). 2004. *Fall 2004 Program Schedule.* Winnipeg: Aboriginal Peoples Television Network.

APTN (Aboriginal Peoples Television Network). 2011a. *Annual Report 2011.* Winnipeg: Aboriginal Peoples Television Network.

APTN (Aboriginal Peoples Television Network). 2011b. "Milestones." https://web.archive.org/web/20160416113412/http://aptn.ca/corporate2/about/milestones.

APTN (Aboriginal Peoples Television Network). 2014. *Communiqué 2014: Sharing Our Stories.* Winnipeg: Aboriginal Peoples Television Network.

APTN (Aboriginal Peoples Television Network). 2016a. "APTN Mission." https://web.archive.org/web/20160229083028/http://aptn.ca/corporate2/.

APTN (Aboriginal Peoples Television Network). 2016b. "Board of Directors." https://web.archive.org/web/20160416113257/http://aptn.ca/corporate2/board-of-directors/.

APTN (Aboriginal Peoples Television Network). 2016c. "Development &

Licensing Eligibility Guidelines." https://web.archive.org/
web/20160416114017/http://aptn.ca/corporate2/producers/indepen-
dent-productions/development-licensing-eligibility-guidelines/.

APTN (Aboriginal Peoples Television Network). 2018. *APTN Communiqué 2018*. Winnipeg: Aboriginal Peoples Television Network.

APTN Conditional Support. 2005. "APTN Licence Renewal." https://web
.archive.org/web/20070211040647/http://www.turtleisland.org/
discussion/viewtopic.php?p=5992.

Asch, Michael. 1993. *Home and Native Land: Aboriginal Rights and the
Canadian Constitution*. Vancouver: UBC Press.

Avison, Shannon. 1996. "Aboriginal Newspapers: Their Contribution to the
Emergence of an Alternative Public Sphere in Canada." Master's thesis,
Concordia University, Montreal.

Banff Centre for the Arts. 1994. *Aboriginal Film and Video Art Alliance—
Native Net: Its National Significance*. Paul D. Fleck Library and Archives,
Banff, Alberta.

Barclay, Barry. 2003. "Celebrating Fourth Cinema." *Illusions* (35): 7–11.

Barnett, Chelsea. 2016. "In Defence of Sympathy: VR, Empathy, and
Real-World Storytelling." *Alternatives International Journal*, August 2016.
https://www.alterinter.org/?In-Defence-of-Sympathy-VR-Empathy
-and-Real-World-Storytelling.

Beaucage, Marjorie. 1991. "Aboriginal Film & Video Art Alliance: Background History." Marjorie Beaucage Personal Archives, Duck Lake,
Saskatchewan.

Beaucage, Marjorie. 2014a. Interview with Karrmen Crey. July 4, 2014.

Beaucage, Marjorie. 2014b. Interview Follow-Up Email to Karrmen Crey.
July 27, 2014.

Beaucage, Marjorie, and Delegates. 1993. *Storytellers and Media: A Gathering*. Banff, AB: Banff Centre for the Arts.

Berman, Sarah. 2017. "Why an Indigenous Filmmaker Directed a VR Documentary about the Highway of Tears." *Vice*, January 29, 2017. https://
www.vice.com/en/article/5353gd/why-an-indigenous-filmmaker
-directed-a-vr-documentary-about-the-highway-of-tears.

Bowman, Arlene. 1983. "Biah Woman." In *Annual Report: Fiscal Year
1982–1983*. University of California, Los Angeles.

Bowman, Arlene. 1985. *Annual Report 1984/1985*. Los Angeles: UCLA
American Indian Studies Center.

Bowman, Arlene, dir. 1986. *Navajo Talking Picture*. New York: Women
Make Movies.

Bowman, Arlene. 2015a. Email with Karrmen Crey. October 31, 2015.

Bowman, Arlene. 2015b. Interview with Karrmen Crey. July 7, 2015.

Bowman, Arlene. 2015c. Interview with Karrmen Crey. September 9, 2015.

Brady, Miranda J., and John M. H. Kelly. 2017. *We Interrupt This Program: Indigenous Media Tactics in Canadian Culture.* Vancouver: UBC Press.

Bredin, Marian. 1993. "Ethnography and Communication: Approaches to Aboriginal Media." *Canadian Journal of Communication* 18 (3).

Bredin, Marian. 1995. "Aboriginal Media in Canada: Cultural Politics and Communication Practices." PhD diss., McGill University.

Bredin, Marian. 2010. "APTN and Its Audience." In *Indigenous Screen Cultures in Canada,* edited by Sigurjón Baldur Hafsteinsson and Marian Bredin, 69–85. Winnipeg: University of Manitoba Press.

Bredin, Marian. 2012. "Producing Aboriginal Television in Canada: Obstacles and Opportunities." In *Canadian Television: Text and Context,* edited by Marian Bredin, Scott Henderson, and Sarah A. Matheson, 73–93. Waterloo, ON: Wilfrid Laurier University Press.

Broadcaster Magazine. 2014. "APTN and OMNI TV Greenlight Season 2 of Original Canadian Series." February 18, 2014.

Byrd, Jodi A. 2011. *The Transit of Empire: Indigenous Critiques of Colonialism.* Minneapolis: University of Minnesota Press.

Cairns, Alan. 2000. *Citizens Plus: Aboriginal Peoples and the Canadian State.* Vancouver: UBC Press.

Caldwell, John Thornton. 2008. *Production Culture: Industrial Reflexivity and Critical Practice in Film and Television.* Durham, N.C.: Duke University Press.

Campbell, Angie. 2016. Interview with Karrmen Crey. May 3, 2016.

Canadian Communications Foundation. 2022. *The Current.* https://broadcasting-history.com/programming/radio/current.

Cardinal, Gil. n.d. "Playlist: The Aboriginal Voice: The National Film Board and Aboriginal Filmmaking through the Years." National Film Board of Canada. https://www.nfb.ca/playlists/gil-cardinal/aboriginal-voice-national-film-board-/.

Cardinal, Harold. 1974. *The Unjust Society: The Tragedy of Canada's Indians.* New York: Free Press.

Cardinal-Schubert, Joane. 1994. "The Warning Bark (of a Camp Dog)." *Talking Stick* (Spring): 12–14.

CBC Radio. 2016. "Highway of Tears: The Making of a Virtual Reality Documentary from CBC Radio's *The Current.*" *The Doc Project,* YouTube video, 5:16. October 17, 2016. https://youtu.be/69wCtYlfDWA.

CBC Radio. 2017. "*The Current* Transcript for February 1, 2017." https://www.cbc.ca/radio/thecurrent/the-current-for-february-1-2017-vancouver-public-forum-1.3959929/february-1-2017-full-episode-transcript-1.3962242.

Century, Michael. 1993a. Memo to Marjorie Beaucage. March 12, 1993. Paul D. Fleck Library and Archives, Banff, Alberta.

Century, Michael. 1993b. *A Policy Framework for Intercultural Programming.* Paul D. Fleck Library and Archives, Banff, Alberta.

CMF (Canada Media Fund). 2013a. "Performance Envelope." https://web .archive.org/web/20130123013313/http://www.cmf-fmc.ca/funding -programs/convergent-stream/performance-envelope/?setLocale=1

CMF (Canada Media Fund). 2013b. "Re. CMF Policy Guidelines Review." https://web.archive.org/web/20140825004006/https://cmf-fmc.ca/ documents/files/about/ind-outreach/2013-14/responses/Aboriginal -Peoples-Television-Network.pdf

CMF (Canada Media Fund). 2016a. "Envelope Administration–FAQ." https://web.archive.org/web/20160813115653/http://www.cmf-fmc .ca/faq/category/3/envelope-administration/.

CMF (Canada Media Fund). 2016c. *Performance Envelope Manual 2016–2017.* Toronto: Canada Media Fund.

Coates, Ken. 2015. *#IdleNoMore and the Remaking of Canada.* Regina, SK: University of Regina Press.

Communications Network Corporation Act, Statutes of Saskatchewan 1990–91, c. C-16.01. https://www.canlii.org/en/sk/laws/stat/ss-1990 -91-c-c-16.01/latest/ss-1990-91-c-c-16.01.html.

Cook, Sarah, and Sara Diamond. 2012. *Euphoria & Dystopia: The Banff New Media Institute Dialogues.* Banff, AB: Riverside Architectural Press/ABC Art Books Canada.

Cook-Lynn, Elizabeth. 1997. "Who Stole Native American Studies?" *Wicazo Sa Review* 12 (1): 9–28.

Cosentino, Gina, and Paul L. A. H. Chartrand. 2007. "Dream Catching Mulroney Style: Aboriginal Policy and Politics in the Era of Brian Mulroney." In *Transforming the Nation: Canada and Brian Mulroney,* edited by Raymond B. Blake, 294–338. Montreal: McGill-Queen's Press.

Coulthard, Glen Sean. 2014. *Red Skin, White Masks: Rejecting the Colonial Politics of Recognition.* Minneapolis: University of Minnesota Press.

Crey, Karrmen. 2021. "The Aboriginal Film and Video Art Alliance: Indigenous Self-Government in Moving Image Media." *JCMS: Journal of Cinema and Media Studies* 60 (2): 175–80.

Crey, Karrmen. Forthcoming. "'It's Not the What, It's the How': An Interview with Lisa Jackson." In *"The Women, They Hold the Ground": Indigenous Women's Digital Media,* edited by Joanna Hearne and Karrmen Crey. Minneapolis: University of Minnesota Press.

Cronin, J. Keri, and Kirsty Robertson, eds. 2011. *Imagining Resistance: Visual Culture and Activism in Canada.* Waterloo, ON: Wilfrid Laurier University Press.

CRTC (Canadian Radio-Television and Telecommunications Commission). 1999. "Decision CRTC 99–42." https://crtc.gc.ca/eng/archive/1999/db99-42.htm.

CRTC (Canadian Radio-Television and Telecommunications Commission). 2010. "Broadcasting Regulatory Policy CRTC 2010–808." http://www.crtc.gc.ca/eng/archive/2010/2010-808.htm.

CRTC (Canadian Radio-Television and Telecommunications Commission). 2018. "Decision CRTC 2018-340." https://crtc.gc.ca/eng/archive/2018/2018-340.htm.

Cruikshank, Julie. 1994. "Oral Tradition and Oral History: Reviewing Some Issues." *Canadian Historical Review* 75 (3): 403–21.

Csordas, Thomas J. 1999. "Ritual Healing and the Politics of Identity in Contemporary Navajo Society." *American Ethnologist* 26 (1): 3–23.

Cuthand, Doug. 1982. "Indian Government and the Future within Confederation." *Saskatchewan Indian* (April 1982): 46–50.

Cuthand, Doug, dir. 1995. *Stay in School.* Regina, SK: Tapwe Ci Productions/Saskatchewan Communications Network.

Cuthand, Doug. 1997. "Saskatchewan Loses Esteemed Health Advocate." *Saskatchewan Indian* (Winter 1997): 21.

Cuthand, Doug. 1999. "Remembering Dief the Man From Prince Albert." *Toronto Star,* August 25, 1999.

Cuthand, Doug, dir. 2001. *Donna's Story.* Montreal: National Film Board of Canada. https://www.nfb.ca/film/donnas_story/.

Cuthand, Doug. 2005. *Tapwe: Selected Columns of Doug Cuthand.* Penticton, BC: Theytus Books.

Cuthand, Doug. 2015. Interview with Karrmen Crey. January 27, 2015.

d'Auray, Michelle. 1991. *Aboriginal Film and Video Makers' Symposium.* Montreal: National Film Board of Canada.

David, Jennifer. 2012. *Original People, Original Television: The Launching of the Aboriginal Peoples Television Network.* Ottawa: Debwe Communications.

Deger, Jennifer. 2006. *Shimmering Screens: Making Media in an Aboriginal Community.* Minneapolis: University of Minnesota Press.

de la Peña, Nonny, Peggy Weil, Joan Llobera, Elias Giannopoulos, Ausiàs Pomés, Bernhard Spanlang, Doron Friedman, Maria V. Sanchez-Vives, and Mel Slater. 2010. "Immersive Journalism: Immersive Virtual Reality for the First-Person Experience of News." *Presence* 19 (4): 291–301.

Deloria, Philip J. 2004. *Indians in Unexpected Places.* Lawrence: University Press of Kansas.

Cuthand, Doug, 1988. "Indian Control of Indian Education: A Brief History." *Saskatchewan Indian* (September 1988): 18–19. Deloria, Philip J. 1998. *Playing Indian.* New Haven, CT: Yale University Press.

Demay, Joel. 1991. "Clarifying Ambiguities: The Rapidly Changing Life of the Canadian Aboriginal Print Media." *Canadian Journal of Native Studies* 11 (1): 95–112.

Department of Justice. 2021. "The Canadian Constitution." Last modified September 1, 2021. http://www.justice.gc.ca/eng/csj-sjc/just/05.html.

de Rosa, Maria. 2002. "Studio One: Of Storytellers and Stories." In *North of Everything: English-Canadian Cinema Since 1980*, 328–41. Edmonton: University of Alberta Press.

Dessart, George. n.d. "Public Service Announcements." Museum of Broadcast Communications. https://web.archive.org/web/20160612164941/https://www.museum.tv/eotv/publicservic.htm.

Diamond, Sara. 1992. "Invitation to First Nations Filmmakers' Alliance Steering Committee." Paul D. Fleck Library and Archives, Banff, Alberta.

Dillon, Grace L. 2012. *Walking the Clouds: An Anthology of Indigenous Science Fiction.* Tucson: University of Arizona Press.

Doty, Ainsley. 2017. "Exploring the Highway of Tears." *Medium,* December 8, 2016. https://medium.com/secret-location/exploring-the-highway-of-tears-c6e1153f60bf.

Dowell, Kristin L. 2013. *Sovereign Screens: Aboriginal Media on the Canadian West Coast.* Lincoln: University of Nebraska Press.

Druick, Zoë. 2007. *Projecting Canada: Government Policy and Documentary Film at the National Film Board.* Montreal: McGill-Queen's Press.

Dunlevy, T'Cha. 2011. "Reel Injun Continues Making Waves; Peabody Award Is Just the Latest Accolade for Montreal-Made Documentary on Native Life." *Montreal Gazette,* April 11, 2011.

Dussault, Rene, and Georges Erasmus. 1996. *Report of the Royal Commission on Aboriginal Peoples, Volume 3—Gathering Strength.* Ottawa: Canada Communication Group.

Edwards, Leigh H. 2013. *The Triumph of Reality TV: The Revolution in American Television.* Santa Barbara, Calif.: Praeger.

Eisner, Ken. 2003. "Shadow and Light: First Nations Women Filmmakers." In *Women Filmmakers: Refocusing,* edited by Jacqueline Levitin, Judith Plessis and Valerie Raoul, 394–403. Vancouver: UBC Press.

Ellis, Elizabeth. 2019. "Centering Sovereignty: How Standing Rock Changed the Conversation." In *Standing with Standing Rock: Voices from the #NoDAPL Movement,* edited by Jaskiran Dhillon and Nick Estes, 172–97. Minneapolis: University of Minnesota Press.

Erasmus, Georges. 1989. "Introduction: Twenty Years of Disappointed Hopes." In *Drumbeat: Anger and Renewal in Indian Country,* edited by Boyce Richardson, 1–42. Toronto: Summerhill Press.

Evans, Michael Robert. 2008. *Isuma: Inuit Video Art.* Montreal: McGill-Queen's Press.

Faris, James C. 1996. *Navajo and Photography: A Critical History of the*

Representation of an American People. Albuquerque: University of New Mexico Press.

Film Studies Association of Canada. n.d. "Links to Film Studies and Related Programs at Colleges and Universities in Canada." Accessed November 17, 2022. http://www.filmstudies.ca/resources/film-studies-in-canada.

First Nations Film and Video Art Alliance. 1993. *Pathways to Success: National Aboriginal Project.* Paul D. Fleck Library and Archives, Banff, Alberta.

First Nations Filmmakers Alliance. 1992. "Discussion Paper for 'Making It:' Issues and Recent Developments in the First Nations Film and Video Community." Presented at 'Making It:' A Symposium for First Nations Filmmakers and Videographers, Regina, Saskatchewan, October 8, 1992.

FNSP (First Nations Studies Program). n.d. "First Nations Studies at UBC." UBC First Nations Studies Program, accessed July 29, 2016. https://fnis .arts.ubc.ca/

Foster, Adrian. 2012. "Artist-Run Organizations and the Restoration of Indigenous Cultural Sovereignty in Toronto, 1970–2010." In *Well-Being in the Urban Aboriginal Community: Fostering Biimaadiziwin, a National Research Conference on Urban Aboriginal Peoples,* edited by David Newhouse, 22–41. Toronto: Thompson Educational Publishing.

Foster, Alethea J. 2008. "Aboriginal Presence in the Mainstream Media: Issues and Journalists." Master's thesis, University of Regina, Saskatchewan.

Foucault, Michel. 2007. *Security, Territory, Population: Lectures at the Collège de France 1977–1978.* Edited by Arnold I. Davidson. Translated by Graham Burchell. New York City: Palgrave MacMillan.

Fournier, Suzanne, and Ernie Crey. 1997. *Stolen from Our Embrace: The Abduction of First Nations Children and the Restoration of Aboriginal Communities.* Vancouver: Douglas & McIntyre.

Gaertner, David. 2015. "Indigenous in Cyberspace: CyberPowWow, God's Lake Narrows, and the Contours of Online Indigenous Territory." *American Indian Culture and Research Journal* 39 (4): 55–78.

Gagnon, Monika Kin. 1999. *Other Conundrums: Race, Culture, and Canadian Art.* Vancouver: Arsenal Pulp Press.

Gauthier, Jennifer L. 2010. "Dismantling the Master's House: The Feminist Fourth Cinema Documentaries of Alanis Obomsawin and Loretta Todd." *Post Script—Essays in Film and the Humanities* 29 (3): 27–43.

Ginsburg, Faye. 1991. "Indigenous Media: Faustian Contract or Global Village?" *Cultural Anthropology* 6 (1): 92–112.

Ginsburg, Faye. 1993. "Aboriginal Media and the Australian Imaginary." *Public Culture* 5 (3): 557–78.

Ginsburg, Faye. 1994a. "Culture/Media: A (Mild) Polemic." *Anthropology Today* 10 (2): 5–15.

Ginsburg, Faye. 1994b. "Embedded Aesthetics: Creating a Discursive Space for Indigenous Media." *Cultural Anthropology* 9 (3): 365–82.

Ginsburg, Faye. 1995. "The Parallax Effect: The Impact of Aboriginal Media on Ethnographic Film." *Visual Anthropology Review* 11 (2): 64–76.

Ginsburg, Faye. 2003. "Indigenous Media: Negotiating Control over Images." In *Image Ethics in the Digital Age,* edited by Larry Gross, Jonathan Katz, and Jay Ruby, 295–312. Minneapolis: University of Minnesota Press.

Ginsburg, Faye. 2007. "Shooting Back: From Ethnographic Film to Indigenous Production/Ethnography of Media." In *A Companion to Film Theory,* edited by Toby Miller and Robert Stam, 295–322. Malden, Mass.: Blackwell.

Ginsburg, Faye. 2012. "Australia's Indigenous New Wave: Future Imaginaries in Recent Aboriginal Feature Films." Adriaan Gerbrands Lecture, Foundation for Ethnology, Leiden, Holland.

Gittings, Christopher E. 2002. *Canadian National Cinema. Ideology, Difference and Representation.* London: Routledge.

GLAM Collective. n.d. "About Us." Accessed November 17, 2022. https://glamcollective.ca/About-Us.

Goldberg, Lesley. 2022. "'Rutherford Falls' Canceled at Peacock." *Hollywood Reporter,* September 2, 2022. https://www.hollywoodreporter.com/tv/tv-news/rutherford-falls-canceled-peacock-1235211299/.

Goldhar, Kathleen, and Josh Bloch. 2016. "Explore B.C.'s Notorious Highway of Tears in New Virtual Reality Documentary." *CBC,* October 17, 2016. https://www.cbc.ca/news/canada/british-columbia/current-virtual-reality-highway-of-tears-1.3806459.

Government of Canada. 2002. "Behind the Diary: Politics, Themes, and Events from King's Life—Mackenzie King and Spiritualism." Accessed July 31, 2016. https://web.archive.org/web/20160731160100/http://www.collectionscanada.gc.ca/king/023011-1070.08-e.html.

Government of Canada. 2022. "Canadian Film or Video Production Tax Credit." Last modified August 8, 2022. https://www.canada.ca/en/canadian-heritage/services/funding/cavco-tax-credits/canadian-film-video-production.html.

Guelph Mercury. 2006. "Getting Mileage Out of Moose Jokes; Montreal-Based Sitcom Gives Canadian Natives a Chance to Show Different Side of Talent." July 13, 2006, F12.

Hafsteinsson, Sigurjón Baldur. 2008. "Unmasking Deep Democracy: Aboriginal Peoples Television Network (APTN) and Cultural Production." Ph.D. diss., Temple University, ProQuest (AAT 3300354).

Hafsteinsson, Sigurjón Baldur. 2010. "Aboriginal Journalism Practices as Deep Democracy: APTN National News." In *Indigenous Screen Cultures in Canada,* edited by Sigurjón Baldur Hafsteinsson and Marian Bredin, 53–68. Winnipeg: University of Manitoba Press.

Hampton, Chris. 2017. "Forget 2017—These Indigenous VR Artists Are Imagining Canada's Future 150 Years from Now." *CBC,* Last modified June 19, 2017. https://www.cbc.ca/arts/forget-2017-these-indigenous -vr-artists-are-imagining-canada-s-future-150-years-from-now -1.4167856.

Hanson, Eric, Daniel P. Games, and Alexa Manuel. 2020. "The Residential School System." Indigenous Foundations. Last modified September 2020. https://indigenousfoundations.web.arts.ubc.ca/residential-school -system-2020/.

Hanuse, Banchi, dir. 2010. *Cry Rock.* Bella Coola, BC: Smayaykila Films. DVD.

Hanuse, Banchi. 2015. Email Interview with Karrmen Crey. April 14, 2015.

Hassan, Robert. 2020. "Digitality, Virtual Reality and the 'Empathy Machine.'" *Digital Journalism* 8 (2): 195–212.

Hawkins, Richard C. 1970. *Report of UCLA Ethnographic Film Project Funded in 1966 by CICS.* Los Angeles Archives, University of California.

Hawthorn, Henry B., and Marc-Adelard Tremblay. 1967. *A Survey of the Contemporary Indians in Canada. A Report on Economic, Political, Educational Needs and Policies: Vol. 2.* Indian Affairs Branch. Ottawa: Department of Indian Affairs and Northern Development.

Hearne, Joanna. 2012. *Native Recognition: Indigenous Cinema and the Western.* Albany: State University of New York Press.

Hearne, Joanna. 2017. "Native to the Device: Thoughts on Digital Indigenous Studies." *Studies in American Indian Literatures* 29 (1): 3–26.

Hearne, Joanna. Forthcoming. "'The Child in Me Has Survived': An Interview with Buffy Sainte-Marie." In *"The Women, They Hold the Ground": Indigenous Women's Digital Media,* edited by Joanna Hearne and Karrmen Crey. Minneapolis: University of Minnesota Press.

Hjort, Mette. 2013. "Introduction: More than Film School—Why the Full Spectrum of Practice-Based Film Education Warrants Attention." In *The Education of the Filmmaker in Africa, the Middle East, and the Americas,* edited by Mette Hjort, 1–22. New York: Palgrave Macmillan.

Hogarth, David. 2002. *Documentary Television in Canada: From National Public Service to Global Marketplace.* Montreal: McGill-Queen's University Press.

Huhndorf, Shari M. 2021. "Scenes from the Fringe: Gendered Violence and the Geographies of Indigenous Feminism." *Signs: Journal of Women in Culture and Society* 46 (3): 561–87.

Humphreys, Fran. 1999. "Canada Celebrates 20 Years of TV in Banff." *Video Age International* 19 (5): 28.

Igloliorte, Heather, Julie Nagam, and Carla Taunton. 2016. "Transmissions: The Future Possibilities of Indigenous Digital and New Media Art." *Public (Toronto)* 27 (54): 5–13.

Ignace, Marianne. 2011. "'Why Is My People Sleeping?': First Nations Hip Hop Between the Rez and the City." In *Aboriginal Peoples in Canadian Cities: Transformations and Continuities,* edited by Craig Proulx and Heather Howard-Bobiwash, 203–26. Waterloo, ON: Wilfrid Laurier University Press.

imagineNATIVE. 2021. "2021 Industry Days." Last modified September 3, 2021. https://festival.imaginenative.org/2021-industry-days/.

imagineNATIVE Film + Media Arts Festival. 2017. "*2167:* Indigenous Storytelling in VR." YouTube video, 1:25:20. October 25, 2017. https://youtu.be/g7dTlB2ZjbY.

Indian Chiefs of Alberta. 1970. "Foundational Document: Citizens Plus." Published in *Aboriginal Policy Studies* 1, no. 2 (2011): 188–281.

Indigenous Foundations. 2009. "The White Paper, 1969." Accessed November 17, 2022. https://indigenousfoundations.arts.ubc.ca/the_white_paper_1969/.

Indigenous Screen Office. 2022. "About ISO." Accessed September 6, 2022. https://iso-bea.ca/who-we-are/about-iso/.

Inuit Broadcasting Corporation. n.d. "Inuit Film and Video Archives." Accessed April 3, 2017. https://web.archive.org/web/20170403063711/http://www.building4dreams.ca/about-ifva.

Jackson, Lisa. n.d. "Lisa Jackson: Filmmaker." Accessed August 19, 2022. https:// lisajackson.ca.

James, David E. 2005. *The Most Typical Avant-Garde: History and Geography of Minor Cinemas in Los Angeles.* Berkeley: University of California Press.

Jiwani, Yasmin, and Mary Lynn Young. 2006. "Missing and Murdered Women: Reproducing Marginality in News Discourse." *Canadian Journal of Communication* 31 (4): 895.

Kesler, Linc. 2003a. "FNSP 310–Theory Seminar Syllabus." University of British Columbia.

Kesler, Linc. 2003b. "FNSP 320–Research Methods Syllabus." University of British Columbia.

King, Sarah. 2017. "In/consequential Relationships: Refusing Colonial Ethics of Engagement in Yuxweluptun's *Inherent Rights, Vision Rights.*" *BC Studies* (193): 187.

Knopf, Kerstin. 2010. "Aboriginal Media on the Move: An Outside Perspective on APTN." In *Indigenous Screen Cultures in Canada,* edited by

Sigurjón Baldur Hafsteinsson and Marian Bredin, 87–104. Winnipeg: University of Manitoba Press.

Knowles, Ric. 2009. "Inter-Cultural-Performance." *Canadian Theatre Review* 139: 3–5.

Koven, Mikel J. 2007. "Most Haunted and the Convergence of Traditional Belief and Popular Television." *Folklore* 118 (2): 183–202.

KPMG LLP. 2014. *Financial Statements of Aboriginal Peoples Television Network Incorporated, Year Ended August 31, 2014*. Winnipeg, MB: Aboriginal Peoples Television Network.

Kymlicka, Will. 1995. *Multicultural Citizenship: A Liberal Theory of Minority Rights*. Oxford: Oxford University Press.

Kymlicka, Will. 2010. *The Current State of Multiculturalism in Canada and Research Themes on Canadian Multiculturalism 2008–2010*. Ottawa: Citizenship and Immigration Canada.

Lempert, William. 2014. "Decolonizing Encounters of the Third Kind: Alternative Futuring in Native Science Fiction Film." *Visual Anthropology Review* 30 (2): 164–76.

Leuthold, Steven. 1998. *Indigenous Aesthetics: Native Art, Media, and Identity*. Austin: University of Texas Press.

Levin, Dan. 2016. "Dozens of Women Vanish on Canada's Highway of Tears, and Most Cases Are Unsolved." *New York Times,* May 24, 2016.

Lewis, Randolph. 2006. *Alanis Obomsawin: The Vision of a Native Filmmaker*. Lincoln: University of Nebraska Press.

Lewis, Randolph. 2012. *Navajo Talking Picture: Cinema on Native Ground*. Lincoln: University of Nebraska Press.

L'Hirondelle, Cheryl. 2016. "Re:lating Necessity and Invention: How Sara Diamond and the Banff Centre Aided Indigenous New Media Production (1992–2005)." *Public* 54: 25–35.

Limbrick, Peter. 2010. *Making Settler Cinemas: Film and Colonial Encounters in the United States, Australia, and New Zealand*. New York City: Palgrave MacMillan.

Litt, Paul. 2016. *Trudeaumania*. Vancouver: UBC Press.

Mackey, Eva. 1999. *The House of Difference: Cultural Politics and National Identity in Canada*. London: Routledge.

MacLeod, Douglas. 1996. "Preface." In *Immersed in Technology: Art and Virtual Environments*, edited by Mary Anne Moser and Douglas MacLeod, ix–xiii. Cambridge, Mass.: MIT Press.

Mamber, Stephen. 1972. "Cinema Vérité in America: Part II—Direct Cinema and the Crisis Structure." *Screen* 13 (3): 114–36.

Mander, Jerry. 1992. *In the Absence of the Sacred: The Failure of Technology and the Survival of the Indian Nations*. San Francisco: Sierra Club Books.

Marr, Carolyn J. n.d. "Assimilation Through Education: Indian Boarding

Schools in the Pacific Northwest." American Indians of the Pacific Northwest Collection. Accessed November 17, 2022. https://content .lib.washington.edu/aipnw/marr.html#top.

Martinez, Cristóbal. n.d. "Bio." Accessed November 18, 2022. https:// cristobalmartinez.net/.

Masayesva, Victor. 2005. "Indigenous Experimentation." In *Transference, Tradition, Technology: Native New Media Exploring Visual & Digital Culture,* edited by Melanie A. Townsend, Dana Claxton, and Steve Loft, 164–77. Banff, AB: Walter Phillips Gallery Editions.

Maskegon-Iskwew, Ahasiw. 1994. "The Moccasin Telegraph Goes High-Tech." *Talking Stick,* Spring 1994.

Mather, Elsie. 1995. "With a Vision Beyond Our Immediate Needs: Oral Traditions in an Age of Literacy." In *When Our Words Return: Writing, Reading, and Remembering Oral Traditions from Alaska and the Yukon,* edited by Phyllis Morrow and William Schneider, 13–26. Logan: Utah State University Press.

McCall, Sophie. 2011. *First Person Plural: Aboriginal Storytelling and the Ethics of Collaborative Authorship.* Vancouver: UBC Press.

McMaster, Gerald, and Lee-Ann Martin, eds. 1992. *INDIGENA: Contemporary Native Perspectives in Canadian Art.* Vancouver: Craftsman House.

McMillan, Alan, and Eldon Yellowhorn. 2009. *First Peoples in Canada.* Vancouver: Douglas & McIntyre.

McSorley, Tom. 2006. "The Centre Cannot Hold: The Cinema of Atlantic Canada." In *Self Portraits: The Cinemas of Canada Since Telefilm,* edited by Tom McSorley and André Loiselle, 271–80. Ottawa: Canadian Film Institute/Institut canadien du film.

Meadows, Michael. 2005. "Journalism and Indigenous Public Spheres." *Pacific Journalism Review* 11 (1): 36–41.

Medak-Saltzman, Danika. 2017. "Coming to You from the Indigenous Future: Native Women, Speculative Film Shorts, and the Art of the Possible." *Studies in American Indian Literatures* 29 (1): 139–71.

Michaels, Eric. 1986. *The Aboriginal Invention of Television in Central Australia, 1982–1986: Report of the Fellowship to Assess the Impact of Television in Remote Aboriginal Communities.* Canberra: Australian Institute of Aboriginal Studies.

Michaels, Eric. 1994. *Bad Aboriginal Art: Tradition, Media, and Technological Horizons.* Minneapolis: University of Minnesota Press.

Milloy, John. 2008. *Indian Act Colonialism: A Century of Dishonour, 1869–1969.* May 2008. National Centre for First Nations Governance. https://fngovernance.org/wp-content/uploads/2020/09/milloy.pdf

Myers, Lisa. 2014. *Of the Moment in the Moment.* Toronto: VTape. https://

www.vtape.org/wp-content/uploads/2011/10/Of-the-MomentIn-the
-Moment.pdf.

Myers, Lisa. 2018. "Marjorie Beaucage: Retrospective." imagineNATIVE.
Accessed September 24, 2018. https://web.archive.org/web/
20180924094844/https://imaginenative.org/2018-marjorie-beaucage
-retrospective.

Nakamura, Lisa. 2020. "Feeling Good about Feeling Bad: Virtuous Virtual
Reality and the Automation of Racial Empathy." *Journal of Visual Culture* 19 (1): 47–64.

Nation to Nation. n.d. "About." accessed November 17, 2022. https://www
.cyberpowwow.net/about.html.

NFB (National Film Board of Canada). n.d. "Our World." Accessed September 28, 2010. http://web.archive.org/web/20100928121752/http://
films.nfb.ca/ourworld/aboutourworld.php.

National Inquiry into MMIWG (Missing and Murdered Indigenous
Women and Girls). 2017. *Interim Report: Our Women and Girls are Sacred.* Ottawa: Privy Council Office.

National Inquiry into MMIWG (Missing and Murdered Indigenous
Women and Girls). 2019. *Reclaiming Power and Place: Final Report of the National Inquiry into Missing and Murdered Indigenous Women and Girls.* Vancouver: Privy Council Office.

NationTalk. 2012. "imagineNATIVE's Stolen Sisters Digital Initiative." Last
modified August 10, 2012. https://nationtalk.ca/story/imaginenatives
-stolen-sisters-digital-initiative

Native Women's Association of Canada. 2010. *What Their Stories Tell Us: Research Findings from the Sisters in Spirit initiative.* Akwesasne.

Nichols, Bill. 1992. *Representing Reality: Issues and Concepts in Documentary.* Bloomington: Indiana University Press.

Nichols, Bill. 2010. *Introduction to Documentary.* Bloomington: Indiana
University Press.

Noriega, Chon A. 2000. *Shot in America: Television, the State, and the Rise of Chicano Cinema.* Minneapolis: University of Minnesota Press.

Nothof, Anne. 2012. "Representations of the Self and the Other in Canadian Intercultural Theatre." In *Selves and Subjectivities: Reflections on Canadian Arts and Culture,* edited by Veronica Thompson and Manijeh Mannani, 1–12. Athabasca, AB: Athabasca University Press.

Okada, Jun. 2015. *Making Asian American Film and Video: History, Institutions, Movements.* New Brunswick, NJ: Rutgers University Press.

Orthner, Carmen Pauls. 2009. "Aboriginal Column Pulled from Regina
Newspaper." *Saskatchewan Sage,* 1. April 1, 2009. ProQuest.

Ostler, Jeffrey, and Nick Estes. 2019. "The Supreme Law of the Land:

Standing Rock and the Dakota Access Pipeline." In *Standing with Standing Rock: Voices from the #NoDAPL Movement*, edited by Jaskiran Dhillon and Nick Estes, 96–100. Minneapolis: University of Minnesota Press.

Pack, Sam. 2000. "Indigenous Media Then and Now: Situating the Navajo Film Project." *Quarterly Review of Film and Video* 17 (3): 273–86.

Pack, Sam. 2007. "Watching Navajos Watch Themselves." *Wicazo Sa Review* 22 (2): 111–27.

Palmater, Pamela. 2016. "Shining Light on the Dark Places: Addressing Police Racism and Sexualized Violence against Indigenous Women and Girls in the National Inquiry." *Canadian Journal of Women and the Law* 28 (2): 253–84.

Peach, Ian. 2011. "The Power of a Single Feather: Meech Lake, Indigenous Resistance and the Evolution of Indigenous Politics in Canada." *Review of Constitutional Studies* 16 (1): 1–29.

Petrie, Duncan. 2010. "Theory, Practice, and the Significance of Film Schools." *Scandia* 76 (2): 31–46.

Petrie, Duncan J., and Rod Stoneman. 2014. *Educating Film-Makers: Past, Present and Future*. Bristol, UK: Intellect Books.

Phillips, Carol. 1992. Memo to Michael Century. Paul D. Fleck Library and Archives, Banff, Alberta.

Phillips, Carol. 1993. Memo to Graeme McDonald. Paul D. Fleck Library and Archives, Banff, Alberta.

Pick, Zuzana. 1999. "Storytelling and Resistance: The Documentary Practice of Alanis Obomsawin." In *Gendering the Nation: Canadian Women's Cinema*, edited by Kay Armitage, Kass Banning, Brenda Longfellow, and Janine Marchessault, 76–93. Toronto: University of Toronto Press.

Pick, Zuzana. 2003. "This Land Is Ours—Storytelling and History in Kanehsatake: 270 Years of Resistance." In *Candid Eyes: Essays on Canadian Documentaries*, edited by Jim Leach and Jeannette Sloniowski, 181–96. Toronto: University of Toronto Press.

Proulx, Craig. 2010. "Aboriginal Hip Hoppers: Representin' Aboriginality in Cosmopolitan Worlds." In *Indigenous Cosmopolitans: Transnational and Transcultural Indigeneity in the Twenty-First Century*, edited by Maximilian Christian Forte, 39–61. Bern: Peter Lang.

Raboy, Marc. 1990. *Missed Opportunities: The Story of Canada's Broadcasting Policy*. Montreal: McGill-Queen's Press.

Raheja, Michelle H. 2013. *Reservation Reelism: Redfacing, Visual Sovereignty, and Representations of Native Americans in Film*. Lincoln: University of Nebraska Press.

Raynauld, Vincent, Emmanuelle Richez, and Katie Boudreau Morris. 2018. "Canada Is #IdleNoMore: Exploring Dynamics of Indigenous Political and Civic Protest in the Twitterverse." *Information, Communication & Society* 21 (4): 626–42.

Red, Crissy. 2016. Interview. Edited by Karrmen Crey. October 16, 2016.

Reichwein, PearlAnn, and Karen L. Wall. 2020. *Uplift: Visual Culture at the Banff School of Fine Arts.* Vancouver: UBC Press.

Research Office of the Canada Council for the Arts. 2008. *Arts & Culture in Canada Fact Sheet: Aboriginal Arts in Canada.* Ottawa: Canada Council for the Arts.

Retzlaff, Steffi. 2006. "Power Over Discourse: Linguistic Choices in Aboriginal Media Representations." *Canadian Journal of Native Studies* 26 (1): 25–52.

Rezolution Pictures, Inc. 2016. "About Us." Accessed May 15, 2016. https://web.archive.org/web/20160515200259/http://rezolutionpictures.com/about-us/.

Rezolution Pictures, Inc. n.d.a. "*Indians + Aliens.*" Accessed November 17, 2022. http://rezolutionpictures.com/portfolio_page/indians-aliens/.

Rezolution Pictures, Inc. n.d.b. "Rez Rides." Accessed November 17, 2022. http://rezolutionpictures.com/portfolio_page/rez-rides/.

Robertson, Clive. 2006. *Policy Matters: Administrations of Art and Culture.* Toronto: YYZ Books.

Robertson, Mark Cronlund, and Carmen Anderson, L. 2011. *Seeing Red: A History of Natives in Canadian Newspapers.* Winnipeg: University of Manitoba Press.

Robinson, Dylan. 2015. "Reconciliation Relations." *Canadian Theatre Review* 161: 60–63.

Roth, Lorna. 2005. *Something New in the Air: The Story of First Peoples Television Broadcasting in Canada.* Montreal: McGill-Queen's Press.

Royal Canadian Mounted Police. 2014. "Missing and Murdered Aboriginal Women: A National Operational Overview." Last modified May 27, 2014. https://www.rcmp-grc.gc.ca/en/missing-and-murdered-aboriginal-women-national-operational-overview.

Royal Canadian Mounted Police. 2016. "Project E-PANA." Last modified December 13, 2016. https://bc-cb.rcmp-grc.gc.ca/ViewPage.action?siteNodeId=23&languageId=1&contentId=27048.

Royal Commission on Aboriginal Peoples. 1993. *Partners in Confederation: Aboriginal Peoples, Self-Government, and the Constitution.* Privy Council Office. Ottawa: Royal Commission on Aboriginal Peoples.

Royal Commission on Aboriginal Peoples. 1996. *Report of the Royal Commission on Aboriginal Peoples, Volume 3: Gathering Strength.* Ottawa: Royal Commission on Aboriginal Peoples.

Rupert, Robert. 1983. "Native Broadcasting in Canada." *Anthropologica* 25 (1): 53–61.

Russell, Dan. 2011. *A People's Dream: Aboriginal Self-Government in Canada.* Vancouver: UBC Press.

Ryan, Allan J. 1999. *The Trickster Shift: Humor and Irony in Contemporary Native Art.* Seattle: University of Washington Press.

Saha, Anamik. 2018. *Race and the Cultural Industries.* Malden, Mass.: Polity Press.

Schouls, Timothy. 2005. *Shifting Boundaries: Aboriginal Identity, Pluralist Theory, and the Politics of Self-Government.* Vancouver: UBC Press.

SCN (Saskatchewan Communications Network). 2007. *SCN Annual Report 2006–2007.* Regina: Saskatchewan Communications Network.

Silverman, Jason. 2002. "Uncommon Visions: The Films of Loretta Todd." In *North of Everything: English-Canadian Cinema Since 1980,* edited by William Beard and Jerry White, 376–89. Edmonton: University of Alberta Press.

Singer, Beverly R. 2001. *Wiping the War Paint Off the Lens: Native American Film and Video.* Minneapolis: University of Minnesota Press.

Skawennati. n.d. "CPW 2K: A Chatroom Is Worth a Thousand Words by Skawennati." Accessed November 17, 2022. https://www.cyberpowwow.net/STFwork.html.

Smith, Linda Tuhiwai. 1999. *Decolonizing Methodologies: Research and Indigenous Peoples.* London: Zed Books.

Steven, Peter. 1993. *Brink of Reality: New Canadian Documentary Film and Video.* Toronto: Between the Lines.

Stewart, Michelle. 2007. "The Indian Film Crews of *Challenge for Change*: Representation and the State." *Canadian Journal of Film Studies = Revue canadienne d'études cinematographiques* 16 (2): 49–81.

Taner, Shona. 1999. "The Evolution of Native Studies in Canada: Descending from the Ivory Tower." *Canadian Journal of Native Studies* 19 (2): 289–319.

Tinic, Serra. 2009. "Borders of Production Research: A Response to Elana Levine." In *Production Studies: Cultural Studies of Media Industries,* edited by Vicki Mayer, Miranda J. Banks, and J. T. Caldwell, 167–72. New York: Routledge.

Todd, Loretta. 1990. "Notes on Appropriation." *Parallelogramme* 16 (1): 24–33.

Todd, Loretta. 1992. "What More Do They Want?" In *INDIGENA: Contemporary Native Perspectives in Canadian Art,* edited by Gerald McMaster and Lee-Ann Martin, 71–79. Vancouver: Craftsman House.

Todd, Loretta. 1994. "We Dream Who We Are." *Talking Stick,* 7–8.

Todd, Loretta. 1996. "Aboriginal Narratives in Cyberspace." In *Immersed in Technology: Art and Virtual Environments,* edited by Mary Anne Moser, 179–94. Cambridge, Mass.: MIT Press.

Todd, Loretta. 2005a. "Aboriginal Narratives in Cyberspace." In *Transfer-*

ence, Tradition, Technology: Native New Media Exploring Visual & Digital Culture, edited by Melanie A. Townsend, Dana Claxton, and Steve Loft, 152–63. Banff, AB: Walter Phillips Gallery Editions.

Todd, Loretta. 2005b. "Polemics, Philosophies and a Story: Aboriginal Aesthetics in the Media of This Land." In *Transference, Tradition, Technology: Native New Media Exploring Visual & Digital Culture,* edited by Melanie A. Townsend, Dana Claxton, and Steve Loft, 104–24. Banff, AB: Walter Phillips Gallery Editions.

Todd, Loretta. 2014. Interview with Karrmen Crey. August 8, 2014.

TRC (Truth and Reconciliation Commission) of Canada. 2015a. *Canada's Residential Schools: The History, Part 1, Origins to 1939. The Final Report of the Truth and Reconciliation Commission of Canada.* Montreal: McGill-Queens University Press for the TRC.

TRC (Truth and Reconciliation Commission) of Canada. 2015b. *Truth and Reconciliation Commission of Canada: Calls to Action.* Winnipeg: TRC of Canada.

Tsinhnahjinnie, Hulleah J. 1998. "When Is a Photograph Worth a Thousand Words?" Accessed September 1, 2016. http://www.hulleah.com/9to5/1000words.htm.

Turner, Terence. 1992. "Defiant Images: The Kayapo Appropriation of Video." *Anthropology Today* 8 (6): 5–16.

UCLA American Indian Studies Center. 1980. *Five Year Report 1975–1980.* UCLA: American Indian Studies Center.

Valaskakis, Gail. 2005. *Indian Country: Essays on Contemporary Native Culture.* Waterloo, ON: Wilfrid Laurier University Press.

Vancouver Police Department, Sisterwatch Project, and Women's Memorial March Committee. 2011. *The Tragedy of Missing and Murdered Aboriginal Women in Canada: We Can Do Better.* Vancouver: Vancouver Police Department.

Warner, Michael. 2002. *Publics and Counterpublics.* New York City: Zone Books.

Waugh, Thomas, Ezra Winton, and Michael Brendan Baker, eds. 2010. *Challenge for Change: Activist Documentary at the National Film Board of Canada.* Montreal: McGill-Queen's Press.

Wayland, Sarah V. 1997. "Immigration, Multiculturalism and National Identity in Canada." *International Journal on Group Rights* 5: 33–58.

Webb, Ernest, prod. 2013. *Indians + Aliens.* Season 1, episode 1, "Matthew." Aired September 3, 2013. Rezolution Pictures Inc.

White, Jerry. 2002. "Alanis Obomsawin, Documentary Form and the Canadian Nation(s)." In *North of Everything: English-Canadian Cinema Since 1980,* edited by William Beard and Jerry White, 364–75. Edmonton: University of Alberta Press.

White, Jerry. 2006. "A Typically Canadian Cinema: Filmmaking in Alberta, Its Institutions and Authors." In *Self Portraits: The Cinemas of Canada Since Telefilm*, edited by André Loiselle and Tom McSorley, 297–319. Ottawa: Canadian Film Institute/Institut canadien du film.

Williams, Kenneth. 1997. "New TV Awards." *Windspeaker*, June 1997, 11.

Wong, Tia. 2009. "Eyeing Resistance: Alanis Obomsawin's Third Cinema/ Gaze/World." *Cinephile: The University of British Columbia's Film Journal* 5 (1): 51–55.

Worth, Sol, and James Adair. 1972. *Through Navajo Eyes: An Exploration in Film Communication and Anthropology*. Bloomington: Indiana University Press.

Zolf, Dorothy. 1986. "Educational Broadcasting: A Problem of Divided Jurisdiction." *Canadian Journal of Communication* 12 (2): 21–49.

Index

Page numbers in italics represent photos.

Karrmen Crey is Stó:lō from Cheam First Nation and is associate professor in the School of Communication at Simon Fraser University.

Printed in the USA
CPSIA information can be obtained
at www.ICGtesting.com
CBHW071101091224
18400CB00026B/6